THE NEXT FRONTIER OF RESTAURANT MANAGEMENT

CORNELL HOSPITALITY MANAGEMENT: BEST PRACTICES

The large body of research published by scholars in the dynamic field of hospitality management has been slow to find its way into the classroom and the strategic, managerial, and operating practices of the hospitality industry. In the new series Cornell Hospitality Management: Best Practices, Cornell University Press will publish short books that present, in distilled form, current research findings on best practices in the hospitality industry. As recognized experts, the volume editors are ideally qualified to identify the best available research and present it in a thoughtful and coherent way that serves both the pedagogical needs of the classroom and the practical needs of the hospitality industry. The first books in the series will address hospitality branding, human resource management, finance, operations and revenue management, food and beverage management, and design.

CORNELL
HOSPITALITY
MANAGEMENT
BEST PRACTICES

Edited by CHEKITAN S. DEV

THE NEXT FRONTIER OF RESTAURANT MANAGEMENT

Harnessing Data to Improve Guest Service and Enhance the Employee Experience

EDITED BY ALEX M. SUSSKIND
AND MARK MAYNARD

CORNELL UNIVERSITY PRESS
ITHACA AND LONDON

Chapters 1 & 2: © Cornell University, 2007; Chapter 3: © Alex M.
Susskind, K. Michele Kacmar & Carl P. Borchgrevink, 2018; Chapter 4:
© Alex M. Susskind & Anthony Viccari, 2011; Chapter 5: © Alex M.
Susskind, 2014; Chapter 6: © Cornell University, 2007; Chapter 7:
© Cornell University, 2009; Chapter 8: © Cornell University, 2014;
Chapter 9: © Cornell University, 2015; Chapter 10: © Cornell
University, 2016

First published 2019 by Cornell University Press

Library of Congress Cataloging-in-Publication Data

Names: Susskind, Alex M., editor. | Maynard, Mark, 1967– editor.
Title: The next frontier of restaurant management : harnessing data to
    improve guest service and enhance the employee experience / edited by
    Alex M. Susskind and Mark Maynard.
Description: 1st edition. | Ithaca [New York] : Cornell University
    Press, 2019. | Series: Cornell hospitality management | Includes
    bibliographical references and index.
Identifiers: LCCN 2018053224 (print) | LCCN 2018054426 (ebook) |
    ISBN 9781501736520 (pdf) | ISBN 9781501736537 (epub/mobi) |
    ISBN 9781501736506 (cloth) | ISBN 9781501736513 (pbk.)
Subjects: LCSH: Restaurant management.
Classification: LCC TX911.3.M27 (ebook) | LCC TX911.3.M27 N49
    2019 (print) | DDC 647.95068—dc23
LC record available at https://lccn.loc.gov/2018053224

CONTENTS

PREFACE

This book is designed to introduce ideas and concepts studied in the restaurant industry through articles published by Cornell University's School of Hotel Administration. In the chapters below, Alex M. Susskind provides an introduction, summary, and interpretation of each concept presented in the article, and Mark Maynard provides executive commentary. Mark's insights into the best practices of restaurant management are based on his years of experience with Union Square Hospitality Group (USHG), and he offers his own take on each of the concepts presented and how and why they are or are not important for tomorrow's marketplace.

This book is intended to speak to three audiences: undergraduate hospitality and service-focused business programs, executive education programs, and restaurant managers/trainers. For the undergraduate market, in addition to courses in foodservice/restaurant management, this book will serve courses in entrepreneurship, services marketing, and management. For executive education, it will provide leaders from within and outside hospitality management with a framework to address key managerial issues and concerns in their own businesses. Last, due to the practical nature of the book, restaurant managers and those responsible for delivering training in restaurants will find the material useful for enhancing their existing knowledge base and giving them an understanding of what drives a restaurant's success.

With Mark's extensive commentary, all of the content addressed in the chapters that follow will be related to management insights and current market trends coming from an executive of one of the world's best-known restaurant companies. The success of USHG is a result of visionary leaders like Danny Meyer and his team of leaders, including Mark; encapsulating those insights is a key value of this book.

The articles take a cross section of research that affects what Alex and Mark view as the fundamental elements of restaurant success going forward. They address service process management in great detail, along with complaint management, design and ambiance elements of creating the guest and employee experience, and technology (including both consumer-based user characteristics and preferences and operation-based systems and processes). They conclude with a discussion of the human function that is the foundation of the business of restaurants.

THE NEXT FRONTIER OF
RESTAURANT MANAGEMENT

INTRODUCTION

Our Evolving Service Environment

ALEX M. SUSSKIND AND MARK MAYNARD

Welcome!

There are many sources of information out there that vie for your attention, and there are many publications covering the restaurant industry that provide a view into certain aspects of the business. In this book, we offer insights from both the practical world of running restaurants and the academic world of studying, analyzing, and interpreting the many data points that can help describe the guest experience and the business environment for managers and employees. Information is power, and it is a leader's job to use that information to create ways to wow guests while ensuring that our staff and investors (and we!) reap the financial rewards necessary to sustain the business. Competition is fierce, and guests are savvier than ever. So what can you do about it? How will you ensure that you and your business thrive? And why is this important in the first place?

Over the course of this book, we aim to answer these questions as we tackle a few areas that we believe are key to ensuring success. As service expectations increase, guests become more interactive, compensation models change, and technology advances, it is imperative that our businesses evolve to remain relevant and competitive.

We feel that our approach to this subject matter is unique: Alex will use his decades of experience with academic research and teaching to bring a data-driven point of view to the conversation, and Mark will offer commentary and examples from his two decades as a leader within the hospitality industry. While we approach these subjects from different ends of the spectrum, it has been refreshing to work together as we seek to achieve a common understanding. We hope you find valuable tools and insights in the coming pages that will help you navigate your journey, whether you're a student, a seasoned educator, or a manager or owner of a business within our industry.

Throughout this book, we have chosen to share some insights in the first person when we felt it would make the subject matter more meaningful and personal. In general, Alex presents the chapter subject matter and the research we have used as the basis of the chapter, along with an academic appraisal of the research findings. Mark then discusses how his experience working in restaurants either supports or challenges the outcome of the research.

Mark: One of the things I love most about the restaurant industry is the diversity of people working in it. It's an industry that is as welcoming to people with high school diplomas as it is to people with Ph.Ds. Regardless of our résumé, we learn to work together to make our guests happy. Many of us grew up in restaurants and rose through the ranks without any formal training. Restaurants were not necessarily our first career path, but they provided for us while we pursued our passion outside of hospitality. I, for example, studied and pursued a career in landscape architecture before choosing to commit full-time to restaurants. But since I was sixteen, work in restaurants, hotels, and bars has provided for me—whether I was bussing tables at a seasonal seaside restaurant as a teenager, serving bagels to college students like me in Ithaca, or working as a maître d' at one of New York's most iconic restaurants—an appreciation for and commitment to this incredible business. For people traveling this path, colleagues and mentors taught important skills and lessons about how to take care of people and, ultimately, how to run a business. Coming from diverse backgrounds, we had to be adaptable and versatile as we learned on the job. Yet what we lacked at the outset was the quantitative training to help us navigate a profit and loss statement, create a marketing plan, or analyze data that would help us spot trends beyond anecdotal evidence.

Fortunately, business schools spend a lot of time teaching the back-end of our industry and excel at parsing data, introducing new technologies and innovating well beyond what a single operator could tackle. The approach tends to be abstract and academic, as one may expect, with an emphasis on global trends, the economy, and larger-scale issues facing our industry. Some schools do focus on service delivery and the guest experience; however, the emphasis at most universities tends to be more theoretical than practical. In contrast to the people who "landed" in the industry, those individuals who tend to be attracted to business schools specializing in hotels and restaurants love figuring out what makes business tick, from the greeting at the front door to the financial modeling of a new development and everything in between.

Of course, there are no absolutes in my over-generalization: most of us have benefited from a combination of formal training and practical experience; in order to compete and succeed, we need to appreciate, understand, and deploy both perspectives.

Throughout my career, I have witnessed mutual skepticism between people who prefer either the academic or practical approach. In fact, early in my career, I contributed to a prejudice against academics because I had risen through the ranks. This sort of insecurity and narrow-mindedness can lead to a lack of understanding among those who have traveled different roads, and the unfortunate consequence is that the two groups miss an opportunity to learn from each another. I firmly believe that there is a place for both approaches and that the sooner we integrate them, the better our industry will be. This book takes a step toward that integration, using academic research as a foundation and integrating it with day-to-day learnings from the front lines.

As you read, be mindful of your perspective and try to be self-aware enough to know your preconceived notions. Approach the subjects with an open mind and form your own opinions. We sincerely hope that you will find things here that speak to you. Here's to an exciting journey ahead!

Part I

SERVICE CLIMATE

What Matters Most?

ALEX M. SUSSKIND AND MARK MAYNARD

Alex: Service climate gets a fair amount of attention from academics. Over the years, it has been identified through research that all of the constituents in a service organization contribute to the co-creation of a service experience, and each constituent has an interconnected stake in the process. Many service-based businesses, including brick-and-mortar retail and grocery, healthcare, and restaurants in particular, are high-contact businesses. In high-contact businesses the consumers (guests) and the members of the organization have a fair amount of interaction in order to deliver and consume the service experience. In restaurants much of this production, interaction, and consumption takes place within the four walls of the restaurant (with exceptions noted for off-site catering, takeaway, and delivery services).

As noted above, service delivery is co-created through a service climate and is made up of and affected by three main constituents: managers and owners, employees, and guests. Managers and owners (not always one and the same but henceforth referred to as "management") set the stage for the service experience. Management designs and creates the restaurant concept and offerings, secures the resources needed (people, products, operational conditions, and money [PPOM]), sets the standards to execute processes, and evaluates performance along the way to ensure that PPOM are being used optimally to the benefit of all. Employees are an important part of the service process and influence the climate as well. As the primary point of contact for the guests, employees are charged with the tasks and the responsibility of executing and delivering products and service to their guests and meeting the expectations of management and their guests at the same time. Because service delivery in restaurants is mainly the responsibility of the employees, they act as mediators between management's expectations for the service delivery (standards and processes) and the guest experience. Guests are the ultimate consumer of the products and services management creates and represent the top line of the income statement—that is, the revenue stream. If guests don't like the concept or execution of that concept, they will spend their dollars elsewhere. There is sufficient competition in the restaurant business to safely say that each guest truly matters not just for the money they spend today but for the potential money they will spend long into the future.

To detail and describe the importance of understanding a climate for service, we selected three articles from the *Cornell Hospitality Quarterly* for this part, two of which I cowrote. The first article, "How Organizational Standards and Coworker Support Improve Restaurant Service" (Susskind, Kacmar, & Borchgrevink, 2007), is an early replication of the Guest-Server-Exchange Model (GSX; Susskind, Kacmar, & Borchgrevink, 2003) using a restaurant sample, which examines the connection between line-level employees' perceptions of the work they do as service providers and guest satisfaction. The second article, "Guest Satisfaction and Restaurant Performance" (Gupta, McLaughlin, & Gomez, 2007), looks at the guests' reactions to their service experiences in restaurants and various outcome metrics normally considered by management as a gauge of performance. The last article, "The Relationship of Service Providers' Perceptions of Service Climate to Guest Satisfaction, Return Intentions, and Firm Performance" (Susskind, Kacmar, & Borchgrevink, 2018), is a further extension of the GSX model that combines the ideas from the first two articles to examine the connection between employees' reactions to their work as service providers and guest satisfaction and organizational performance, measured as sales per seat. The ideas in each article build on one another, so we address each one in turn.

The first article, "How Organizational Standards and Coworker Support Improve Restaurant Service," introduces the GSX model. The GSX model, which is built on the premise that all constituents in the service process are connected and influence one another, outlines and identifies the parts of the service climate that influence service delivery for each of the constituents. The GSX model is a variant of the Service Profit Chain, which shows standards, created to produce service quality and influence positive employee behavior and attitudes, that create value for customers, breed loyalty among customers, and ultimately drive firm growth and profitability.[1]

Much like the Service Profit Chain, the GSX begins with standards for service. In the GSX model, standards are measured as employees' beliefs that there are strong standards in place in the organization. As noted above, management sets these standards, and employees are responsible for executing them; getting a read on employees' perceptions of standards is important to ensure those standards are perceived correctly (i.e., truly exist as far as your employees are concerned), are understood, and can be executed. The next part of the GSX model looks at how well employees believe they receive support from both their coworkers and their supervisors. Perceived support is an important part of a service climate because there are so many moving parts in the process; for service delivery to be executed properly, line-level staff need support from their peers and supervisors. What the research shows is that standards for service are strongly connected to perceptions of both coworker support and supervisory support. This means that when employees believe the organization has a strong set of standards in place, they also report that they receive strong levels of support from both their coworkers and supervisors to perform their work. One could say that the standards create the need for support and provide the mechanism for support to be shared as needed.

Mark: I couldn't agree more with the research, though it's important to remember that standards are necessary for both technical deliverables and behavior guidelines. In my experience, businesses with the happiest guests have clear standards for both technical service delivery and overall employee behavior, which is more challenging to quantify. It's tough to measure how genuine, engaged, creative, or curious one is, but these are the very traits that tend to resonate with guests. Did my server understand what I really want, did my bartender customize my experience based on my likes, did that reservationist understand the agenda for my lunch reservation? Setting a standard for these sorts of skills is potentially more important than setting a standard for wine knowledge or the ability to expedite a busy lunch service. That said, standards in both hard and soft skills are imperative.

It is sometimes falsely assumed by managers that employees do not like clear standards and high expectations. Some managers believe that "riding" the staff can have negative effects on staff morale, and these managers believe that leading by example is the only way to achieve excellence. I have always found that point of view to be condescending and insulting. When I was a host at Union Square Cafe (USC), I wanted to know what success looked like to my supervisor, and I worked hard to deliver that, making some mistakes and learning from them along the way. The management team's clear (and very high) standards made me a better employee, and the guest benefited. It's no surprise, then, that USC garnered countless accolades, because we leveraged the technical standards necessary for excellent service delivery while not forgetting that guests really remember the fun things, like how a room feels, how the food tastes, and whether or not the team is on the guest's side. This point was driven home when we did an all-employee survey about how to improve the employee experience at Union Square Hospitality Group (USHG). In the results from Porchlight (USHG's first bar concept), one of the most common requests was that management challenge the team more consistently and expect more from each employee. It was a real eye-opener, and it reinforced the belief that people want to work for something meaningful and become champions in the process. As a result, we vastly improved our education program so employees could learn more about the hundreds of spirits we serve. At the request of the employees, we also began to share more financial information about the business so that each team member could understand how his or her actions affect the top line and bottom line. The enthusiasm was quickly contagious, and the guest experience improved as the team became more engaged.

Alex: Moving along in the GSX, "guest orientation" appears next. Guest orientation is a measure of employees' commitment to their guests. In the GSX model, support functions from both coworkers and supervisors are connected to guest orientation, basically showing that when employees have the support from colleagues, they have higher job satisfaction and tend to place higher value on the importance of the guest in the service equation. In the tests of the GSX model, these relationships were only partially supported: the connection between coworker support and guest orientation was statistically significant, but the relationship between supervisory support and guest orientation was not. At first, we were perplexed by these findings in our research (Susskind et al., 2003, 2007, 2018). What we came to realize and firmly believe is that on the front lines of service organizations, the most important support front line–level employees receive comes from peers. Line-level staff work side by side, serving, cooking, bartending, cleaning, and the like. All these functions are needed for the service experience to be successful. It is that interaction with their peers that helps them be successful in delivering service, which then allows service staff to build a level of commitment to their guests. This does not mean, however, that support from supervisors is not important; in fact, supervisory support is viewed as being strongly connected to the presence of standards, showing that employees recognize the connection to standards and their supervisors. It is our belief that if managers set the stage properly for employees to do their work and properly engage and monitor behavior, a positive service climate will emerge for the staff and management.

Mark: I wholeheartedly agree with Alex's conclusion that a positive service climate results when managers lay the groundwork for employees to do their jobs, engage with the employees, and monitor behavior . . . with a couple of caveats: hiring, onboarding, and training are arguably the most important part of any leader's job. While we do set the standards, the most important thing we create and foster is culture. So, if we set clear expectations for behavior and we make consistent hiring decisions to support that culture, we will be successful in what Alex has mentioned. Yes, employees derive much of their motivation from their peers, but employees need to be surrounded by the right peers who embody and support the culture. For decades, I have seen what happens when we do a poor job with hiring. While our track record is incredibly good, it is easy to fall into old patterns to "fill the hole," especially when the business has been short-staffed for an extended period of time. As I write this, our industry is experiencing an epidemic of understaffing, and it is no surprise that chefs and general managers may be prone to making bad or hasty hiring decisions. Invariably, the staff will make our mistakes very clear, and the wrong employee can cast a pall over an otherwise healthy team. While we may not want to admit it, human nature is a strong force, and I have seen many subtle examples of peer-to-peer "freezing out" of team members who do not live up to our cultural standards. In the front of house, this may take the shape of not picking up shifts when an employee needs a particular day off or not helping with sidework. In the back of house, it can manifest itself in not helping a struggling line cook during service or not getting mise en place from the walk-in for a colleague when in need. This behavior may seem harsh, and it is never something management condones, but it is a natural part of human nature. It is our job as leaders to make sure we select the right plants for the garden, avoid introducing invasive weeds, and do everything we can to help everyone flourish.

Several years ago, when I was the general manager of Blue Smoke and Jazz Standard, I lamented to Richard Coraine, then the COO of USHG, that I was feeling overwhelmed and needed to delegate more. He encouraged me but cautioned, "I don't want you to delegate hiring. You have created a very strong culture here, and new employees need to hear directly from you what is expected of them. It's not as strong if they hear those expectations secondhand. They need to hear it from you first, and the other managers can support your mission." I took that to heart, and I have shared that wisdom with the general managers who have reported to me over the years.

Alex: Staff and management are only one side of the equation or two sides of the triangle. The last part of the GSX model is guest satisfaction. If you have standards in place that are properly executed, along with the support needed for your staff, you build a strong focus on guest service and hence a climate for service. Guest orientation was shown to be a strong indicator of guest satisfaction in the GSX, indicating that service providers' commitment to their guests is connected to higher levels of guest satisfaction. These findings bring to mind a quote from Danny Meyer. He was quoted in an interview that was printed in the May 31, 2012, issue of *Wine Spectator Magazine*: "I'm watching the staff. Are they having fun with each other, helping each other out? If they're having fun, the customers will have fun." That quote pretty much sums up the GSX model in the article "How Organizational Standards and Coworker Support Improve Restaurant Service."

The article "Guest Satisfaction and Restaurant Performance" takes a different perspective to identify how a well-functioning restaurant performs. Instead of looking at the connection between employees and guests as the GSX does, the authors look at the connection between guests' behaviors, preferences, and reactions to their restaurant experience and organizational performance. In their work, they set out to determine how well guests' behaviors and attitudes can predict restaurant performance. To do so, they created two models that utilized the existing guest satisfaction measurement system in the restaurant and paired it with operational data shared by the restaurant company.

The first model looked at twenty attributes of the guest experience measured by the guest satisfaction survey and the connection to guests' reports of their desire to return the restaurant in the next thirty days (a common repeat-patronage intention measure used by operators). In effect, they calculated the probabilities that a given attribute could be connected to the guests' desire to return to the restaurant. Ultimately, they classified the attributes as high- versus low-performing (as rated by guests) and high-impact versus low-impact (leverage) on a guest's desire to return to the restaurant. The high-leverage, low-performance category highlights attributes that have the largest relative influence but are rated lower by the guests. This category is one that managers should pay the most attention to because it identifies weaknesses in execution that could negatively affect a guest's desire to return. In this category are "food tasting delicious," perceived "cost appropriateness," and service being "timely," prompt," and "attentive." These attributes touch on elements of food, service, and value. Conversely, the low-leverage, high-performance category highlights attributes that have a small relative influence but are rated higher by the guests. This category includes "clean and dry table," "prompt seating," "server appearance" and being "friendly," and "food portion size." These five attributes touch on different elements of food, service, and value dimensions of the restaurant experience for the guests. Only two attributes were classified as high-leverage, high-performance items: "cheerful greeting" and "food presentation." Only two attributes, "food quality" and "temperature of the food," were classified as low-leverage, low-performance items. These analyses highlight the complexity of the restaurant experience and the number of moving parts that are produced, delivered, and consumed. Being able to identify and specifically target parts of the service experience that influence guests' reactions, satisfaction, and desire to return is a useful management tool. One could say that as the concepts are created, menus are developed and standards are written explicitly for guests. This type of analysis helps identify strengths and weaknesses in execution through the guests' eyes. As an example, from this analysis, "food tasting delicious" is a high-leverage item that is performing lower than the other attributes, but perceived "food quality" and "temperature of food" were also classified as lower-performing attributes but with a lower impact on repeat-patronage intentions; yet the same guests reported the food presentation as a high performer, with a high connection to repeat-patronage intentions. An operator could see that all of these food-related elements are connected, but guests reacted to them differently. It seems that the food overall would require some attention and that there is too much variance in how it is being produced, served, and hence perceived by the guests. The challenge arises around how to tackle the process of making improvements. If the preparation, taste, presentation, and service of the food are monitored for consistency, the variance would decrease, and it would then be possible to determine which of the factors (if any), is a more important driver of performance.

Mark: As I have considered the research surrounding guests' intentions to return, it seems clear that guest expectations are an important driver of guest satisfaction. Things like "food presentation" and "food portion size" can be in the eyes of the beholder. It is management's responsibility to tell the story of the restaurant so that guests can understand what they are signing up for when they make a reservation or walk through the front door. A guest's expectations for price and presentation would be understandably different between a fine dining and casual restaurant, and I would argue that most reasonable people will expect more from a $20 burger at an upscale restaurant than a $10 burger at a greasy spoon. But the data also supports that universal attributes such as "cheerful greeting" will transcend the level of establishment. Gone are the days when people would accept being treated poorly at a "hot" fancy restaurant. Similarly, even casual, family-oriented restaurants are expected to put some thought into plate presentation. The democratization of food culture has educated the consumer so much that there are no shortcuts in our industry, whether we run a QSR (quick-service-restaurant) or a three-star restaurant. But both types of restaurants can provide incredible perceived value that transcends the price of the meal . . . assuming the guest knows what to expect.

Alex: The second model in "Guest Satisfaction and Restaurant Performance" was developed to examine the relationship between repeat-patronage intentions, restaurant characteristics, and marketing efforts on guest counts. The authors used three restaurant brands to test their models. What they found overall is that guests' repeat-patronage intentions were a significant predictor of guest counts (measured as main courses sold). While television marketing, number of seats, and lot size were also found to have a notable influence on guest counts, the effects were not consistently strong across the three brands. The finding that guests' reports of a desire to return to the restaurant are connected to sales is an important finding but not by itself. From the first model described above, it was shown that guest satisfaction with specific restaurant attributes was connected to repeat-patronage intentions; hence, happy guests report that they want to return. The second study showed that repeat-patronage intentions were connected to sales. This paper highlighted three very important elements that operators pay attention to and measure (guest satisfaction, repeat-patronage intentions, and sales) but did not connect the three items together directly. That is where the third and final article in this part comes in.

"The Relationship of Service Providers' Perceptions of Service Climate to Guest Satisfaction, Return Intentions, and Firm Performance" was designed by my coauthors and me to build on the previous research that measured service climate, guest satisfaction, repeat-patronage intention, and performance using the GSX model. Since the GSX was introduced and described in the first article, there is no need repeat that introduction here. It is important to note that before "The Relationship of Service Providers' Perceptions" was produced, we first tested and replicated the GSX model by considering unit-level sales as the ultimate outcome variable in the model.[2] In our research we gathered sales data from 51 restaurants across 3 different restaurant chains and surveyed a total of 639 employees and 561 guests. In the 2018 replication of the GSX, the goal was to add a measure of organizational performance to the model to show that elements of climate in the restaurants were a key driver of success. In so doing, the 2018 version of the GSX model used data from three sources: guests, employees, and restaurant sales per seat. The 2018 GSX model replicated the findings from the 2007 version (see Susskind, Kacmar, & Borchgrevink, 2018), and the new model showed that guest satisfaction was strongly connected to sales as expected, with guest satisfaction explaining 26% of the variance in sales. This set of findings was a fine addition to our knowledge of service process management, but given what we know about the connection of guest satisfaction to repeat-patronage intentions and repeat-patronage intentions connection to sales, we felt that the GSX model needed to be further expanded to include the influence guests' desire to return to the restaurant. So that is what we did.

To see how repeat-patronage intentions added to our understanding of the GSX model, we undertook another study. In the second 2018 GSX study we used a sample of 80 restaurants from a single restaurant chain and captured responses from 990 employees and 879 guests across those 80 restaurants. The extended 2018 GSX once again replicated the previous model with two modifications: a link between guest satisfaction and repeat-patronage intentions and a link between repeat-patronage intentions and unit-level sales were added. The new model, just like the 2007 and the first 2018 versions, worked well. The connection between guest satisfaction and repeat-patronage intentions was strong and significant, showing that satisfied guests were more likely to return. The connection between repeat-patronage intentions and unit-level sales was also strong and significant, showing that repeat-patronage intentions are solidly connected to sales. Repeat-patronage intentions in the new 2018 GSX model explained 55% of the variance in unit-level sales, an increase of 29% over the previous 2018 model, which just considered the link between guest satisfaction and unit-level sales performance.

So what does all this mean? We know that guest satisfaction is important and that clear, meaningful standards that employees can understand and believe in are the key to making guests happy. Making guests happy is no easy task due to the complexity of the restaurant experience. The food, service, and environment need to be just right and consistent over time for each and every guest. Once guests are happy, the stage is set for them to come back. The research shows that making guests happy is important, but the GSX model has now uncovered a new nuance to consider:

"Happy guests are important, but happy guests who want to return are more important." Being able to explain 55% of the variance in unit-level sales through repeat-patronage intentions is a significant finding. It also reminds us that the GSX model was still unable to explain 100% of the variance. That means that many other factors, such as weather, unemployment, the economy, and location, to name a few, still play a role in the success of a business and should not be ignored.

This was the first study in the restaurant space to connect all these elements using multilayer data, with data from employees, guests, and the restaurants themselves. As shown in the 2007 GSX model, only employees and guests were surveyed; in Gupta, McLaughlin, and Gomez's (2007) models, only data from the guests and the restaurant were considered. As we strive to better understand service experiences, research will continue to uncover new elements that help create better service experiences and the environment in which they are delivered.

Mark: Getting back to human nature, I have observed that when things go well (sales are rising, guests are returning), we naturally feel proud of what we have accomplished, and we give ourselves credit for making smart decisions that improved the business. But when year-over-year sales dip, we frequently start looking at exogenous factors, like tourism, weather, and the economy. These will always be factors, but the studies clearly confirm that most of our success or failure is based on our ability to make guests happy so that they will want to return. One other challenge is that most of us don't have professionals studying our business and providing us with detailed analyses. So we rely on intuition and basic accounting. It can be incredibly frustrating at times, but it's imperative that management always looks at the business from a guest perspective. Every morning, I walk through the front door of Porchlight before we open. When I walk in, I take in everything, from the cleanliness of the sidewalk to the smell of the vestibule to the sound of the lo-boy refrigerators behind the bar. And this is before I've even turned on the lights! During service, I love seeing our managers listening to the music level, checking the lights, and observing how our guests are interacting with one another. Successful managers take time to feel the room, not just solve problems. Every service has a unique vibe, and that energy is affected by everything we do, from cooking food to shaking cocktails to describing the specials. Stepping back and taking time to think like a guest helps us notice things before anyone else does. What we do with that information is what sets apart successful leaders from the rest of the pack.

But it's not just managers who need to think like guests. It's every employee, from the server who presents the menu to the porter who cleans the windows. We put this philosophy in action at Union Square Cafe, after about twelve years in business. At that time, the leadership team at USC began to ask how we could ensure that the restaurant remain relevant in an ever-crowded scene. We created a mantra, "Dynamic, not dinosaur," to remind ourselves that evolution was the antidote to extinction. To support our mantra, we launched an employee dining survey wherein we gave each employee a generous voucher to use at the restaurant within a period of two weeks. Each employee and a guest would experience USC as a "normal" guest or critic would, from making a reservation under an assumed name to walking in and being seated. The staff serving those "critics" could not inform the kitchen or bar team that an employee was dining. Of course, the front-of-house (FOH) team would eventually know who was in the dining room once they arrived, but the team took the mission very seriously, and they also had a ton of fun. Within 24 hours of the meal, the employee would complete a highly detailed survey about the experience, and the management team compiled the data and shared it with the team at an all-staff meeting a month later. What we found is that people were incredibly proud of what we do, and they could really appreciate why guests loved us so much. But they also gave us mountains of feedback about how we could better serve our guests, from improving how we answered the phone (time on hold was a huge complaint) to the temperature of the room (too cold), to the organization of the wine list (as with many long-running restaurants, the format has changed many times over the years). But there were other, even more impactful (and expensive) things that the team told us, like that the menu itself seemed tired and outdated, that the back bar looked worn, and that the chairs were wobbly. So, over the next year, Danny and the partners invested in refreshing the restaurant so that it could reflect the USC of the day, not a memory of what it had once been. This campaign galvanized the team, and everyone seemed to walk a bit taller that year. Guests began to notice, too, and we received many comments that "something seems different, but I'm not quite sure what," which is precisely the response we were looking for. We didn't want to shock people or draw too much attention to what we were doing. Like getting a new hairstyle, we remained the same at the core but subtly different on the outside. Fortunately for us, the *New York Times* restaurant critic William Grimes also noticed. In his glowing 1999 review he said that the restaurant "treats guests very well. It makes them feel welcome. It caters to their every whim in an openhanded, Midwestern manner, which disguises a disciplined, highly professional understanding of service." We could not have been more proud, and as the general manager of the restaurant at the time, this sentence was (and remains) one of the highlights of my career. He got it!

And yet, after congratulating the team the next morning, Danny reminded us that we would need to earn it even more moving forward. Being reanointed by the *New York Times* after 14 years in business would only increase guest expectations. And so it goes. We got back on the horse, remained highly critical of ourselves, and strove each day to be more hospitable, more punctual, more consistent, and more engaged with our guests. Our chosen industry is incredibly complex and exhausting, but, at the end of it all, our mission is to make guests so happy that they have no choice but to return. Challenge, accepted!

Notes

1. J. L. Heskett, T. O. Jones, G. W. Loveman, W. E. Sasser Jr., & L. A. Schlesinger (1994), Putting the service-profit chain to work, *Harvard Business Review*, 72(2), 164–174.

2. Alex M. Susskind, K. Michele Kacmar, & Carl P. Borchgrevink (2018), Guest-Server-Exchange Model (GSX) and organizational performance: A look at the connection between service climate and unit-level sales in multiunit restaurants, *Journal of Hospitality and Tourism Research*, 42(1), 100–110. Awarded "JHTR Best Paper Award 2017" by ICHRIE.

1

How Organizational Standards and Coworker Support Improve Restaurant Service

Alex M. Susskind, K. Michele Kacmar, and Carl P. Borchgrevink

Restaurant service is a process that is mutually created by three groups of individuals: managers (including owners), workers, and guests (Susskind, Kacmar, & Borchgrevink, 2003). Because service is complex, the process is influenced by guest-related variables, such as demographics or behavior; service-provider variables, such as demographics, behavior, mood, and emotion; and the context, such as the organizational environment, structure, leadership, and coworkers (Ford & Etienne, 2003).

As a method of describing how service providers and guests respond to the service process, Hogan, Hogan, and Busch (1984) used the term service orientation in the 1980s. They described service orientation as "a set of attitudes and behaviors that affects the staff of any organization and its guests" (167). In the 1990s, Schneider, White, and Paul (1998, 153) described service orientation as service practices that assess "the degree to which an organization emphasizes, in multiple ways, meeting guest needs and expectations for service quality." These definitions, termed customer orientation or guest orientation, have been applied to the hospitality business to represent the extent to which service providers are committed to their guests (Susskind, Kacmar, & Borchgrevink, 2003; Susskind et al., 2000). Regardless of the specific term, the underlying concept is that line-level employees have an important influence on the guest's experience. Exactly how service-oriented behavior and attitudes among line-level employees translate into guest satisfaction is less clear, particularly regarding restaurant experiences.

The Guest—Server Exchange (GSX) Model

To highlight this important area of guest service research for restaurant operators, we present in this article a test of a model of guest-server interaction in a group of chain restaurants (adapted from Susskind, Kacmar, & Borchgrevink, 2003; Susskind et al., 2000). In the model presented here, we suggest that organizational standards for service form the foundation and guidelines for service providers to perform their jobs. Based on those standards, service providers then receive support from their coworkers and supervisors, which has the effect of creating a positive service atmosphere. That positive service atmosphere fosters guest satisfaction.

The model begins with employees' perceptions of organizational standards for service delivery (as shown in figure 1.1). Standards for service delivery are antecedents to employees' perceptions of coworkers' and supervisors' support. That support in turn leads to service workers' guest orientation. Last, frontline service workers' guest orientation promotes guests' reported satisfaction with their service experience.

Organizational Standards

Organizational standards for service delivery are a key influence on employees' behavior and outcomes in organizations. Standards in this context consist of (1) organizational goals and objectives; (2) managerial expectations for job performance; and (3) the implicit importance placed on those goals, objectives, and performance demands (Litwin & Stringer, 1968). In service organizations, line-level employees are responsible for the bulk of interaction with guests. Frontline employees thus constitute the direct link between an organization's operational mission and its guests (Grisaffe, 2000). Consequently, an organization must have

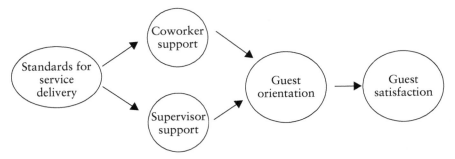

Figure 1.1. Proposed model of the guest service processes and
organizational outcomes

standards in place to guide, direct, and monitor the service behavior of
line-level employees and those who supervise them (Susskind, Kacmar, &
Borchgrevink, 2003; Susskind et al., 2000).

Standards for service are an important part of an organization's mission because they provide the foundation on which services are produced,
delivered, and evaluated. Research has shown that managerial philosophies and values behind an organization's internal business practices influence the actions of both service personnel and guests (Grisaffe, 2000). In
that regard, support from managers can improve employees' well-being
and performance (Schmit & Allscheid, 1995).

A study by Armeli and colleagues (1998) found that employees' perceptions of organizational support are stronger when employees believe
they are being guided by a strong set of standards (see also Eisenberger
et al., 1997; Susskind, Kacmar, & Borchgrevink, 2003; Susskind et al.,
2000). While the strong presence of standards has been shown to promote
the GSX, additional support is needed, as standards alone do not guarantee appropriate service.

Perceptions of Support

If standards set the stage for desired performance, service personnel will
likely use them as a guide. Support functions in service-based organizations have been shown to come from two main sources: (1) support from
coworkers and (2) support from supervisors or management (Susskind,
Kacmar, & Borchgrevink, 2003; Susskind et al., 2000). Separating support

functions into coworker and supervisory parts emphasizes the fact that line-level employees and their supervisors play distinct but essential support roles in the GSX. In this framework, coworker support is defined as the extent to which employees believe their coworkers provide them with work-related assistance to aid them in carrying out their service-related duties (Susskind, Kacmar, & Borchgrevink, 2003; Susskind et al., 2000). By the same token, supervisory support is defined as the extent to which employees believe that their supervisors offer them work-related help in performing their jobs as service workers (Susskind, Kacmar, & Borchgrevink, 2003; Susskind et al., 2000). In the model shown in figure 1.1, we propose that standards act as a reminder for both coworkers and supervisors to support service providers. Consequently, we can conclude that having standards in place motivates service providers (employees and supervisors) to support one another in their work.

Guest Orientation

For our purposes, we use the definition of guest orientation that focuses on the importance that service providers place on their guests' needs and the extent to which service providers are willing to put forth time and effort to satisfy their guests (Kelley, 1992). By this definition, guest orientation is a key part of guest service, is influenced by interaction with the constituents of a service experience (e.g., guests, coworkers, and superiors) (Brady & Cronin, 2001), and represents a service provider's level of commitment to his or her guests (Susskind, Kacmar, & Borchgrevink, 2003; Susskind et al., 2000). Service providers who are proactive, anticipate their guests' needs, and are willing to go the extra mile for their guests would be considered guest-oriented. Service providers who receive support from their coworkers and superiors while performing their duties are likely to show a stronger commitment to the service process and their guests, particularly when the supportive actions of others are based on the organization's standards for service delivery (Susskind, Kacmar, & Borchgrevink, 2003; Susskind et al., 2000).

Guest Satisfaction

The end point of the model, guest satisfaction, is the desired outcome for service-related businesses, because of its contribution to profitability. To our surprise, only a limited number of research studies have examined the direct connection between employees' and guests' perceptions of the service process (see, for example, Brady & Cronin, 2001; Johnson, 1996; and Susskind, Kacmar, & Borchgrevink, 2003). With this study, we examine the connection between service providers' attitudes and perceptions of their work-related duties and how those attitudes are connected to their guests' satisfaction with their service experiences. When service providers are committed to their role in the service process, they are more likely to consistently offer their guests better service.

Study Details and Data Analyses

We studied a total of 324 service employees from twenty-five units of a Midwestern restaurant chain over a two-month period. Forty percent of the line-level participants were male, their median age was twenty-two (ranging between seventeen and forty-five),[1] and they had worked for the company at the time of the survey for a median of just under twelve months (ranging from one month to ten years).[2] To assess guest satisfaction in the restaurants, an average of eleven guests were surveyed from each of the twenty-five units we surveyed. In total, we collected 271 usable responses from guests. We surveyed an average of 12 employees from each of the twenty-five units (ranging from 6 to 24 employees per unit).

We evaluated the line-level employees' perceptions of standards using a questionnaire that had four items for service delivery, three items for coworker support, four items for supervisory support, and five items for guest orientation. Survey questions used 5-point Likert-type scales with anchors ranging from strongly agree (5) to strongly disagree (1). The questionnaire items used and the scale reliabilities (Cronbach's a) at the individual level are reported in the appendix. We then surveyed each restaurant's guests using a six-item questionnaire. (Again, see the appendix for the items used and the scale reliabilities.) The responses to employee and guest data were aggregated to the organizational level. We made no attempt to match specific guest reactions to specific employees because multiple employees served each guest and some guests were in the restaurant during a shift change.

Data Aggregation

To offer sufficient support to aggregate these variables to the organizational level we examined the rWG(J) statistic to determine within-organization agreement (James, Demaree, & Wolf, 1984). This technique offers a measure of reliability within and across the units to ensure that aggregation of the data to the unit level is possible and appropriate. The rWG(J) was computed for each scale, in each of the twenty-five units. The employees' responses from the twenty-five units aggregated to the organizational level exceed the recommended cutoff of .60 (James, 1982). The statistics are as follows: rWG(4) = .78 for standards for service delivery, rWG(3) = .77 for coworker support, rWG(4) = .73 for supervisor support, and rWG(5) = .92 for guest orientation. Likewise, the guest satisfaction data yielded from the 271 guests from the twenty-five units were well suited to aggregation, indicating a high level of agreement (rWG(6) = .96).

Path Analysis

The path model presented in figure 1.2 was analyzed using least-squares static-path analysis to examine the direct and indirect effects of relationships presented in the model (Hunter & Hamilton, 1995). Although path analysis does not establish causal relationships with certainty, it does provide quantitative interpretations of potential causal relationships

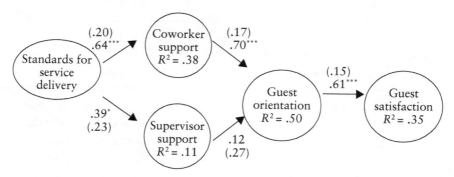

Figure 1.2. Model of guest service processes and organizational outcomes.
Note: The standard errors for the path coefficients appear in parentheses; the model was tested at the unit level. *p < .05. ***p < .001.

(Borchgrevink & Boster, 1998). In this case, the presence of service-delivery standards was treated as the exogenous variable in the model, with coworker support, supervisory support, guest orientation, and guest satisfaction treated as the endogenous variables. The support functions were presented as mediators of the relationship between standards and guest orientation, and guest orientation was presented as a mediator between the support functions and guest satisfaction.

The path model was assessed for fit with the following specifications: (1) global chi-square tests for the sum of squared error for the model are nonsignificant; (2) each path linkage in the model is tested for significance at the $p < .05$ level; and (3) sampling error analyses were conducted for each unspecified path in the model to rule out any misspecifications (Borchgrevink & Boster, 1998).

Study Results and Discussion

Test of the Proposed Model

The test showed that the hypothesized model produced a good fit to the data, $\chi2 (5) = 1.55$, $p = .90$. The descriptive statistics and correlations of the variables presented in the model are reported in table 1.1.[3] In all twenty-five restaurants surveyed, employees and guests reacted similarly to the service environment they mutually created. This study shows that

TABLE 1.1. Descriptive statistics and correlations from the final aggregated scales at the organizational level

	M	SD	1	2	3	4	5
1. Standards for service delivery	3.64	0.38	[.68]				
2. Coworker support	3.77	0.43	.43*	[.74]			
3. Supervisor support	3.47	0.47	.64**	.08	[.68]		
4. Guest orientation	4.23	0.39	.49*	.63**	.24	[.91]	
5. Guest satisfaction	3.38	1.03	.48*	.59**	.30	.62**	[.96]

Note: N = 25. The rWG(J) aggregation statistic (James, Demaree, & Wolf, 1984) is presented along the diagonal in brackets and represents the average across the 25 units in the company. *$p < .05$. **$p < .01$.

employees who reported high service standards indicated a strong presence of coworker support but a weaker level of supervisor support, which was then related to their perceptions of a guest orientation. In restaurants where employees reported a high level of guest orientation, guests reported a higher level of guest satisfaction with service. These findings confirm the results from a previously reported study that examined a broader range of service-based organizations (including restaurants, hotels, and retail stores) (Susskind, Kacmar, & Borchgrevink, 2003).

A clear set of relationships emerged from the analyses. Guest satisfaction was related directly or indirectly to a number of service-related factors (as shown in table 1.1). Some of these factors are under management's control (notably, standards for service delivery and supervisory support), while others rest solely with the frontline service providers (including coworker support and guest orientation).

The test of the model in figure 1.2 revealed three notable findings. First, perceptions of standards for service lay the foundation for how individuals view their jobs as service providers. In the model, support functions proved to be mediators of the relationship between standards for service and guest orientation. This means that standards alone are not sufficient to foster a guest orientation. The support and direction that emerge from standards are important to building a guest orientation among staff members. When perceived standards for service delivery were high, the findings showed that employees reported higher levels of support from both coworkers and supervisors. It should be noted, however, that the influence of standards on supervisor support was weaker than was the influence of standards on coworker support.[4] What this suggests is that standards for service are fostered among coworkers more notably than are the standards among supervisors or managers. This observation is consistent with how the front line of a restaurant works. Although managers are present on the floor, the servers are the ones who must execute the service standards enunciated by managers. Although support from managers is weaker in the model than is support from coworkers, manager support is not insignificant and represents an important piece of the GSX.

Second, coworker support was significantly related to a server's guest orientation, while supervisor support was not.[5] These findings suggest that the perceived presence of supportive coworkers in a service environment leads employees to a higher level of commitment to their guests. Once again, our findings indicate that restaurant employees need a supportive group of peers to help them perform service-related duties, while effusive supervisory support is not essential to a guest orientation. We suspect that coworker support contains distinctive elements that do not exist in the interaction of superiors and subordinates. This finding further reflects line-level employees' essential role in the GSX, since they are the ones interacting the most with guests. The observed relationships involving coworker and supervisor support indicate that servers view support functions relating to coworkers differently than they view support functions connected with their managers and supervisors (see Susskind, Kacmar, & Borchgrevink, 2003). This finding confirms our belief that perceptions of support in a service environment come from multiple sources and that each type of support plays a different, but necessary role.

Last, guest satisfaction with service was strongly related to high levels of guest orientation, as reported by the servers and the guests in the restaurants.[6] This is a result that all restaurateurs would believe to be true; service providers who demonstrate a strong commitment to their guests will make their guests happier than those servers who are less guest-focused. These findings suggest that when guest-oriented employees fulfill their role as service providers, they deliver excellent service to their guests, and in turn guests notice the service and report high satisfaction.

The study shows that standards account for about 38% of the variance in coworker support and 11% of the variance in supervisor support. We think that this is a promising finding for operators. That is, about half of the influence in support functions can be attributed to the reported presence of standards for service. The strong presence of standards is a key to developing cooperative behavior among servers. Of equal importance is the relationship between support functions and guest orientation; 50% of the variance in guest orientation in this model is attributed to support functions, the bulk of which comes from coworkers. This suggests that camaraderie and support among the service staff is a key influence of being committed to guest service, with managerial and supervisory support being viewed as a peripheral element. Last, more than a third of the variance in guest satisfaction could be accounted for by servers' levels of guest orientation. This finding suggests that a large part of the guests' experience is influenced by the service they receive, but other elements (such as food, comfort, and ambience) likely have considerable influence on guest satisfaction as well. This model provides a good framework for operators to focus on elements in the GSX that lead to enhanced guest satisfaction.

Managerial Implications

For service standards to guide and direct employees, those standards need to be developed and articulated in a way that is generally accepted, clear, and understood by all employees. Training and organizational activities should emphasize the standards' specific goals and underlying rationale to ensure that they can be consistently achieved (Litwin & Stringer, 1968). Servers will likely disregard standards that are viewed as unattainable or not pragmatic. Given the strong connection between standards and coworker and supervisor support, training, development, and management efforts should emphasize service standards whenever possible.

Another implication of our study relates to the role of the supervisor. Our study found that while supervisory support was an outgrowth of standards, support from the supervisor was not directly linked to service employees' reported guest orientation. This suggests that while the supervisor has an important role to play in clarifying and specifying service standards for employees and dealing with the service process at large, when it is time for service to occur, the supervisor should recognize that line-level workers make or break the experience for the guest under normal circumstances. Therefore, supervisors should maintain a strong focus on the service standards as a way of helping line-level people deliver on those standards.

Our model suggests that a shared understanding of service standards, teamwork, and a guest orientation are important influences on guest satisfaction. Gaining a better understanding of how each element operates within the restaurant is a way to improve guests' service experiences.

Limitations

When designing the study, we knew that we would have to aggregate the data for each restaurant because we had no good way of collecting data that matched the results of individual employees and guests. Thus, the guests were not assessing their satisfaction with a specific employee but instead with their overall dining experience. The problem is that we then have a sample of just twenty-five restaurants. The sample size is a limitation, but one that we would face even if we surveyed two or three times as many restaurants in the chain without matched employee-and-guest data. Limitations notwithstanding, this type of design and sampling methodology is common among field studies and studies of groups and teams where a single organization or a limited set of organizations is used. For example, Schneider et al. (2005) recently surveyed fifty-six departments in a national grocery chain, in a survey that drew a response rate of 40%. Researchers should continue to maximize sample size in their studies whenever possible but should not lose sight of the rich data that are available from smaller organizations, departments, or teams.

Last, while guest orientation accounted for roughly one-third of the variance in guest satisfaction in the restaurants we sampled, two-thirds of the variance remains unexplained through our model. This means that a guest-oriented service staff has a sizeable influence on guest satisfaction, but other factors that were not measured here have even greater influence on how guests react to their dining experiences. These influences should be identified and addressed in future studies.

Next Steps

The findings of this study highlight several directions for future research. First, it would be useful to test this model using additional guest-outcome measures such as intention to return, value perceptions, and satisfaction with other dimensions of the restaurant experience such as food, comfort, or ambience. Additionally, using measures of performance beyond guest satisfaction, such as employee performance or firm performance, could also shed more light on the pieces of the model presented here. Second, although it would be difficult to secure a matched sample of employee, managerial, and guest responses, it would be prudent to do so, to test this model entirely at the individual level of analysis.

In conclusion, this research shows the strong connection of employee behavior and attitudes with guest satisfaction. Given the dynamic nature of restaurant experiences, developing a better understanding of the elements that can be controlled and managed to improve the service process and perceived outcomes for guests is a key to improving restaurant performance.

Appendix: Listing of the Guest Service Attitude Questions

Standards for Service Delivery Items ($\alpha = .87$)

1. The managers believe that well-trained guest-service employees are the key to providing excellent guest service in our restaurant.
2. In the restaurant I work for, we set very high standards for guest service.
3. Our management believes that no job is done so well that it couldn't be done better.
4. The managers believe that if we are happy, excellent guest service will result.

Coworker Support Items ($\alpha = .94$)

1. I find my coworkers very helpful when performing my guest-service duties.
2. When performing my service duties, I rely heavily on my coworkers.
3. My coworkers provide me with important work-related information and advice that make performing my job easier.

Supervisor Support Items ($\alpha = .95$)

1. I find my supervisor very helpful in performing my guest-service duties.
2. When performing my service duties, I rely heavily on my supervisor.
3. My supervisor provides me with important work-related information and advice that make performing my job easier.
4. I can count on my supervisor to do the "right thing" when serving guests.

Guest Orientation Items ($\alpha = .80$)

1. When performing my job, the guest is most important to me.
2. It is best to ensure that our guests receive the best possible service available.
3. If possible, I meet all requests made by my guests.
4. As an employee responsible for providing service, guests are very important to me.
5. I believe that providing timely, efficient service to guests is a major function of my job.

Guest Satisfaction with Service Items ($\alpha = .93$)

1. Overall, I am happy with the service I just received.

2. The employee(s) who assisted me seemed interested in providing excellent service.
3. The employee(s) who assisted me appeared happy to serve me.
4. The employee(s) performed their duties as I anticipated.
5. The employee(s) who assisted me appeared to be cold and distant.
6. This restaurant's employees really focus on guest service.

Source: Adapted from Susskind, Kacmar, & Borchgrevink, 2003.

Notes

Original citation: Susskind, A. M., Kacmar, K. M., & Borchgrevink, C. P. (2007). How organizational standards and coworker support improve restaurant service. *Cornell Hotel and Restaurant Administration Quarterly* 48(4): 370–379.

1. Median age = 22 (standard deviation = 5.14 years); mean age = 24.55.

2. Median tenure = 12 months (standard deviation = 20.32 months); mean = 18.76 months.

3. To allay concerns over multicollinearity among the variables, as suggested by Nunnally and Bernstein (1994), we performed a principal-components factor analysis using a varimax rotation with the individual-level data. The results show that the items loaded consistently on each of the four factors with no notable cross-loadings. The total variance explained by the measurement model was 75.72%. The scales are highly correlated, but based on the factor analyses, multicollinearity seems not to be a concern among these data. A copy of the factor analysis is available upon request from the first author.

4. $\beta = .64$, $p < .001$, $R2 = .38$ for the path between standards and coworker support; and $\beta = .39$, $p < .05$, $R2 = .11$ for the path between standards and supervisory support.

5. $\beta = .70$, $p < .001$, for the path between coworker support and customer orientation; and $\beta = .12$, $p = $ n.s. for the path between supervisory support and customer orientation with a combined $R2 = .50$ on customer orientation.

6. $\beta = .61$, $p < .001$, for the path between customer orientation and customer satisfaction, with an $R2 = .35$.

References

Armeli, S., Eisenberger, R., Fasolo, P., & Lynch, P. (1998). Perceived organizational support and police performance: The moderating influence of socioemotional needs. *Journal of Applied Psychology*, 83: 288–297.

Borchgrevink, C. P., & Boster, F. J. (1998). Leader-member exchange and interpersonal relationships: Construct validity and path model. *Journal of Hospitality & Leisure Marketing*, 5(1): 53–80.

Brady, M. K., & Cronin, J. J. (2001). Customer orientation: Effects on customer service perceptions and outcome behavior. *Journal of Service Research*, 3: 241–251.

Eisenberger, R., Cummings, J., Armeli, S., & Lynch, P. (1997). Perceived organizational support, discretionary treatment, and job satisfaction. *Journal of Applied Psychology, 82:* 812–820.

Ford, W. S. Z., & Etienne, C. N. (2003). Can I help you? A framework for interdisciplinary research on customer-service encounters. *Management Communication Quarterly, 7:* 413–441.

Grisaffe, D. (2000). Putting customer satisfaction in its place: Broader organizational research perspectives versus measurement myopia. *Journal of Consumer Satisfaction, Dissatisfaction, and Complaining Behavior, 13:* 1–16.

Hogan, J., Hogan, R., & Busch, C. M. (1984). How to measure service orientation. *Journal of Applied Psychology 69:* 167–73.

Hunter, J. E., & M. A. Hamilton. (1995). *PATH: A program in BASICA.* East Lansing: Michigan State University.

James, L. R. (1982). Aggregation bias estimates of perceptual agreement. *Journal of Applied Psychology, 67:* 219–229.

James, L. R., Demaree, R. G., & Wolf, G. (1984). Estimating within-group interrater reliability with and without response bias. *Journal of Applied Psychology, 69:* 85–98.

Johnson, J. (1996). Linking employee perceptions to customer satisfaction. *Personnel Psychology, 49:* 831–852.

Kelley, S. W. (1992). Developing customer orientation among service employees. *Journal of the Academy of Marketing Science, 20:* 27–36.

Litwin, G. H., & Stringer, R. A. Jr. (1968). *Motivation and organizational climate.* Boston: Harvard University Graduate School of Business.

Nunnally, J. C., & Bernstein, I. H. (1994). *Psychometric theory.* 3rd ed. New York: McGraw-Hill.

Schmit, M. J., & Allscheid, S. P. (1995). Employee attitudes and customer satisfaction: Making theoretical and empirical connections. *Personnel Psychology, 48:* 521–536.

Schneider, B., Eirhart, M. G., Mayer, D. M., Saltz, J. L., & Niles-Jolly, K. (2005). Understanding organization-customer links in service settings. *Academy of Management Journal, 48:* 1017–1032.

Schneider, B., White, S. S., & Paul, M. C. (1998). Linking service climate and customer perceptions of service quality: Test of a causal model. *Journal of Applied Psychology, 83:* 150–163.

Susskind, Alex M., Borchgrevink, Carl P., Kacmar, K. Michele, & Brymer, Robert A. (2000). Customer service employees' behavioral intentions and attitudes: An examination of construct validity and a path model. *International Journal of Hospitality Management, 19*(1): 53–77.

Susskind, A. M., Kacmar, K. M., & Borchgrevink, C. P. (2003). Customer service providers' attitudes relating to customer service and customer satisfaction in the customer-server exchange (CSX). *Journal of Applied Psychology, 88*(1): 179–187.

2

Guest Satisfaction and Restaurant Performance

Sachin Gupta, Edward McLaughlin, and Miguel Gomez

Companies and organizations in virtually every industry employ customer-satisfaction measures for the straightforward reason that satisfied customers are essential for a successful business. Despite what seems like agreement on the importance of customer satisfaction, however, there is little consensus on the details of what constitutes satisfaction or even how to quantify the difference customer satisfaction makes. Also in debate are how customer satisfaction should be measured, with what frequency, and at what level of aggregation, as well as how such measures are or should be linked with a firm's performance. What is more, some empirical evidence suggests that the relationships between customer satisfaction, customer loyalty (repeat business), and a firm's performance are tenuous at best.

The study described in this article attempts to address the key issue in customer satisfaction, namely, the relationships between customer satisfaction, customers' repeat-purchase intentions, and restaurant performance. Much research, both theoretical and empirical, has examined how customer satisfaction may be related to organizational goals and business performance. In this study, we employ a large data set from a national restaurant chain to construct models that describe the factors that influence customers' likelihood of repeat purchase. We then link this purchase likelihood, along with other variables, to restaurant sales.

Linking Customer Satisfaction with Performance

The relationships we study are part of a framework referred to as the service-profit chain (this concept was developed by Heskett et al., 2004). In this framework there are certain attributes of the dining experience that affect customer satisfaction. Next, higher customer satisfaction should lead to increased probability of repeat purchase, which in turn should result in greater restaurant sales. In this section, we review earlier work that measured the customer satisfaction and performance links in the restaurant sector.

The empirical literature on this topic with regard to restaurants dates from the past twenty years. A few studies were conducted in the late 1980s and the 1990s focusing mostly on attributes of the dining experience that determine customer satisfaction (see, e.g., Knutson, 1988; Davis & Vollmann, 1990; Dubé, Renaghan, & Miller, 1994; and Kivela, Inbakaran, & Reece, 2000). More recently, however, researchers started addressing the links between customer satisfaction and performance, emphasizing the way satisfaction affects customers' repeat purchases (examples of recent contributions include Sulek & Hensley, 2004; Söderlund & Öhman, 2005; and Cheng, 2005). Next, we review the main findings on the drivers of customer satisfaction, the links between such drivers and repeat-purchase intentions, and the influence of customer satisfaction on restaurant performance.

Drivers of Customer Satisfaction

Many researchers have explored the underlying factors that result in customer satisfaction. Knutson (1988) discussed principles that managers should follow to meet or exceed customer expectations, such as employee greeting, restaurant atmosphere, speed of service, and convenience. Fitzsimmons and Maurer (1991) constructed a managerial tool to measure the attributes driving customer satisfaction. Other studies have identified numerous factors that influence customer satisfaction with a dining experience, including waiting time, quality of service, responsiveness of frontline employees, menu variety, food prices, food quality, food-quality consistency, ambience of the facilities, and convenience (Davis & Vollmann, 1990; Dubé, Renaghan, & Miller, 1994; Kivela, Inbakaran, & Reece, 2000; Sulek & Hensley, 2004; Iglesias & Yague, 2004; and Andaleeb & Conway, 2006).

Customer Satisfaction and Repeat-Purchase Intentions

Determining satisfaction is not sufficient, however, because one needs also to establish the link between satisfaction and repeat purchases, which are an important source of restaurants' profits. Thus, studies have addressed the links between customer satisfaction with various restaurant attributes and repeat-purchase intentions (for instance, see Sulek & Hensley, 2004; Söderlund & Öhman, 2005; and Cheng, 2005). While these studies often find strong links, the importance of a particular attribute varies according to the type of restaurant and the type of customer (for a detailed analysis, see Cheng, 2005). For instance, food quality is the critical attribute influencing repeat-purchase intentions in full-service restaurants, while waiting time is the most important attribute in quick-service restaurants (research focusing on full-service restaurants includes Sulek & Hensley, 2004 and Clark & Wood, 1998; research on fast-food restaurants is from Davis & Vollmann, 1990). When Kivela, Inbakaran, and Reece (2000) conducted an extensive survey of diners of various restaurants, they found that first and last impressions have the greatest impact on repeat-purchase intentions, followed by excellence in service and food quality. This literature concludes that different classes of restaurant businesses should implement different managerial strategies to compete and succeed (Cheng, 2005). Most studies that show strong links between customer satisfaction and repeat-purchase intentions typically employ cross-sectional data. Nevertheless, marketing researchers argue that one should take into account the dynamic properties of such links (see, for example, Rust & Zahorik, 1993; Bernhardt, Donthu, & Kennett, 2000).

Repeat-Purchase Intentions and Sales Performance

The general conclusion of these studies is that higher levels of customer satisfaction lead to an increase in customers' repeat purchases and improved financial performance (Mittal & Kamakura, 2001). However, evidence regarding the link between customer satisfaction and a restaurant's performance remains ambiguous. Anderson, Fornell, and Rust (1997), for instance, found no correlation between customer satisfaction and productivity in service firms as a group or among restaurants in particular. In contrast, Bernhardt, Donthu, and Kennett (2000) employed data from a national chain of quick-service restaurants and found a positive association between changes in customer satisfaction and changes in sales performance. They argued that researchers and managers should take into account the dynamic properties of this link because there is a time horizon for the influence of customer satisfaction on restaurant performance. Söderlund and Öhman (2005) found another dimension in addition to time. They concluded that the correlations between (1) repeat-purchase intentions and customer satisfaction and (2) repeat-purchase intentions and actual repeat purchases are sensitive to the particular measure of repeat-purchase intentions employed. Overall, the restaurant literature calls for further empirical research on the links between customer satisfaction and firm performance (Söderlund & Öhman, 2005).

In the study described in this article, we address at the same time all three elements of the link between customer satisfaction and performance, namely, customer satisfaction, repeat-purchase intentions, and firm performance. Our model considers the dynamic nature of the aforementioned relationships and identifies the lag structure among the three constructs. Finally, our study fills a gap in the empirical literature that focuses on the restaurant sector by linking customer satisfaction to restaurant performance.

Study Goals and Data Sources

We set out to determine the principal drivers of customer satisfaction in a restaurant chain and, subsequently, to determine how customer-satisfaction data can be most effectively used to improve the chain's performance. In particular, our goals were the following: (1) to identify the customer-experience attributes that cause customers to come back to a restaurant; (2) to prioritize those customer experience attributes in terms of their effect on customers' likelihood to come back; and (3) to identify the relationships between likelihood to come back, and guest count or restaurant sales, and quantify the effect of changes in "come-back" scores on restaurant performance.

We acquired a large data set from a national restaurant company that has more than three hundred outlets in locations covering roughly one-half of the United States. This company's three restaurant divisions record total sales of approximately $1,000,000 per day. This rich data set contained several distinct parts. First, we had data from more than eighty thousand guest surveys regarding guests' detailed and overall restaurant experience spanning the period September 2005 to April 2006. Second, the data set also contained detailed information on various indices of daily individual restaurant performance, such as guest counts, sales, and margin. Third, we collected data on a series of restaurant characteristics to refine our analysis for the three restaurant concepts, including number of restaurant seats, lot square footage, and building square footage. Fourth, we measured the available marketing activity during the time that our guest-satisfaction survey was conducted. Included here were weekly data on TV and radio advertising by market, direct marketing activity, number of free-standing inserts (FSIs), and outdoor marketing activity. Although we attempted to gather monthly data on unemployment rates, Consumer Price Index, and hourly wage rates, these data are not available at a level that coincides with the restaurants' locations, except for the unemployment rate. Unemployment data are available by zip code from the US Department of Labor, Bureau of Labor Statistics.

Analysis and Interpretation

We constructed two separate models. The first explores the relationship of guest satisfaction with twenty-one distinct attributes of the dining experience, defined by the guest-satisfaction survey, and guests' overall intention to return to the restaurant. This is done both at an aggregate level for five major attribute groups and at a more detailed level for the entire list of fifteen attributes. The second model captures the relationship between restaurant performance (number of entrées sold) and customers' reported likelihood to return for a repeat visit (which we term the "comeback score"), along with several additional control variables described below.

Model 1: Intention to Come Back

The goal of this model is to quantify the relationship between guests' perception of each of the twenty attributes of their current dining experience and their intention to return (that is, to come back) to this restaurant in the subsequent thirty days. Data for this model were obtained from the guest-satisfaction survey. The variables in the model are defined in table 2.1.

We treat intention to come back as the dependent variable. Since this variable takes only two values (0 or 1), we employed logit models for analysis. "Model 1 Overall" uses the overall ratings of the five major attributes as explanatory variables, while "Model 1 Detailed" uses the fifteen detailed attributes within each of the five major attributes as explanatory variables. (See appendix A for the technical details of the model and its estimation procedures.)

Model Validity   The key metric for model validation here is the face validity of estimated attribute effects. We expect to see positive effects on "comeback" of each of the major attributes in Model 1 Overall, and each of the detailed attributes in Model 1 Detailed. Thus, each of the estimated model parameters is expected to be positive. We also assess statistical significance of each of the estimated parameters at the 5% level.

Interpretation of Effects   First, we define an attribute's score as the percentage of surveys in the sample that rate the attribute positively. Similarly, we define the comeback score as the percentage of surveys in the sample that are positive with respect to their intention to come back in the succeeding thirty days.

We use the elasticity of the comeback score with respect to an attribute score as the measure of how large is the effect of changes in an attribute score on the comeback score. Needless to say, whether the attribute score improves or deteriorates determines whether the elasticities are positive or negative. We distinguish between an "up elasticity" and a "down elasticity." An up elasticity of an attribute is the change in the comeback score when the attribute score improves by 1 percentage point, all other attributes remaining unchanged. For example, if the current comeback score

TABLE 2.1. Guest satisfaction survey questions and variable names for model of comeback (response categories: yes or no)

Question number	Question text	Short text	Variable name
1	When you arrived, were you greeted promptly and made to feel welcome?	Greeting: overall	G0
2	Was the greeting you received cheerful, friendly and attentive?	Greeting: cheerful friendly attentive	G1
3	And did we seat you at your table as quickly as possible?	Greeting: seated quickly	G2
4	Overall, were you pleased with the level of your service?	Service: overall	G3
5	Was the food served in a timely manner?	Service: food served in timely manner	G4
6	Was the server attentive to your needs and did they check back with you often?	Service: attentive	G5
7	Was your server's appearance neat and clean?	Service: server appearance	G6
8	Did a server approach your table promptly and offer to take your order?	Service: prompt approach and take order	G7
9	Was your server friendly?	Service: friendly	G8
10	Were you completely satisfied with the quality of your food?	Food: overall	G9
11	Was the food served exactly as you ordered it?	Food: accurate order	G10
12	And the food, was it delicious?	Food: delicious	G11
13	Was your food served at the proper temperature?	Food: temperature	G12
14	Was the presentation of the meal appealing?	Food: presentation	G13
15	Do you feel that you received a good value for the money you spent?	Value: overall	G14
16	Was the total cost appropriate for the food and service you received?	Value: cost appropriate	G15
17	Were the menu prices too high?	Value: prices too high	G16
18	Were you pleased with the amount of food you were served?	Value: food portion	G17
19	Was the interior of the restaurant clean, comfortable and inviting?	Restaurant: overall	G18
20	Was your table clean and dry?	Restaurant: table clean and dry	G19
21	Did your visit make you want to come back again soon?	Comeback	G20

is 94%, and the food overall score is 92%, an up elasticity of .30 for food overall means that if the food overall score increases to 93%, the comeback score is predicted to increase to 94.3%. A down elasticity is defined analogously as the predicted impact on comeback score of a 1 percentage point decrease in the attribute score. Up and down elasticities are computed by simulation, separately for each attribute. Elasticities can be compared across attributes to assess the relative importance of attributes' effects on comeback.

Model 2: Restaurant Performance and Comeback

Next we develop a model to assess the impact of the comeback score on restaurant performance. The performance of each restaurant is measured using weekly guest counts, that is, the number of entrées sold on each business day, summed within each week. Comeback score is computed as the average score within each restaurant for each week, to make the data comparable with guest counts. To illustrate, a comeback score for a particular restaurant equaling 90% would mean that 90% of the respondents in a particular week reported that they intended to come back in the following thirty days.

We considered the following key issues in developing the model:

1. We expect that the guest count in any restaurant-week is affected by the comeback scores in the same restaurant-week, as well as in several recent weeks. The number of prior weeks that is relevant depends on the intervisit frequency of restaurant guests, which is not known from these data files. After some trial and error, we concluded that up to seven prior weeks of comeback scores may influence the guest count in any week. It is possible that comeback scores older than seven weeks might also affect guest counts, but a longer time-series of data than were available to us would be needed to model such effects reliably.

   We aggregate the lagged comeback scores (that is, the scores in prior weeks) into two variables, as follows. The average comeback score over the current week (call it week t) and the past three weeks (weeks t-1, t-2, and t-3) is called lag_comeback_1. The average comeback score over the four weeks preceding week t-3 (namely, weeks t-4, t-5, t-6, and t-7) is called lag_comeback_2. These two variables are among those that we used to predict guest counts in week t.

2. To allow for nonlinearity in the possible effects, we specified a multiplicative model (also called log-log). In this model, the effects of log(lag_comeback_1) and log(lag_comeback_2) on log(guest counts) are linear. (Details of this model are provided in appendix B.)

3. Because of the client's organization structure, we developed separate models for the company's three restaurant divisions (concepts A, B, and C). Within each of these groups, data are pooled across restaurants to estimate the model, since there is insufficient data at the restaurant level for reliable estimation of model effects. Restaurant characteristics, such as number of seats and lot square footage, are included in the model to control for differences in guest counts arising from these differences.

   Since we expect local prosperity to be related to the decision to eat out in a restaurant, the model included the effects of monthly unemployment rates for the zip code in which a restaurant appears. While the estimated effect was as we expected (that is, higher local unemployment is correlated with lower restaurant guest counts), data for April 2006 were unavailable. As a consequence, we omitted unemployment rates in the final model.

4. Differences in guest counts over time may also arise due to marketing activities. Therefore, we include in the models TV and radio advertising as well as free-standing insert (FSI) and direct marketing (DM) activities.

Marketing Activities   Data on the following four types of marketing activities were available to us for each restaurant-week: TV total rating points (TRPs), radio TRPs, drop of an FSI, and drop of a DM piece. The marketing data are merged with the guest-count data. For each of the marketing activities, we also know the effective weeks. For instance, an FSI may have carried a coupon that was valid for four weeks. Each marketing initiative is defined as being "active" in each week it was effective. Although in certain weeks there may be more than one FSI or more than one DM piece, we define these two promotional activities to be binary—each activity is either present or it is absent. We had no way to measure the quality or effectiveness of any given FSI or DM piece.

Effects of radio and TV advertising on guest counts are assumed to persist for up to four weeks from the time of the campaign. In the model, this is accommodated by allowing guest counts in week t to be influenced by values of TV TRPs and radio TRPs in weeks t, t-1, t-2, and t-3. To that end, we created the following two variables for TV: TV1, which is the sum of TV TRPs for weeks t and t-1, and TV2, which is the sum of TV TRPs for weeks t-2 and t-3. We did the same thing for radio.

In future modeling efforts, it may be useful to include the characteristics or attributes of different marketing instruments, such as campaign details for TV and radio and the face value of coupons for FSI or DM pieces. However, currently these more detailed marketing attributes were not available to us. Not all marketing activities were employed for all three restaurant groups. Concept A restaurants did not have DM activity, concept B did not purchase radio advertising, and concept C did not use TV advertising or DM. The model specifications for the three groups of restaurants are accordingly different. (Again, see appendix B for the technical details of the model and its estimation procedures.)

The variables in the model are as follows:

- Guest_count: The average daily number of entrées sold (note that the model is based on weekly data, but this variable is defined as daily guest counts);
- Lag_comeback_1: The average comeback score in weeks t, t-1, t-2, and t-3;
- Lag_comeback_2: The average comeback score in weeks t-4, t-5, t-6, and t-7;
- TV1: The sum of TV TRPs in weeks t and t-1;
- TV2: The sum of TV TRPs in weeks t-2 and t-3.;
- Radio1: The sum of radio TRPs in weeks t and t-1;
- Radio2: The sum of radio TRPs in weeks t-2 and t-3;
- FSI: 1 if there was at least one active FSI in week t, 0 otherwise; and
- DM: 1 if there was at least one active DM piece in week t, 0 otherwise.

Model Validity   We assessed the validity of each model via the overall fit of the model (R2 and F-statistic), face validity of estimated parameters, and statistical significance of the estimated parameters. In terms of face validity, we expect all estimated effects to be positive.

Interpretation of Effects   In the multiplicative model, the estimated effects of lag_comeback_1 and lag_comeback_2 are interpretable as elasticities.

Thus, δ1 is an estimate of the percentage change in daily guest_ count in week t when lag_come-back_1 changes by 1%. (Note that this definition of an elasticity is slightly different from the elasticity in the logit model.) Similarly, γ1 through γ4 are elasticities of the various TV and radio TRPs. Since FSI and DM are binary (or, indicator) variables that only take values 0 or 1, their effects are interpreted differently. In particular, exp(γ5) is a multiplier that measures the multiplicative factor by which guest_count is predicted to increase when FSI is 1 compared with when FSI is 0. Similarly, exp(γ6) is the multiplier for DM. For ease of interpretation, we translate all elasticities into incremental guest counts, relative to the current average guest count.

Results

We have 80,845 surveys available in the sample. In figure 2.1 we show the average response to the five overall attribute questions, while in figure 2.2 we show the results of the fifteen detailed attribute questions, along with the question on intention to come back. As shown in figure 2.1, approximately 95% of guests responded that their visit made them "want to come back in the next 30 days."

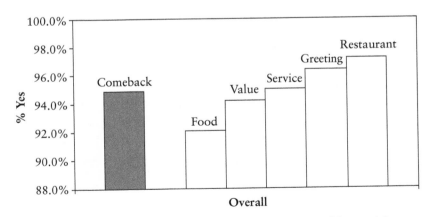

Figure 2.1. Mean overall attributes. *Note:* The interpretation of the remaining attributes is the same. For the overall attributes, "overall food quality" has the lowest satisfaction level (92%), while a "clean, comfortable and inviting restaurant" has the highest satisfaction ratings (97%).

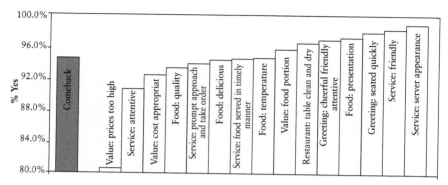

Figure 2.2. Mean specific attributes

For the overall attributes, "overall food quality" has the lowest satisfaction level (92%), while "a clean, comfortable and inviting restaurant" has the highest satisfaction ratings (97%). For the detailed attributes, the value-attribute measuring the perceived value in the level of menu prices scored lowest in respondent satisfaction (80.5%), while the attribute describing server appearance as being "neat and clean" recorded the highest satisfaction rating (greater than 98%).[1]

In table 2.2 we show descriptive statistics of the three restaurant groups. Concept A is the leader in several of these key measurements. It has the largest number of restaurants of the three groups (145), the largest average guest count per day (496), the largest average sales per day per restaurant, and the greatest seating capacity measured in average number of seats per restaurant (165). However, despite having a smaller daily guest count and smaller average daily restaurant sales, concept B has both a larger average lot size (49,027 sq. ft.) and a larger average building size (4,307 sq. ft.). Except for average building size and weeks with active FSIs, concept C has the lowest numbers of all three groups. It has fewer restaurants (48), fewer customers per day (323), lower average daily sales ($3,113), fewer seats per restaurant (4,218), and smaller lot size (27,637 sq. ft.).

Marketing activity is allocated quite differently across the three restaurant divisions. Concept B displays more advertising intensity relative to the other two concepts. Concept B uses about three-quarters more (76%) TV TRPs in an average week than does concept A (264 vs. 150), while

TABLE 2.2. Descriptive statistics of the restaurant data

	Concept A	Concept B	Concept C
Number of restaurants	145	104	48
Average guest count per day per restaurant	496	360	323
Average sales ($) per day per restaurant	3,984	3,220	3,113
Average number of seats (range)	165 (96–220)	152 (106–208)	144 (94–230)
Average lot size (square feet)	33,462	49,027	27,637
Average building size (square feet)	3,833	4,307	4,218
Average weekly TV TRPs	150	264	0
Average weekly radio TRPs	15	0	10
Percentage of weeks with active FSIs	37.7	80.0	83.5
Percentage of weeks with active DM pieces	0	20.9	0

Note: TRPs = total rating points; FSI = free-standing inserts; DM = direct marketing.

concept C uses no TV at all. Moreover, concept B exhibits over twice the FSI frequency of concept A (80.0% of weeks with active FSIs versus 37.7%), while concept C is higher still at 83.5% of weeks with active FSIs. Additionally, concept B relies on various direct mail promotions (20.9% of weeks record an active DM activity), while the other two regions do not employ DM marketing. The one exception where concept B is not the most advertising intensive is in radio advertising. Concept B employs no radio advertising while concept A and concept C use modest amounts (15 TRPs for concept A and 10 TRPs for concept C).

Overall Comeback Score

All five overall attributes have positive and significant effects on the comeback score. The significance of effects is particularly impressive because of the limited range of variation of attribute perceptions, as indicated in figures 2.1 and 2.2 (e.g., the maximum proportion of negative responses in figure 2.2

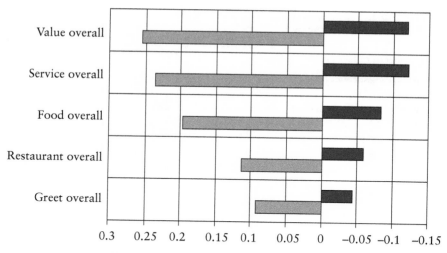

Figure 2.3. Up (shaded light) and down (shaded dark) elasticities of comeback: Overall attributes

is 8%). In figure 2.3 we show the elasticities of the five attributes. Effectively, these elasticities measure the responsiveness of overall comeback scores to changes in the overall attributes. Thus, when the elasticity of value overall is .26, for instance, the overall comeback score is predicted to increase from the current 95% to 95.26%. By the same token, when the elasticity is –.12, we expect the overall comeback score to decrease from 95% to 94.88%). It is worthwhile noting that the order of magnitude for "up and down" elasticities is the same. Whether the attribute score is increased or decreased by 1 percentage point, the magnitude of change in the overall comeback score is greatest for overall value, followed by services overall, food overall, restaurant overall, and greeting overall.

Effects of Detailed Attributes on Intent to Return

All fifteen detailed attributes have statistically, significant effects on the comeback score. As shown in figure 2.4, elasticities of the detailed attributes are interpreted in the same manner as with the overall attributes. When the elasticity of "food delicious" is .26, for instance, the overall comeback score is predicted to increase from the current 95% to 95.26%.

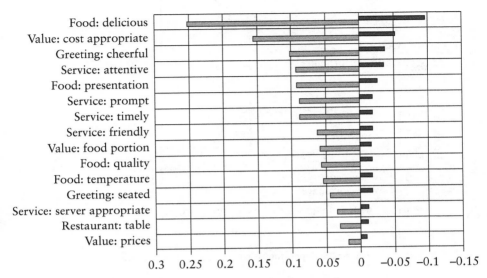

Figure 2.4. Up (shaded light) and down (shaded dark) elasticities of comeback:
Detailed attributes

A down elasticity works in the same way. If the elasticity is –.09 for "food delicious," we expect the likelihood of returning to decline from 95% to 94.91%. We note that "food delicious" has the greatest elasticity values at .26 and –.09, and the "value: cost appropriate" is not far behind with elasticity values of .16 and –.06. In contrast, the attribute with the smallest elasticity in either direction is "value: prices" at .02 and –.01.

Our results allow us to combine two of our key findings—satisfaction levels and elasticities—into an opportunity matrix, as shown in figure 2.5. This 2 × 2 matrix locates the detailed attributes according to how satisfied guests are with each particular attribute—we call this performance—and the elasticity associated with each, which is a measure of how guest count responds to an attribute.

Placement of each attribute in one of the quadrants of this matrix shows at a glance areas in need of improvement, or opportunity. For example, the satisfaction rating of "food: delicious" is a little less than average (below 95% shown by the vertical arrow) but the elasticity is quite high (.26), placing the attribute in the quadrant of low performance–high responsiveness.

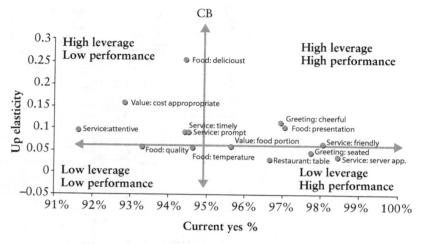

Figure 2.5. Opportunity matrix. *Note:* CB=comeback.

Thus, efforts to improve the performance of "food: delicious" may represent an area of opportunity for restaurants since guest-count responsiveness is strong. Conversely, server appearance is associated with quite a high level of satisfaction as reported by guests (98.5%) but the guest-count responsiveness is quite low (.04). Further improvements in server appearance are not likely to generate much response in overall guest counts.

Results of Model 2

In table 2.3 we show parameter estimates of model 2 for each of the three restaurant groups. These are the estimated effects of changes in each variable on restaurant performance (measured as average daily number of entrées sold, which we call guest counts). The confidence that we can have in these estimates is in part indicated by the extent to which each of these independent variables is a significant predictor of guest counts. We can be reasonably certain that the most significant of these predictors, indicated in bold (significant at a 5% level), really make a difference in guest counts. For example, in the concept B model, six of the eight variables are highly significant predictors of restaurant guest counts. Because our sample was quite large—at least for concept A and concept B—small differences in the reported numbers can be detected as influencing guest counts.

TABLE 2.3. Untransformed parameter estimates (and standard errors) of model 2

	Concept A	Concept B	Concept C
Log(lag_comeback_1)	.307 (.080)	.411 (.208)	−.100 (.104)
Log(lag_comeback_2)	.301 (.082)	.327 (.117)	.010 (.100)
Log(TV1+1)	*.010 (.005)*	**.011 (.004)**	—
Log(TV2+1)	−.002 (.003)	**.010 (.003)**	—
Log(radio1+1)	.008 (.011)	—	.001 (.007)
Log(radio2+1)	−.014 (.009)	—	−.004 (.007)
FSI	−.025 (.027)	−.001 (.027)	**.087 (.032)**
DM	—	.026 (.022)	—
Log(seats)	*.077 (.042)*	**.213 (.040)**	*.123 (.057)*
Log(lot_sqft)	.001 (.001)	**.021 (.002)**	.003 (.004)
Number of observations	3,082	2,377	953

Note: Bold = most reliable (significant at 5 percent). Italics = less reliable (significant at 10 percent). Neither italics nor bold = least reliable (not significant at 10 percent). FSI = free-standing insert; DM = direct marketing.

Considering only statistically significant effects, we can now predict the effects of a 1-percentage-point increase in the comeback score on guest counts as follows. In the average concept A restaurant, the guest count is predicted to increase by 1,100 per year, which is computed as the average guest count per day (see table 2.2) times the elasticity of comeback (496 × 0.608% = 0.307 + 0.301; see table 2.3) times 365 days in a year. Analogously, in the average concept B restaurant, the guest count is predicted to increase by 970 per year, which is computed as the average guest count per day (see table 2.2) times the elasticity of comeback (360 × 0.738% = 0.411 + 0.327; see table 2.3) times 365 days in a year. The estimated effects of the comeback score on guest counts in concept C restaurants are not statistically reliable.

The effects of TV advertising on guest counts can be quantified in a similar fashion. We consider the impact of a 10% increase in TV TRPs on guest counts. For concept A restaurants, only TV1 has a significant effect. Taking the effect of TV2 to be zero, we predict that the increase in guest counts for the average restaurants will be 181 per year, which is given by the average guest count per day (see table 2.2) times the elasticity of TV1 times the 10% increase in TV TRPs (496 × 0.010% × 10%;

see table 2.3) times 365 days in a year. Similarly, for the average concept B restaurant, the predicted increase in guest count per year is 276, which is computed as the average guest count per day (see table 2.2) times the elasticity of TV (360 × 0.021% = 0.011 + 0.010; see table 2.3) times 365 days in a year.

The effects of radio advertising are found to be statistically insignificant in both concept A and concept B restaurants. The multiplier effect of an additional effective FSI week is computed for the average concept C restaurant as 1.091 (= exp[0.087]; see table 2.3). This implies that daily guest count in a restaurant is predicted to increase on a one-time basis by 9.1% with the insertion of an additional FSI week in the media plan. The effects of direct marketing are uniformly not significant.

Managerial Implications and Further Work

The chief implication for this chain's three restaurant concepts is that its managers need to stick to the knitting. The factors that had the greatest influence on whether a guest would return are those at the core of restaurant operation, namely, delicious food, an appropriate cost, a cheerful greeting, and attentive service. Doing well on these factors, particularly serving delicious food at an appropriate cost, has the almost certain effect of encouraging your guests to return. Failure on these attributes does not seem fatal but will certainly diminish the likelihood that a guest will return.

More to the point, our study has quantified the connection between intent to return and actual traffic counts. Even considering the caveat that our data cover a relatively brief time span, our models show that this relationship is distinct for each restaurant concept, and we can offer no blanket rule. One restaurant concept alone (concept A) could count on gaining another 1,100 customer visits per year just by boosting its customers' comeback score by 1 percentage point. While this is a seemingly modest 0.6% increase in traffic, or an average of about $25.00 per day, this still means an increase of approximately $1.3 million ($25 × 145 restaurants × 365 days) just from ensuring an excellent performance that will boost intent to return.

Looking at the opportunity matrix, it is clear that this restaurant company has the possibility of taking advantage of our findings, because its performance was low for appropriate cost and attentive service, and it could pay more attention to its food quality.

Further Study

The data provided for this study were rich and allowed for the analysis reported here. However, the complexities of the models, particularly the sales-performance model (model 2), require data over a longer period of time than were available to us. With longer series of data, we could produce more robust models and gain greater insight into a restaurant's strategic options. Moreover, in the future, opportunities exist to improve the data quality by modifications to the guest-satisfaction survey design.

Appendix A: Model Specification and Estimation

The mathematical form of Model 1: Overall is as follows:

$$\text{Prob(comeback} = 1) = \exp(\alpha + \beta 1 F0 + \beta 2 S0 + \beta 3 R0 + \beta 4 V0 + \beta 5 G0) \; 1 + \exp(\alpha + \beta 1 F0 + \beta 2 S0 + \beta 3 R0 + \beta 4 V0 + \beta 5 G0) \text{ and}$$
$$\text{Prob(comeback} = 0) = 1 - \text{Prob(comeback} = 1).$$

The mathematical form of Model 1: Detailed is analogous, with the fifteen detailed attributes taking the place of the overall attributes as explanatory variables.

The parameters of these models are estimated by pooling data across surveys. Thus, if there are N complete surveys available, there are N observations in the data set used to estimate each of the two models. The estimation method we employed is maximum likelihood.

Appendix B: Model Specification

The general form of the multiplicative model for guest counts is as follows:

$$\text{Guest\_countrt} = \alpha(\text{lag\_comeback\_1rt})\delta 1(\text{lag\_ comeback\_2rt})\delta 2$$
$$(\text{TV1rt} + 1)\gamma 1 \; (\text{TV2rt} + 1)\gamma 2(\text{Radio1rt} + 1)\gamma 3 \; (\text{Radio2rt} + 1)$$
$$\gamma 4(\gamma 5)\text{FSIrt}(\gamma 6)\text{DMrt(Seatsr)}\tau 1 \; (\text{Lot\_sqftr})\tau 2$$

where the subscript r indicates restaurant r, and subscript t indicates week t. As noted previously, specific marketing activities are omitted in the models for each of the three restaurant groups.

We transform, or log-linearize, the model by taking natural logarithm of both sides of the model. Data are pooled across restaurants and weeks, within each restaurant group. The parameters of the model are estimated using ordinary least squares.

Notes

Original citation: Gupta, S., McLaughlin, E., & Gomez, M. (2007). Guest satisfaction and restaurant performance. *Cornell Hospitality Quarterly 28*(3): 284–298.

1. For the attribute "prices: too high," the "no" responses are shown in figure 2.2, in contrast with all other attributes for which the proportion of "yes" responses is shown.

References

Andaleeb, S.S., & Conway, C. (2006). Customer satisfaction in the restaurant industry: An examination of the transaction-specific model. *Journal of Services Marketing, 20*(1): 3–11.

Anderson, E. W., Fornell, C., & Rust, R. T. (1997). Customer satisfaction, productivity, and profitability: Differences between goods and services. *Marketing Science, 16*(2): 129–145.

Bernhardt, K. L., Donthu, N., & Kennett, P. A. (2000). A longitudinal analysis of satisfaction and profitability. *Journal of Business Research, 47*(2): 161–171.

Cheng, K. (2005). A research on the determinants of consumers' repurchase toward different classes of restaurants in Taiwan. *Business Review, 4*(2): 99–105.

Clark, M. A., & Wood, R. C. (1998). Consumer loyalty in the restaurant industry—A preliminary exploration of the issues. *International Journal of Contemporary Hospitality Management, 10*(4): 139–144.

Davis, M. M., & Vollmann, T. A. (1990). A framework for relating waiting time and customer satisfaction in a service operation. *Journal of Services Marketing, 4*(1), 61–69.

Dubé, L., Renaghan, L. M., & Miller, J. M. (1994). Measuring customer satisfaction for strategic management. *Cornell Hotel and Restaurant Administration Quarterly, 35*(1): 39–47.

Fitzsimmons, J. A., & Maurer, G. B. (1991). A walk-through audit to improve restaurant performance. *Cornell Hotel and Restaurant Administration Quarterly, 31*(4): 94–99.

Heskett, J. L., Jones, T. O., Loveman, G. W., Sasser, W. E., & Schlesinger, L. A. (2004). Putting the service-profit chain to work. *Harvard Business Review, 72*(2): 164–174.

Iglesias, M. P., & Yague, M. J. (2004). Perceived quality and price: Their impact on the satisfaction of restaurant customers. *International Journal of Contemporary Hospitality Management, 16*(6): 373–379.

Kivela, J., Inbakaran, R., & Reece, J. (2000). Consumer research in the restaurant environment, part 3, Analysis, findings, and conclusions. *International Journal of Contemporary Hospitality Management, 12*(1): 13–30.

Knutson, B. J. (1988). Ten laws of customer satisfaction. *Cornell Hotel and Restaurant Administration Quarterly, 29*(3): 14–17.

Mittal, V., & Kamakura, W. A. (2001). Satisfaction, repurchase intent, and repurchase behavior: Investigating the moderating effect of customer characteristics. *Journal of Marketing Research, 38*(1): 131–142.

Rust, R. T., & Zahorik, A. J. (1993). Customer satisfaction, customer retention, and market share. *Journal of Retailing, 69*(2): 193–215.

Söderlund, M., & Öhman, N. (2005). Assessing behavior before it becomes behavior: An examination of the role of intentions as a link between satisfaction and repatronizing behavior. *International Journal of Service Industry Management, 16*(2): 169–185.

Sulek, J. J., & Hensley, R. L. (2004). The relative importance of food, atmosphere, and fairness of wait: The case of a full-service restaurant. *Cornell Hotel and Restaurant Administration Quarterly, 45*(3): 235–247.

3

The Relationship of Service Providers' Perceptions of Service Climate to Guest Satisfaction, Return Intentions, and Firm Performance

Alex M. Susskind, K. Michele Kacmar, and Carl P. Borchgrevink

Researchers have a continuing interest in uncovering ways to better understand the connection between service workers, guests, and organizational outcomes. In service-based organizations, employees and guests cocreate the service experience, which consists of both tangible and intangible factors (Mayer, Ehrhart, & Schneider, 2009; Schneider, White, & Paul, 1998). This set of interactions in the cocreation of service experiences has been framed and developed in several ways by researchers. First, the evolution of exchanging goods and services in a service-based economy has been well defined by Vargo and Lusch (2004). In their work, Vargo and Lusch identified how intangible elements of product and service delivery have become more important to businesses and how the cocreation of value and relationship building with consumers has moved to the forefront in our economy. Second, the service-profit chain (Heskett, Jones, Loveman, Sasser, & Schlesinger, 1994) posits that profitability for a firm emerges from customer loyalty, which is a product of employee productivity, employee satisfaction, and employee commitment to their work. Finally, the guest-server exchange (GSX; Susskind, Kacmar, & Borchgrevink, 2003, 2018) shows that a positive climate for service is connected to guest satisfaction and ultimately firm performance.

Research examining the GSX, broadly defined, has considered (a) employees' reactions to guest service episodes (Bitner, Booms, & Mohr, 1994), (b) service or guest orientation (Brady & Cronin, 2001), (c) organizational factors and boundary conditions that influence guest service processes and perceptions of a climate for service (Hong, Liao, Hu, & Jiang, 2013; Mayer et al., 2009; Schneider et al., 1998; Shaw, Dineen, Fang, & Vellella, 2009; Susskind et al., 2003, 2018; Vandenberghe et al., 2007), (d) the connection between employee and guest affect (Schneider, Ehrhart, Mayer, Saltz, & Niles-Jolly, 2005; Susskind et al., 2003; Vandenberghe et al., 2007), and to a lesser extent, (e) the relationship between guest evaluations of service experiences and the connection to firm financial performance (Anderson, Fornell, & Mazvancheryl, 2004; Emery & Barker, 2007; Grizzle, Lee, Zablah, Brown, & Mowen, 2009; Hong et al., 2013; Schneider et al., 2005; Susskind et al., 2018; Zeithaml, 2000).

To consolidate our understanding of the research in this domain, Hong et al. (2103) conducted a meta-analysis to better define the elements that affect and are outcomes of a service climate. Hong et al. (2013) found that a service climate was driven mainly by HR practices and company leadership, such that the foundations of how a company does business is a key driver of service climate. We view these dimensions as similar to standards for service in the GSX. Hong et al. (2013) also found that employee attitudes and service performance emerge from a service climate and influence customer satisfaction. Again, we view this portion of the model similar to the connection of guest orientation and guest satisfaction in the GSX (Susskind et al., 2003, 2018). The last portion of the model in Hong et al. (2013) showed a connection between customer satisfaction and financial outcomes for the firm. This portion of the model is also consistent with the GSX model (Susskind et al., 2018).

Although many studies have looked at a combination of service providers' reactions to their work, guests' reactions to service experiences, and the relationship to firm performance in one way or another, very few studies have examined all three elements concurrently (employees, guests, and financial performance). With the 58 studies used by Hong et al. (2013) for their meta-analysis, only four studies measured employees,

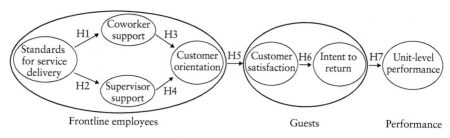

Figure 3.1. Hypothesized model of the guest service process and firm outcomes

guests, and financial performance concurrently. In addition, we found that the majority of the research in this domain is relying on proxies of organizational financial performance, not true financial performance (cf. Rego, Morgan, & Fornell, 2013; Schneider et al., 2005; Yavas, Babakus, & Ashill, 2010).

To address this gap in the current literature, we replicate and extend the GSX model (cf. Susskind et al., 2003, 2018) by concurrently measuring employees' reactions to a climate for service, guests' reactions to their service experience, and unit-level performance represented as sales. Specifically, in our replication and extension, we measure a climate for service (cf. Schulte, Ostroff, Shmulyian, & Kinicki, 2009) as the combination of (a) known standards for service, (b) support functions for service, and (c) guest orientation among line-level service providers. We then examine the connection between service providers' perceptions of their climate for service and their guests' satisfaction and intentions to return. Finally, we examine the connection between guests' reactions to their service experiences and firm performance represented as unit-level sales. These proposed relationships are presented as figure 3.1 and build upon the work of Susskind et al. (2003, 2018) and Schneider et al. (2005) and are based on the meta-analytic findings of Hong et al. (2013).

Replicating and Extending the GSX

Of particular interest are two new links added to the GSX model that have not been tested. Specifically, previous marketing research has shown a connection between customer satisfaction and repurchase intentions

(Anderson & Sullivan, 1993; Gupta, McLaughlin, & Gomez, 2007; Mittal & Kamakura, 2001; Rust, Zahorik, & Keiningham, 1995), and several studies have shown that repurchase behavior was a stronger predictor of firm performance than customer satisfaction (Gupta & Zeithaml, 2006; Kamakura, Mittal, de Rosa, & Mazzon, 2002; Towler, Lezotte, & Burke, 2011). In an effort to further clarify the relationship between guest outcomes and firm performance, we propose that guests' return intentions are directly connected to firm performance and hence mediate the relationship between guest satisfaction and unit-level sales.

Method

Participants and Procedure

We surveyed 990 servers and bartenders working in 80 full-service restaurants of a chain restaurant company based in the southeastern United States. We sampled an average of 12.38 employees from each restaurant. The 80 restaurants we examined ranged from 160 to 210 seats in size (M = 196.70, SD = 10.07), with monthly sales per seat (using a 3-month average) ranging from US$740.00 to US$1,610.56 (M = US$979.97, SD = US$186.52).

The participants were 55% female, between the ages of 17 years and 50 years (M = 23.87, SD = 6.03), having worked for the company when surveyed on average 22.31 months. We gathered guest outcome data at the unit level through the responses of 879 guests, producing an average of 10.98 guests sampled per restaurant. The responses from the guests were aggregated to the unit level along with the responses from employees and combined with the monthly sales per seat from each of the 80 restaurants.

We sampled line-level employees during their work shifts by asking them to complete a questionnaire regarding their attitudes and perceptions of their work and work environment. We visited the restaurants on several subsequent occasions to capture the guest outcome data, and we received the unit-level sales data for the appropriate time period from the corporate headquarters after we secured the employee and guest data. Employees and guests were not matched to a specific service experience.

Measurement and Analyses

Line-Level Employees   Using the survey measures developed by Susskind et al. (2003), we evaluated the line-level employees' perceptions of standards for service delivery (α = .82), coworker support (α = .94), supervisory support (α = .95), and guest orientation (α = .84). The participants were asked to indicate their level of agreement with each question on a five-choice metric with anchors ranging from strongly agree = 5 to strongly disagree = 1. All the employee survey measures were aggregated to the unit level. A sample standards for service item is "In the organization I work for, we set very high standards for guest service," a sample coworker support item is "I find my coworkers very helpful in performing my guest service duties," a sample supervisory support item is "I find my supervisor very helpful in performing my guest service duties," and a sample guest orientation item is "When performing my job, the guest is most important to me."

Guests   Guest satisfaction was measured using six items developed by Susskind et al. (2003) using the five-choice response categories applied to the scales completed by the employees (α = .95). A sample guest satisfaction item is "Overall, I am happy with the service I just received." Guests' intent to return was measured with a single item asking them their intent to return to the restaurant within the next 30 days, on 5-point scale with 1 = definitely will not return, 2 = probably would not return, 3 = not sure, 4 = probably will return, and 5 = definitely will return. As with the guest satisfaction items, the single-item measure was aggregated to the unit level. The complete list of survey items used in our study can be found in Susskind et al. (2003, 2018).

Data Aggregation   In their study, Hong et al. (2013) reported that the level of analysis (i.e., team, branch/unit) did not moderate service climate variables and the outcomes, suggesting that the level of analysis chosen should match the data and sample. To inform our decision about testing our model at the unit level, we calculated and examined the intraclass correlations, ICC(1) and ICC(2), of the variables in the model. The ICC(1) estimates the proportion of variance in the participants that could be accounted for through differences in their unit affiliation and the ICC(2) estimates the reliability of measurement at the unit level (Bliese, 2000).

The ICC(1) and ICC(2) levels were consistent with estimates reported in prior studies of this type (cf. Lam & Mayer, 2014; Schneider et al., 2005): ICC(1) = .17 and ICC(2) = .73 for standards for service delivery, ICC(1) = .20 and ICC(2) = .69 for coworker support, ICC(1) = .24 and ICC(2) = .62 for supervisor support, and ICC(1) = .22 and ICC(2) = .85 for guest orientation.

Similarly, the guest satisfaction and intent to return data showed that the guests' responses across the 80 restaurants were well suited to aggregation, indicating a high level of unit-level agreement, ICC (1) = .23, ICC (2) = .84 and ICC (1) = .19, ICC (2) = .88. The descriptive statistics and correlations of the variables aggregated to the unit level are reported in table 3.1. Based on these analyses, we aggregated the data to the unit level.

Structural Equation Modeling The model presented as figure 3.1 was estimated using LISREL 8.12a (Jöreskog & Sörbom, 1993), with a maximum likelihood routine based on a covariance matrix. To account for measurement error, we fixed the proportion of error variance assigned to each factor based on the scale reliabilities and the relevant variance associated with each factor (Hayduk, 1987). Specifically, we set (a) the paths from the latent variables to the indicators as the square root of the scale reliability at the unit level and (b) the error variance to the variance of the scale multiplied by one minus the reliability. We allowed the error terms

TABLE 3.1. Descriptive statistics and correlations from the final aggregated scales at the unit level. (N = 80.)

	M	SD	(1)	(2)	(3)	(4)	(5)	(6)	(7)
1. Standards for service delivery	3.66	.37	—						
2. Coworker support	3.80	.42	.62**	—					
3. Supervisor support	3.55	.45	.38**	.36**	—				
4. Guest orientation	4.29	.37	.63**	.69**	.34**	—			
5. Guest satisfaction	3.52	.97	.45**	.61**	.34**	.68**	—		
6. Intent to return	3.50	1.01	.45**	.55**	.35**	.66**	.90**	—	
7. Unit-level sales (per seat)	979.97	186.52	.35**	.38**	.13	.45**	.60**	.68**	—

$**p < .01$.

to correlate among those specified in the model with no unspecified relationships in the path model correlated in the model.

Results

The initial model estimation revealed that the fully mediated hypothesized model produced a very good fit to the data ($\chi 2[14] = 14.62$, p = .40). The fit statistics confirmed the nonsignificant $\chi 2$ result, comparative fit index (CFI) = .99, normed fit index (NFI) = .96, root mean square error approximation (RMSEA) = .02. All of the paths were positive and significant at the p < .01 level with the exception of the path between supervisory support and guest orientation (H4). Sampling error analysis revealed no unspecified links in the model that warranted further consideration. Based on the findings of Susskind et al. (2003, 2018) and Hong et al. (2013), we did not test for effects moderation in the model as their research identified that the variables under study here were best represented as mediated.

Employees reporting high levels of standards for service delivery indicated a strong presence of both coworker (path = .88, p < .001) and supervisor support (path = .58, p < .01), providing support for Hypothesis 1 and Hypothesis 2. The relationship between coworker support and guest orientation was strong and significant (path = .89, p < .001; supporting Hypothesis 3), whereas the relationship between supervisory support and guest orientation was not significant (path = .02, ns; not supporting Hypothesis 4). Service employees' guest orientation was strongly and significantly related to guest satisfaction (path = .77, p < .001), supporting Hypothesis 5. Hypothesis 6 was supported as guest satisfaction was strongly and significantly related to guests' intention to return to the restaurant in the next 30 days (path = .99, p < .001). Finally, guests' intention to return was significantly connected to unit-level sales (path = .74, p < .001), supporting Hypothesis 7. In the model, the R2 =.55 for unit-level sales, showing guests' reported intention to return explained 55% of the variance in sales. Finally, "a necessary component of mediation is a statistically and practically significant indirect effect" (Preacher & Hayes, 2004, p. 717). In figure 3.2, the indirect path from standards, through coworker support, guest orientation, guest satisfaction, and return intentions to sales per seat was significant (.45, p < .05), further supporting the

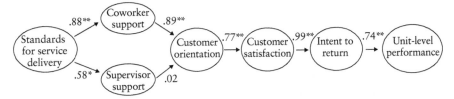

Figure 3.2. Estimated model of guest service process and firm outcomes. *Note:* Path coefficients presented are completely standardized and all links in the model were tested at the organizational level. *$p < .05$. **$p < .01$.

mediated model. The indirect effect through supervisory support in the model was not significant, consistent with prior tests of the GSX (Susskind et al., 2018).

Discussion

In this investigation, we studied a set of frontline-level employees, guests, and sales data from 80 full-service restaurants within a single chain restaurant company. Through our study, we were able to confirm and extend the findings of Susskind et al. (2003, 2018) and Hong et al. (2013), showing that line-level employees' positive perceptions of a service climate bundle were connected to guests' positive perceptions of their service experience, framed as a guest experience climate bundle, which were ultimately connected to unit-level sales.

Our study revealed a few notable findings. First, we have confirmed the GSX model and the employee-driven service climate bundle presented in Susskind et al. (2018), showing that standards for service delivery, support from peers and supervisors,[1] and guest orientation as the foundation of guest service delivery. As noted above, it also can be inferred from these findings that standards for service create the starting point for coworkers and supervisors to offer supportive behaviors, and then each type of support takes on a different function in creating and executing a service experience for guests.

Second, as an extension to the GSX, guest satisfaction mediated the relationship between guest orientation and guests' intent to return to the restaurant. Based on role theory, this finding shows that as service providers embrace their role in providing service, they are better able to provide their guests with a satisfying service experience, which is then connected to the guests' interest in returning to the restaurant. The addition of return intentions is a notable extension of the research on service climate and guests' reactions to service experiences and shows that a second-service climate bundle exists for guests. Previous studies, with few exceptions (cf. Gupta et al., 2007), have stopped short after measuring guest satisfaction. Understanding the influence of return intentions brings us one step closer to better understanding organizational performance of service organizations, as return intentions offer a more direct assessment of guests' future behavior, or at least their intentions for future behavior (planned behavior).

Finally, with the addition of return intentions and unit-level sales to the GSX model, we have been able to demonstrate that guests' return intentions mediate the relationship between guest satisfaction and unit-level sales. This shows that satisfied guests reported that they are more likely to return to the restaurant, which is then associated with higher unit-level sales.

The extended GSX model shows the mediated relationships presented in figure 3.2 is a sound representation of the data. In the GSX model, return intentions accounted for 55% of the variance in unit-level sales, which is a far greater proportion compared with studies solely looking at guest satisfaction and financial outcomes (cf. Hong et al., 2013). We show that guest satisfaction remains an important outcome of a service climate, but guests' return intentions are a better financial performance indicator.

Directions for Future Work

With the addition of guest return intentions, our extended GSX model explained 55% of the variance in unit-level sales—an improvement from the 26% captured in Susskind et al. (2018). This shows that there is still a fair amount of variance in unit-level sales we have yet to account for. These findings highlight the fact that additional influences should be included in the model to further our understanding of how service-based organizations function. Although we framed the GSX as a set of climate bundles connected to outcomes for the guest and financial outcomes, it is clear that other elements that we did not measure, such as managers' perceptions and attitudes, economic conditions, and competition, may be important to further define our model and highlight additional climate features.

Implications for Management

Our study identifies several elements important for management practice. First, it is clear that the elements of the service climate we measured among employees are strongly connected to guests' reactions regarding their experience in the restaurant. We believe, therefore, that it is important to have clearly articulated standards for service that employees can understand and use to support each other in service delivery. Likewise, as perceptions of support functions from coworkers are strongly connected to guest orientation (a key correlate of guests' satisfaction), managerial efforts to create and/or improve a supportive work environment will go a long way toward creating a guest-focused climate. Finally, we would never say that making your guests satisfied is not important; what we found, however, is that guests' intentions to return to the restaurant were a better predictor of sales than satisfaction. Therefore, management, marketing, and promotion efforts should be built around a satisfying guest experience that can drive repeat visits.

In conclusion, we were able to show how specific service climate bundles and the roles played by employees and guests as they coproduce the service experience are connected to firm performance.

Notes

Original citation: Susskind, A. M., Kacmar, K. M., & Borchgrevink, C. P. (2018). The relationship of service providers' perceptions of service climate to guest satisfaction, return intentions, and firm performance. *Cornell Hospitality Quarterly* 59(4): 390–396.

The author(s) declared no potential conflicts of interest with respect to the research, authorship, or publication of this article. The author(s) received no financial support for the research, authorship, or publication of this article.

1. Consistent with prior tests of the GSX model, supervisor support in the service climate bundle was significantly connected to standards, but not significantly connected to guest orientation.

References

Anderson, E. W., Fornell, C., & Mazvancheryl, S. (2004). Customer satisfaction and shareholder value. *Journal of Marketing*, 68: 172–185.

Anderson, E. W., & Sullivan, M. W. (1993). The antecedents and consequences of customer satisfaction for firms. *Marketing Science*, 12: 125–43.

Bitner, M. J., Booms, B. H., & Mohr, L. A. (1994). Critical service encounters: The employee's viewpoint. *Journal of Marketing, 58*: 95–106.

Bliese, P. D. (2000). Within-group agreement, non-independence, and reliability: Implications for data aggregation and analysis. In K. J. Klein and S. W. J. Kozlowski (Eds.), *Multilevel theory, research, and methods in organizations: Foundations, extensions, and new directions* (pp. 349–381). San Francisco, CA: Jossey-Bass.

Brady, M. K., & Cronin, J. J. (2001). Customer orientation: Effects on customer service perceptions and outcome behaviors. *Journal of Service Research, 3*: 241–251.

Emery, C. R., & Barker, K. J. (2007). Effect of commitment, job involvement, and teams on customer satisfaction and profit. *Team Performance Management, 13*: 90–101.

Grizzle, J., Lee, J., Zablah, A., Brown, T., & Mowen, J. (2009). Employee customer orientation in context: How the environment moderates the influence of customer orientation on performance outcomes. *Journal of Applied Psychology, 94*: 1227–1242.

Gupta, S., McLaughlin, E., & Gomez, M. (2007). Guest satisfaction and restaurant performance. *Cornell Hotel and Restaurant Administration Quarterly, 48*: 284–298.

Gupta, S., & Zeithaml, V. (2006). Customer metrics and their impact on financial performance. *Marketing Science, 25*: 718–739.

Hayduk, L. A. (1987). *Structural equation modeling with LISREL: Essentials and advances.* Baltimore, MD: Johns Hopkins University Press.

Heskett, J., Jones, T., Loveman, G., Sasser, W. Jr., & Schlesinger, L. (1994). Putting the service—profit chain to work. *Harvard Business Review, 72*: 164–174.

Hong, Y., Liao, H., Hu, J., & Jiang, K. (2013). Missing link in the service profit chain: A meta-analytic review of the antecedents, consequences, and moderators of service climate. *Journal of Applied Psychology, 98*: 237–267.

Jöreskog, K. G., & Sörbom, D. (1993). LISREL for Windows 8.12a. Chicago, IL: Scientific Software International.

Kamakura, W. A., Mittal, V., de Rosa, F., & Mazzon, J. A. (2002). Assessing the service-profit chain. *Marketing Science, 21*: 294–317.

Lam, C. F., & Mayer, D. M. (2014). When do employees speak up for their customers? A model of voice in a customer service context. *Personnel Psychology, 67*: 637–666.

Mayer, D. M., Ehrhart, M. G., & Schneider, B. (2009). Service attribute boundary conditions of the service climate-customer satisfaction link. *Academy of Management Journal, 52*: 1034–1050.

Mittal, V., & Kamakura, W. (2001). Satisfaction, repurchase intent, and repurchase behavior: Investigating the moderating effect of customer characteristics. *Journal of Marketing Research, 38*: 131–142.

Preacher, K. J., & Hayes, A. F. (2004). SPSS and SAS procedures for estimating indirect effects in simple mediation models. *Behavior Research Methods, 36*: 717–731.

Rego, L. L., Morgan, N. A., & Fornell, C. (2013). Reexamining the market share-customer satisfaction relationship. *Journal of Marketing, 77*(5): 1–20.

Rust, R., Zahorik, A. J., & Keiningham, T. L. (1995). Return on quality (ROQ): Making service quality financially accountable. *Journal of Marketing, 59*: 58–70.

Schneider, B., Ehrhart, M. G., Mayer, D. G., Saltz, J. L., & Niles- Jolly, K. (2005). Understanding organization-customer links in service settings. *Academy of Management Journal, 48*: 1017–1031.

Schneider, B., White, S. S., & Paul, M. C. (1998). Linking service climate and customer perceptions of service quality: Test of a causal model. *Journal of Applied Psychology, 83:* 150–163.

Schulte, M., Ostroff, C., Shmulyian, S., & Kinicki, A. (2009). Organizational climate configurations: Relationships to collective attitudes, customer satisfaction, and financial performance. *Journal of Applied Psychology, 94:* 618–634.

Shaw, J. D., Dineen, B. R., Fang, R., & Vellella, R. F. (2009). Employee-organization exchange relationships, HRM practices, and quit rates of good and poor performers. *Academy of Management Journal, 52:* 1016–1033.

Susskind, A. M., Kacmar, K. M., & Borchgrevink, C. P. (2003). Customer service providers' attitudes relating to customer service and customer satisfaction in the customer-server exchange (CSX). *Journal of Applied Psychology, 88:* 179–187.

Susskind, A. M., Kacmar, K. M., & Borchgrevink, C. P. (2018). Guest-server exchange model and performance: The connection between service climate and unit-level sales in multiunit restaurants. *Journal of Hospitality & Tourism Research, 42:* 122–141.

Towler, A., Lezotte, D., & Burke, M. (2011). The service climate-firm performance chain: The role of customer retention. *Human Resource Management, 50,* 391–406.

Vandenberghe, C., Bentein, K., Michon, R., Chebat, J., Tremblay, M., & Fils, J. (2007). An examination of the role of perceived support and employee commitment in employee-customer encounters. *Journal of Applied Psychology, 92:* 1177–1187.

Vargo, S. L., & Lusch, R. L. (2004). Evolving to a new dominant logic for marketing. *Journal of Marketing, 68:* 1–17.

Yavas, U., Babakus, E., & Ashill, N. (2010). Testing a branch performance model in a New Zealand bank. *Journal of Services Marketing, 24:* 369–377.

Zeithaml, V. A. (2000). Service quality, profitability, and the economic worth of customers: What we know and what we need to learn. *Journal of the Academy of Marketing Science, 28:* 67–68.

Part II

Complaint Management

A Necessary Evil and an Opportunity to Build Loyalty

Alex M. Susskind and Mark Maynard

Alex: Regardless of how well service-based organizations design, build, and execute their service processes, there will always be times when service delivery does not hit the mark and meet the expectations of guests. When expectations are not met, guests have a choice to make: they can complete and conclude their service experience without addressing the element of the service experience that did not meet their expectations, or they can tell the service provider about what did not meet their expectations. In the first case, the operator will never know what went wrong and will not be given a chance to fix the problem or problems that occurred for that guest in that particular service experience. With unresolved problems or an experience that fell short of expectations, it is likely that guests will leave dissatisfied (from part I, we know how important repeat-patronage intentions are). In the second case, a guest will communicate specifically about a part of the service experience that was not right in some way—they are lodging a complaint—and providing an opening for a resolution.

Complaints are important to manage, and it is necessary to create an environment where guests are comfortable expressing what didn't go well and wherein the staff and management are open and skilled at translating feedback into solutions to resolve unmet expectations. Let's first start by defining what a complaint is. Very simply, a complaint is a *social confrontation* that has been initiated to adjust the perceptions and/or outcomes for someone. In daily life, even the most agreeable people complain about a variety of things, to a variety of people, most of whom they know or with whom they have an established interpersonal relationship. For example, one might complain to a spouse about being late, or to children about being messy, or to friends about politics, or to coworkers or supervisors about some work-related issue. Complaints in daily life are connected to a range of issues and people.

It is important to note that, as a social confrontation, a complaint requires one party to initiate the confrontation, so complaining takes time, thought, energy, and effort. Most people complain only after they are frustrated with something and believe that it is necessary to begin a social confrontation to address the issue. Complaints from acquaintances are difficult enough to manage; what about fielding complaints from people with whom you are less familiar?

Two things make complaints in restaurants challenging for both guests and operators: (1) the timing and structure of the service experience; and (2) the temporary interpersonal connection between the guest and the service provider during the service experience. Restaurants typically serve guests who become more familiar over time as they return more frequently. These people become regular guests, the core customers of the business. Taking care of regulars cannot come at the expense of new guests, who breathe new energy into the operation. Interpersonal interaction with new guests may be for only a few minutes, but each minute matters in the long run. Either way, when a guest is not satisfied with some aspect of a service experience, he or she is likely to complain about it.

As a researcher I have always been interested to learn more about the why, what, and how of complaints in restaurants, and I will highlight and discuss two of my articles that start to answer some of these questions. The first article, "A Look at the Relationship between Service Failures, Guest Satisfaction, and Repeat-Patronage Intentions of Casual Dining Guests" (Susskind & Viccari, 2011), examines how specific dimensions of service experiences (that is, food, service, and ambiance) are connected to guests' processing of and reaction to service failures. The second article, "Communication Richness: Why Some Guest Complaints Go Right to the Top—and Others Do Not" (Susskind, 2015), applies a communication richness framework to complaints to examine the differences in how complaints are lodged by restaurant guests when they are dissatisfied with some aspect of their service experience.

Part I highlighted the importance of guest satisfaction and repeat-patronage intentions and how both elements are connected to a restaurant's success. In particular, the article by Gupta, McLaughlin, and Gomez (2007) showed that guests' satisfaction with various attributes of the restaurant experience (i.e., food, service, value) varied in how well they were perceived by the guests and were shown to have different levels of influence on repeat-patronage intentions. Because these data were collected through a standardized guest satisfaction survey for the chain restaurants, the high-performing and low-performing items were not connected to service success and service failure per se, but they were a report of the guests' satisfaction with those particular attributes of the service experience.

To dig a little deeper, in the first article, "A Look at the Relationship between Service Failures, Guest Satisfaction, and Repeat-Patronage Intentions of Casual Dining Guests," I wanted to see how specific service failures unfolded for guests after they complained and how they related to the outcomes that managers want. To do this I surveyed over 800 restaurant guests who had recently eaten a meal in a full-service casual dining restaurant and had complained about some aspect of their meal while dining. The respondents reported complaints in four general categories: (1) food, (2) service, (3) atmosphere and other, and (4) food and service combined. The guests then reported how severe they thought the service failure was, ranging from very minor to very problematic, allowing me to quantify the extent of the failure by service type. Not all service failures are created equal and will have a different impact on the service experience. I next asked the guests if they were satisfied with the remedy they received after complaining; again, I believe guest satisfaction is an important outcome of a service experience. Last, I asked the guests if they were planning on returning to the restaurant after experiencing the service failure and remedy (again highlighting the importance of repeat patronage from guests).

The results of the study revealed that there were distinct differences in how complaints about food, service, atmosphere, and food and service combined were reacted to by the guests: Complaints about *food alone* and *food and service combined* were both classified by guests as being the most severe; guests reported the lowest level of satisfaction with the remedies offered, and they had lower levels of repeat-patronage intentions. On the one hand, food is a critical element of the service experience, and not delivering on this dimension alone or being combined with failures of service makes it hard to win over guests after the fact; on the other hand, guests rated failures in *service* as being the least critical, easier to remedy, and connected to higher repeat-purchase intentions, showing that guests are much more forgiving of service errors compared to errors made with food or food and service together. Last, complaints about *atmosphere and other* elements were rated moderately severe and led to the greatest level satisfaction with the remedy but to the lowest level of repeat-patronage intentions compared to complaints about food alone, service, or food and service combined. The study showed that, as problems arise in atmosphere, such as noise level, comfort, cleanliness, value, and theme, despite best efforts to help guests navigate the negative experience in the restaurant, the guests are less likely to return. This confirms a long-held belief that all of the big three (food, service, and ambiance) matter, but it is clear that execution failures involving food present an uphill battle for operators.

In the second article, "Communication Richness: Why Some Guest Complaints Go Right to the Top—and Others Do Not," I wanted to look at how complaint communication unfolds and how guests prefer to communicate complaints when they are unhappy with some part of a service experience. I also wanted to explore the underlying factors that influence their choice of communication. Similar to the first study, I surveyed 513 guests who had dined in full-service restaurants and had complained about some element of their experience in the restaurant.

When dealing with complaint management, communication richness is a mechanism that can help explain why people choose different modes of communication to deliver a message. Communication richness is defined by certain characteristics. To allow a message to be delivered by the sender and properly received and interpreted by the receiver, the correct communications channel must be used, along with the appropriate level of richness applied to the delivery. A communication exchange would be considered richer when direct feedback is possible, multiple cues and natural language can be used, and the source or the focus of the communication is understood by both parties. Based on this classification, lodging a complaint via face-to-face communication with a manager in the restaurant would be considered richer than speaking to an employee on the phone, sending a letter or email to a manager, or completing a comment card. Guests have multiple communication channels available to them to complain. In this study I considered four types of communication for complaints in decreasing richness: (1) face-to-face with a manager, (2) face-to-face with an employee, (3) written communication via letter, email, or web, and (4) through an organizationally provided comment card.

To better understand how people choose to complain, we also wanted to learn a little bit more about the why. We know that when something goes wrong with the big three in a restaurant, guests have a choice about whether or not to complain. Is the service failure itself enough to initiate the social confrontation, or are there other factors that influence that decision? I believe that there are at least three elements behind a guest's decision whether to complain and the mode of communication they choose once they have decided to do so. The first is propensity to complain. Each individual is going to have a propensity to complain—that is, a disposition to complain when dissatisfied. Those with a higher disposition toward complaining are likely to complain more and find value in initiating social confrontation to resolve differences in expectations.

Information inadequacy is next. When service failures occur, guests often feel that they do not have complete information about the service failure and the elements that led up to the failure. Think about the last time you were at an airport and your flight was delayed or canceled. Did you receive enough information about what happened and what will happen? Having insufficient information about the service failure is likely to influence your complaint behavior, making a need for information a driver of complaint communication.

Last, frustration is a common correlate of service failures. When something or someone blocks access to something desired or expected, the result will be frustration. People who are more prone to frustration from service failures are also more likely to complain and value using complaints to resolve problems.

The results of the study uncovered some interesting findings for communication richness and its connection to factors that underlie guests' desire to complain. First, I found that those respondents who preferred to communicate their complaints directly, face-to-face to a manager, reported high levels of propensity to complain, information inadequacy, and consumer frustration, supporting a communication richness model. Following that same rationale, I had assumed that face-to-face communication with employees to lodge complaints would be viewed as similar to face-to-face communication with a manager because it is also a rich form of communication. However, the guests with lower levels of propensity to complain, information inadequacy, and consumer frustration preferred to communicate face-to-face with employees, clearly showing that managers and employees are viewed as different avenues as a preferred communication mode to resolve a complaint, depending on how they view the complaint process, complaining, information seeking, and frustration.

A similar pattern emerged for written communication (to management) and leaving feedback on organizationally provided comment cards. Those respondents who preferred to lodge their complaints via written communication to management reported high levels of propensity to complain, information inadequacy, and consumer frustration, similar to those respondents who preferred to complain to managers face-to-face. Those respondents who preferred to lodge their complaints via comment cards reported low levels of propensity to complain, information inadequacy, and consumer frustration, similar to those respondents who preferred to complain to employees face-to-face.

The findings show that those guests who reported high levels of propensity to complain, information inadequacy, and consumer frustration preferred communication with management either face-to-face or in written form, just as those guests who reported low levels of propensity to complain, information inadequacy, and consumer frustration preferred communication with employees face-to-face (rather than management) or to fill out a comment card. The traditional communication richness framework did not entirely apply to this study as expected. What I did find, however is that guests clearly view complaint communication to management differently than they view communication to employees.

Mark: I find complaint management to be one of the most fascinating areas we deal with on a daily basis. There's a lot to unpack in the analysis Alex presents above, so I will address each area as I have experienced it over the last three decades.

While the data show that there are people who are likely to complain and those who are not, it's important to believe, in your heart of hearts, that all of your guests genuinely want you to succeed. After all, they have chosen your place over someone else's.

Even in the face-paced world of New York City restaurants, and despite any reputation New Yorkers may have, most people don't relish confrontation. So when someone chooses to complain in person, I assume that the complainer is uncomfortable and that we have, in some way, let him or her down. When I was in high school, I worked at a place where the chef or manager would decide whether the complaint merited a remedy. The service team had no authority to fix even the smallest issue. It was an incredibly paranoid, pessimistic, and adversarial way to look at business. If you assume your customers are out to hurt you, then you will always be right. But if you operate under the premise that your guests actually love what you do and want to enjoy the fruits of your work, then managing complaints becomes much simpler. Danny Meyer and the USC leaders would give the service team the authority to fix small things on the spot, and the culinary team, led by Michael Romano, were fully onboard. True, it is annoying and disruptive to have a meal sent back, but it is counterproductive to spend time disparaging the guest who "doesn't even know what medium-rare is." It's far better to fix the problem and move on. From my first days at USC, I witnessed this charitable (and very practical) philosophy, and it quickly became part of my DNA.

As with avoiding illness and car crashes, I believe that proactive prevention is the best medicine for potential complaints. We don't need to be perfect, but we need to be acutely aware of what's going on, and we may even need to take some risks to solve problems before they arise.

Consider the following illustration: If a maître d' chooses to seat an unexpected large party, experience may have taught us that the other parties in the dining room will suffer because the kitchen team will get bogged down cooking for the large group. We could pretend nothing happened and hope for the best, or we could be proactive. We may choose to alter the sequence of service on the fly, and the server or manager may approach a series of tables and say, "As you may have seen, we just seated a large party. Would you like to place your order ahead of them so we can ensure that your meal won't be delayed?" This method risks interrupting a conversation and making the decision your guests' problem. But presenting options sincerely and gracefully will put power in the guests' hands while showing that you are on their side. Ultimately, they can tell you what they want. In my opinion, the rewards far outweigh the risks.

There are tons of factors that go into why someone complains in the first place, and one of the biggest is the guests' agenda at that meal. I would argue that a group of good friends will have a lower threshold for complaining than a business dinner in which a salesperson is entertaining a potential client. In the friend scenario, everyone knows one another, and there is little chance that anyone will be uncomfortable (unless the friend is always the one who complains, but that's another story). In the client scenario, the host may not want to be seen as unreasonable, so he or she may choose to remain quiet. So what can we do about it? First off, we need to be aware. As Danny has mentioned for years, if guests are looking at one another, things are more likely to be going well than if guests are looking around. Are they engaged with other people at the table, or is something not right? The issue could be as simple as requesting salt or another napkin, but it could be something more serious, like a steak that is overcooked. Given that servers are typically very busy, I believe the management team should work very hard to catch these sorts of things. It is management's job to look at the big picture and ensure that the entire ecosystem of the dining room is humming. By looking for things that seem out of place or out of balance, we can head off problems, many times before a guest has even noticed. And if those guests aren't looking at one another, there is always the chance that the manager may rescue someone from an uncomfortable situation that has nothing to do with the restaurant, like a first date going poorly. So, take the risk, be proactive, and engage with your guests.

When I left USC to open Blue Smoke, I was not prepared for the number of complaints a new, unfamiliar business could receive. Keep in mind, I had left one of New York's most beloved fine dining restaurants to open a barbecue restaurant and jazz club that was very different than USHG's other restaurants, USC, Gramercy Tavern, Eleven Madison Park, and Tabla. As soon as we opened, we got hit from all sides. Many USHG loyalists couldn't understand why we'd open such a big, loud place with only 50 wines on the wine list and where servers wore jeans and T-shirts. Then, there were the barbecue loyalists, some of whom felt we were trying to be too "fancy." Meanwhile, from its inception, Blue Smoke was always meant to walk the line between fine dining and down-home comfort. Our sequence of service was virtually identical to USC's, but instead of offering artisanal breads, we greeted guests with homemade sliced buttermilk white bread and a selection of pickles. We took our bourbon and beer list just as seriously as Gramercy Tavern took its wine list, and we were incredibly proud. But, as with most new businesses, we fell short much of the time, and we spent much of our first few months fielding complaints. As mentioned in chapter 2, so much of guests' happiness has to do with expectations, and we had to get much better at telling our story. Slowly but surely, we improved at proactively avoiding problems and the complaints that might follow. If we knew there was a USHG regular in the dining room, we would be sure to start a conversation with him or her, pointing out the wines on our list that were also on USC's (and we'd sometimes mention that the same wines were generally 25% less expensive at Blue Smoke!). If we had Southerners at a table asking a lot of questions, we would find out where they were from and what style of barbecue they loved. We also gave a lot of smoker tours, leading guests through our kitchen every night to show them our smoking process. When we opened in 2002, we were only the second NYC restaurant to be serving pit barbecue, so most of our guests had never seen the process. By being proactive, getting to know our guests, and sharing our enthusiasm for what we were doing, we engendered intense loyalty and vastly improved our compliment to complaint ratio. Fortunately for us, social media had not yet been born, so we dealt with most complaints (and compliments) face-to-face. I'll discuss social media in a bit. An important area of complaint prevention relates to the experience at the front door. As the research we present shows, people's dissatisfaction with atmosphere will discourage them from returning, even if the complaint is handled by management. But what if a guest's perception of "atmosphere" could be managed before the guest has even entered the dining room? The maître d' can impact this impression without the guest even knowing. Danny used the term "benevolent manipulation" to describe the power we can have on both the guest experience and the successful running of service. And it all begins at the podium. A great first 30 seconds are incredibly powerful and can help mitigate any potential small issues that may happen during the course of the experience. Here are a few examples to illustrate the point: in every restaurant, management has its idea of the "good" and "bad" tables. But beauty is in the eye of the guest, and it's important not to prejudice him or her. At USC, the balcony was my favorite part of the restaurant, but I was in the minority. From time to time, when we would seat guests there, they would complain that they were being relegated to "Siberia." And those tables were usually the last to be seated. But, when we would offer our guests a choice between the balcony and the other dining rooms, we would have a much better time seating the balcony earlier. We would ask, "Would you prefer a private table or something right in the middle of the action?" To some guests, "private" was the key word, especially if they were on a date or trying to close a business deal. But some guests would translate "in the middle of things" to "loud," while others would hear "prime." Again, same table with a different perception. So, unless there is only one table left, why wouldn't we offer a choice? And even then, there are options. I vividly remember a night when I was maître d' and we were running very late for reservations. A group of three women had made a reservation and requested a corner table. When they arrived, they explained that it was their first time to NYC and were incredibly excited to be dining with us. My heart sank, because we were running at least 30 minutes late for their table. I explained the situation, and I offered them a choice: wait for a corner or dine at one of our bar tables where they could "see all the action." They chose the bar table. As first-timers, they were thrilled to see everyone coming and going, and I made sure the server knew what had just transpired, so she could keep an eye out for any issues. Had we not offered a choice, they would have been upset that they had to wait for their table, even though they had requested it a month in advance. Of course, if they had opted to wait, we would have been sure to make them comfortable and let them know that we were looking out for them. But offering that choice put them in the driver's seat and improved the likelihood of a positive outcome. An hour into their meal, a trio of NYC celebrities walked in, and I offered them the only table we had, a bar table right next to the three women. Everyone was thrilled, especially the three women who were getting a true New York City experience, and me, who couldn't believe how lucky I had just been.

Fast forward to today, and we need to consider that our intense addiction to social media has made everyone's megaphone more powerful than ever before. While social media is maligned by a wide swath of chefs and restaurateurs, it has the potential to improve the guest experience by encouraging (scaring?) restaurant management and staff to act on behalf of the guest. And while most of us in management have at some point been the target of unfair social media criticism, just imagine the potential to spread the great aspects of what we do and tell our stories. Replay some of the scenarios we have outlined above and optimistically think about how they could play out on social media. True, people may be more likely to go online to complain than to compliment, but a few gushing five-star reviews can help put some of those social media complaints into context. The frustration for management is when a guest chooses to complain *only* on social media, without giving us the opportunity to fix the problem in real time. Alex defines a complaint as "a social confrontation that has been initiated to adjust the perceptions and/or outcomes for someone." But is a social media complaint the same thing? Is it really a confrontation, and how can we affect the outcome if it's now hours or days later? Do most guests even expect a reply to a social media post? Successful businesses, including USHG, actively monitor social media to engage with guests, help solve problems, and amplify compliments in real time, given that so many guests now post in-the-moment. But most businesses do not have the time or resources to do this, so any response may be days later, after the complaint has been lingering on the Internet. It's easy to understand why so many business owners have anxiety about social media. It's also no surprise that everyone from the Food Network to South Park has featured online restaurant complaints in some way, given social media's ubiquity.

But how do we tackle social media complaints compared to other methods? While the methods may change (engaging with a guest over social media is more complicated than engaging face-to-face), the same time-tested principles should apply. Use the Golden Rule: treat others as you would want to be treated. Isadore Sharp built the Four Seasons into one of our industry's most respected companies using this philosophy, and many of us have adopted his philosophies and methods. As I mentioned above, USHG has always given front-line employees the authority to fix problems before they grow, so resolving an issue while the guest is still in the dining room is the best way to avoid a social media situation. That said, if a complaint does get posted, remember that a "conversation" on social media can quickly become a barroom brawl, with the unintended consequence of getting sucker-punched by a bystander. Whenever possible, take the discussion offline and ask the complainer to call or email the restaurant. In every public statement, remember to stay true to the philosophy of the business. While it may hurt to hear negative feedback, it is even more hurtful when you descend to a level that confirms their opinions. Take the high road for all to see, and openly try to solve the problem. Ultimately, it will be their choice whether or not to reach out.

Whether the complaint is old-fashioned or new media, think old school and follow the Golden Rule. It may not resolve 100% of issues, but you will have given it your best shot and maintained the reputation of the business in the process.

4

A Look at the Relationship between Service Failures, Guest Satisfaction, and Repeat-Patronage Intentions of Casual Dining Guests

Alex M. Susskind and Anthony Viccari

Most operators of service-based organizations recognize the importance of properly managing service failures as they arise in their operations (Liao, 2007; Kim et al., 2003). Having an understanding of how service failures and service recovery influence guests' perceptions and attitudes of the products and services they consume is an important part of an operator's ability to deliver quality products and services to their guests. We use the term "service failure" broadly to describe the elements of a restaurant experience that act as a precursor to a complaint (in this case, food, service, and atmosphere or other). In many ways service failures offer operators the opportunity to gain insight into how well their operations perform and how to improve their performance based on their guests' reactions to service failures and service recovery (Tax, Brown, & Chandrashekaran, 1998; Wirtz & Mattila, 2004; Kim et al., 2003).

Justice theory is often used to describe how guests evaluate service failures and the subsequent service recovery process. Research on justice theory examines whether individuals believe the outcomes of the service recovery process were fair given the extent of the failure (DeWitt, Nguyen, & Marshall, 2008; Ha & Jang, 2009). Justice relating to satisfaction with complaint handling is commonly viewed as a three-dimensional construct that comprises distributive justice, interactional justice, and procedural justice (Tax, Brown, & Chandrashekaran, 1998; Wirtz & Mattila, 2004). Distributive justice involves a consideration of the tangible benefits and costs of a service recovery process; interactional justice involves the manner in which a guest is treated during the service process; and procedural justice involves the process by which a recovery attempt is conducted. A guest's perception of justice in the recovery process is positively related to repeat-purchase intentions (Liao, 2007). Justice theory demonstrates the pivotal role that service recovery plays in building guest loyalty (DeWitt, Nguyen, & Marshall, 2008; Liao, 2007; Ha & Jang, 2009; Kim et al. 2003; Kim, Leong, & Lee, 2005).

In the context of the justice explanation for guests' reaction to restaurant service recovery, we present and test three main ideas in this article. First, we discuss the types of service failures commonly experienced in restaurants. Next, we define how the severity of service failures influences guests' perceptions and attitudes; and last we discuss how service remedies and guests' repeat-patronage intentions emerge from and are influenced by service failures and the complaint process.

Type of Complaint

While a restaurant experience can be considered a single event, it is composed of several interrelated components that can be evaluated both individually and collectively (Susskind, 2005; Gupta, McLaughlin, & Gomez, 2007; Kim, Leong, & Lee, 2005). Needless to say, food and service are the two key factors influencing a restaurant's success (Susskind, 2002). Several studies have shown that the root cause of service failures in restaurants has an influence on how guests communicate with others regarding their experience, and how guests view and respond to recovery actions (Susskind, 2002, 2005; Spreng, Harrell, & Mackoy, 1995). While the "servicescape" and other tangible elements of a restaurant experience influence guests' experiences in service environments, the physical characteristics of the establishment are likely to be less variable and more objectively evaluated than the product- and service-related elements. For example, the atmosphere of a sports bar is likely to be notably different from that of a luxury restaurant. The features of both the sports bar and the luxury restaurant should be consistent with their concept (e.g., noise, décor, lighting, music, entertainment), but each guest will individually evaluate those elements and determine whether they met their expectations. This is true regardless of how well you address a service failure related to the atmosphere (Bitner, 1992).

Severity of the Service Failure

The severity of a service failure not only varies by episode but also according to the guest's perceptions and expectations, which determine his or her evaluation (Susskind, 2000, 2005; Ha & Jang, 2009; Kim, Leong, & Lee, 2005). The severity of the service failure will likely influence what course of action, if any, the guest will take to address the service failure and should help both guests and service providers determine the remedy that is required to redress the problem (Hoffman, Kelley, & Rotalsky, 1995; Liao, 2007; Spreng, Harrell, & Mackoy, 1995).

Service Remedies and Satisfaction with Outcomes

The nature of the remedy applied by service providers to correct dissatisfying elements of a service experience will also vary according to the specifics of the failure (Richins, 1983). In two studies of restaurant guests' complaints about service experiences, a set of recovery actions was defined by the degree of correction offered by the service provider. Actions such as offering free food, discounts, coupons, or managerial interventions were presented as corrections involving a high degree of effort, while actions such as making adjustments, offering apologies, or doing nothing to correct the problem were presented as low-correction actions (Hoffman, Kelley, & Rotalsky, 1995; Susskind, 2005). These groupings of recovery actions appear to be representative of the range of offerings in service settings where the guest evaluates the service experience before rendering payment, such as in a restaurant or hotel

(Hoffman & Chung, 1999; Sundaram, Jurowski, & Webster, 1997). The degree of correction that is negotiated or offered following a service failure is one key to a successful service recovery, and another is matching the recovery actions to the guests' expectations, since success relies on whether the guest believes the remedy was appropriate to the situation (Liao, 2007).

Repeat-Patronage Intentions

As we have been discussing, a critical element in guests' desire to return to a restaurant following a service failure is whether they feel that they have received fair treatment following a service failure (Goodwin & Ross, 1992; Maxham, 2001). A growing body of research has shown this connection between satisfaction with a service experience or service recovery and repeat-patronage intentions (Davidow, 2000; Davidow & Leigh, 1998; Gupta, McLaughlin, & Gomez, 2007; Smith, Bolton, & Wagner, 1999; Spreng, Harrell, & Mackoy, 1995; Ha & Jang, 2009), not to mention favorable word of mouth (Lewis & McCann, 2004; Maxham, 2001; Yi, 1990; Kim, Leong, & Lee, 2005). We should also point out that it has been reported that the recovery time involved in redressing a service failure has a significant effect on repeat-purchase intent and word-of-mouth referrals. As one might expect, immediate recovery actions resulted in higher return intentions and lower negative word of mouth than a delayed or slower service recovery (Wirtz & Mattila, 2004). These findings highlight the importance of correcting service failures as quickly as possible to build repeat-patronage intentions.

Guests' commitment to an organization is an important influence on their repeat-patronage intentions. In general, guests may be affectively committed, and they desire to continue their relationship as a guest, or they may be calculatively committed, meaning that they continue the relationship because of high switching costs (Mattila, 2004). Restaurant switching costs are minuscule, so calculative commitment is not normally a factor for restaurants. Instead, restaurants may seek to improve affective commitment. Oddly, Matilla found that those who have low affective commitment are more forgiving of a service failure if the restaurant's recovery is well handled. However, she also found that those who have high affective commitment are more likely to return to the establishment after a failure and recovery (Mattila, 2004).

With those sometimes-conflicting studies in mind, this investigation sets out to examine how guests react to service failures by considering four factors:

1. the nature of the complaint lodged (food vs. service vs. other),
2. the severity of the service failure,
3. the outcome of the resolution, and
4. how the service failure and remedy influenced subsequent patronage intentions.

To that end, the following three-part research question is presented and tested:

Research Question: How does the type of service failure (i.e., food, service, or atmosphere or other) experienced by a guest relate to the guests' (a) perception of the severity of the service failure experience, (b) satisfaction with how the service failure was handled by service provider, and (c) intent to return to the restaurant?

Participants and Procedure

To test the three research questions proposed above, 802 restaurant patrons were intercepted at airports, convention centers, and vacation destinations. We avoided collecting data at restaurants to avoid any recency effect. These data were collected over a six-month period as part of a larger study investigating the consumer behavior of leisure and business travelers. Participants were asked to fill out the survey in exchange for a $2.00 gift certificate at a national coffee house chain. Each guest was asked to recall a specific time when they had to make a complaint in a casual-dining restaurant. We then asked whether this complaint involved: (1) food, (2) service, (3) a combination of food and service, or (4) atmosphere or other elements. The participants were asked to rate the severity of the service failure on a 5-point scale, where 1 = very minor and 5 = very problematic.[1] Likewise, we asked respondents to rate how satisfied they were with the complaint remedy or outcome on a 5-point scale ranging from 1 = very dissatisfied to 5 = very

satisfied. Last, the participants were asked to rate the probability of returning to the restaurant following their experience with the failure and remedy, again on a 5-point scale ranging from 1 = definitely will not return to
5 = definitely will return.

Although we had a wide age range among participants (18 to
70 years), our respondents skewed toward youth, with a median age of
28 (mean = 32.74, SD = 14.74), and 58% were female. To provide a context for the participants' perceptions of complaints while dining they were
asked to report how often they dine out each week for their lunch and
dinner meals. The participants ate their lunchtime meals out between zero
and seven times per week on average (mean = 3.07, SD = 2.15, median = 3)
and their dinnertime meals out between zero and seven times per week
(mean = 2.51, SD = 1.94, median = 2). To determine whether dining frequency had any influence in the model, dining frequency for lunch and
dinner were added to the model as covariates. The results indicated that
neither lunch nor dinner dining frequency had a significant effect in the
model and were hence removed from further analyses.

Analyses

The analysis treated the mean values of severity of the complaint, satisfaction with the outcome, and repeat-patronage intentions as the dependent variables as relating to the four categories of complaints (i.e., food,
service, combination of food and service, and atmosphere or other) using
one-way analysis of variance. The main effects were examined to determine whether there was a notable difference in guests' reactions to the
complaint and recovery process based on the nature of the complaint. The
significance of the differences among the complaint types was examined
using a post hoc Duncan's multiple-range test. This procedure examined
the differences for one of the quantitative dependent variables (in this case
severity of complaint, satisfaction with outcome, and repeat-patronage
intentions) by a single-factor independent variable (in this case, the nature
of the complaint). The post hoc tests show which means differ specifically to add in the interpretation of the data (using SPSS for Windows
14.0). A visualization of the relationships is presented in figure 4.1, and
the descriptive statistics and correlations among the dependent variables
are presented as table 4.1.

Summary and Discussion of the Findings

The study revealed that the majority of the guests' complaints stemmed from food-related concerns (42.7%). Complaints involving a combination of food- and service-related concerns ranked second at 26.4%, and service-related complaints ranked third at 25.2%. Complaints about the atmosphere or a topic not directly related to food or service accounted for 5.7% of the guests' complaints.

Severity of the Service Failure

In the examination of Research Question 1a, the reported severity of the service failures was highest for failures involving issues of food and service combined (mean = 4.39) and problems with food alone (mean = 4.30). Complaints relating to atmosphere or an issue not directly related to food or service were reported as moderately severe (mean = 3.96), while the reported severity of problems with service alone was the lowest (mean = 3.16).

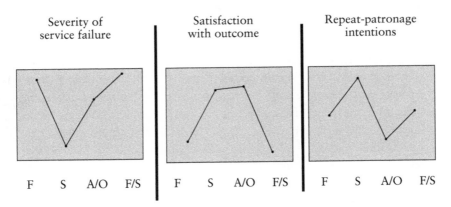

Figure 4.1. Results from the one-way analysis of variance for complaint type
Note: Numbers on the charts are the mean responses for each variable by complaint type: F = food-related, S = service-related, A/O = atmosphere or other, and F/S = a combination of food and service.

TABLE 4.1. Descriptive statistics and correlations among the dependent variables

	Mean (SD)	1.	2.	3.
1. Severity	4.02 (1.18)	—		
2. Outcome	3.47 (1.38)	−.04	—	
3. Repatronage	2.99 (1.28)	−.05	.42**	—

Note: N = 803 using listwise deletion.
**p < .01.

These differences are significant (one-way ANOVA), $F(3, 799) = 59.75$, $p < .001$. Moreover, results from Duncan's multiple-range tests indicated that the weight of food-related problems or a combination of food- and service-related complaints was significantly higher than a complaint relating to the atmosphere, which was in turn significantly higher than complaints relating to service alone at the $p < .05$ level. These findings suggest that errors in service delivery alone are viewed as less problematic to guests when compared to errors involving food or the atmosphere (Susskind, 2002, 2005).

Satisfaction with the Complaint Outcome

The test of Research Question 1b showed the challenges involved in service recovery. Guests who experienced a problem with food and service combined (mean = 3.33) or food alone (mean = 3.39) reported the lowest level of satisfaction with the outcome of the complaint. Satisfaction with the outcome of the complaint for service-related problems alone (mean = 3.70) or the atmosphere (mean = 3.72) was significantly higher. Again, food-related complaints or the combination of food- and service-related complaints appeared to be the most difficult to manage and recover from. Again, the differences in severity from one category to the next is significant (one-way ANOVA), $F(3, 799) = 59.75$, $p < .001$. As with the weight of the complaint, results from Duncan's multiple-range tests indicated that recovery from food-related issues and a combination of food- and service-related complaints were significantly more challenging than a complaint relating to the atmosphere, which was significantly higher than service-related complaints at the p < .05 level.

Repeat-Patronage Intentions

Last, the test of Research Question 1c showed that guests' repeat-patronage intentions varied as a function of type of service failure they experienced. In this case, guests who reported a service-related failure were the most likely to return to the restaurant (mean = 3.32), followed by guests who reported a combination of food- and service-related problems (mean = 2.93) and only food-related problems (mean = 2.88). Oddly, guests who reported problems with the atmosphere or some other non-food- or service-related problem were the least likely to return (mean = 2.59). Similar to the satisfaction with outcome variable noted above, the service-related failures were associated with a higher level of repeat-patronage intentions, when compared with complaints related to food, the combination of food and service, or atmosphere. The one-way ANOVA results revealed significant differences among the means for the satisfaction with outcome variable, $F(3, 799) = 3.48$, $p = .02$. Results from Duncan's multiple-range tests indicated that food-related problems and a combination of food- and service-related complaints were significantly higher than a complaint relating to the atmosphere and a service-related complaint alone at the p < .05 level.

Correlations among the Dependent Variables

To further describe the relationships uncovered through the ANOVA presented above, we examined the correlations among the dependent variables. The correlations revealed that guests' satisfaction with the outcome of their complaint and their repeat-patronage intentions were negatively (but not significantly) related to the severity of the service failure (satisfaction, $r = -.04$, $p = .27$; repeat patronage, $r = -.05$, $p = .12$), suggesting that those guests who experienced more severe service failures reported a lower level of satisfaction with the outcome and a lower desire to return to the restaurant after the service failure. However, one should use caution in interpreting these relationships, because the correlations were small and not statistically significant. Taken together with the results of the one-way ANOVAs, the impact of food-related and food- and service-related complaints was greater to these guests.

Conversely, the association between guests' reported satisfaction with the outcome of their complaint and their repeat patronage intentions following the complaint were positively and significantly related (r = .42, p < .01). This finding highlights the importance of adequately resolving guests' complaints to increase the possibility that they will return to your restaurant after the service failure. We ran a MANOVA to further examine the interrelationships among complaint type and the dependent variables. The multivariate model fit the data quite well, indicating that the type of service failure (i.e., food-related and food- and service-related failures) was associated with higher levels of severity, lower levels of outcome satisfaction, and lower levels of repeat-patronage intentions. The Hotelling-Lawley Trace Statistic was significant (.26, p < .001), yielding the F statistic, $F(9, 2389) = 23.22$, p < .001, $\eta2 = .08$.

Managerial Implications and Conclusion

When looking at what element of the guests' experience led to the service failure, the results showed that problems regarding food alone and a combination of food and service were rated as more severe by the guests, closely followed by complaints regarding the atmosphere or other factors, with service-related complaints alone being viewed as the least severe. This set of findings demonstrates that mistakes made preparing the food and problems with food that are compounded by mistakes made with service are viewed the most critically by guests. On the other hand, while guests appear to be more forgiving of service-related mistakes, failures related to atmosphere were viewed to be nearly as critical as those with food. Problems with the atmosphere of a restaurant are difficult to manage. The results of Research Questions 1b and 1c show a conundrum regarding atmosphere and other non-food issues. Although guests who had problems with the atmosphere reported the highest level of satisfaction with the compliant remedy, they also were the least likely to return to the restaurant. This set of findings suggests that even though errors made in connection with food are the most critical, these problems can be repaired. In addition, it appears that guests in general are more forgiving (or at least less critical) of mistakes involving just service issues. None of these findings indicate that restaurateurs should disregard a failure in any of these categories. Regardless of the severity of the service failure, each one should be carefully addressed and managed to minimize further discomfort to the guest. That said, operators making mistakes with their food are at a greater risk of losing their guests.

An examination of guests' satisfaction with the outcome of the complaints they lodged showed that both service-related and atmosphere-related complaints when remedied lead to higher levels of satisfaction compared to complaints remedied involving problems with the food alone or a combination of food and service. As stated above, it is important to note the weight that food-related service failures carry for restaurant guests.

As supported by the discussions above of both complaint severity and outcome satisfaction, guests who experienced a service-related problem reported the highest level of repeat-patronage intentions (slightly above the midpoint of "not sure I will return"), followed by those who had problems with a combination of food and service and those with mistakes regarding food alone (slightly below the midpoint of "not sure I will return"). The lowest level of repeat-patronage intentions was reported by guests complaining about the atmosphere or other factors not connected with the food or service. We conclude that if elements of the atmosphere are not pleasing to the guest, they are not likely to return, regardless of the remedy.

Readers should keep in mind that this study was conducted among casual-dining restaurant guests. While we believe the ideas presented here probably apply to all segments of the food-service business, we recommend additional work to confirm these results in other types of service-based operations beyond casual dining. Last, the correlational analysis revealed that in general guests who experienced more severe service failures were less satisfied with the outcome and were the least likely to return to the restaurant following the service failure. Likewise, guests who reported that they were satisfied with the outcome from the service failure reported that they were more likely to return to the restaurant. In conclusion, this study demonstrates that when experiencing service failures in restaurants, guests clearly assign different levels of importance to the type of failure and the remedy, and the type of failure and how it is handled influence guests' repeat-patronage intentions.

Notes

Original citation: Susskind, A. M., & Viccari, A. (2011). A look at the relationship between service failures, guest satisfaction, and repeat-patronage intentions of casual dining guests. *Cornell Hospitality Quarterly* 52(4): 438–444.

1. We used single-item measures to assess the guests' reactions to and processing of the service failures they reported, because the use of single-item measures has been shown to be effective, with strong test–retest reliabilities when the survey items gather information about more objective elements, such as the reporting of facts (see Dollinger & Malmquist, 2009).

References

Bitner, M. J. (1992). Impact of physical surroundings on employees and customers in service organizations. *Journal of Marketing*, 56 (April): 57–71.

Davidow, M. (2000). The bottom line impact of organizational responses to customer complaints. *Journal of Hospitality and Tourism Research*, 24: 473–490.

Davidow, M., & Leigh, J. H. (1998). The effects of organizational complaint responses on consumer satisfaction, word of mouth activity, and repurchase intentions. *Journal Consumer Satisfaction, Dissatisfaction and Complaining Behavior*, 11: 91–102.

DeWitt, T., Nguyen, D. T., & Marshall, R. (2008). Exploring customer loyalty following service recovery: The mediating effects of trust and emotion. *Journal of Service Research*, 10(3): 269–280.

Dollinger, S. J., & Malmquist, D. (2009). The reliability and validity of single-item self-reports: With special relevance to college students' alcohol use, religiosity, study and social life. *Journal of General Psychology*, 136: 231–141.

Goodwin, C., & Ross, I. (1992). Consumer responses to service failures: Influence of procedural and interactional fairness perceptions. *Journal of Business Research*, 25: 149–163.

Gupta, S., McLaughlin, E., & Gomez, M. (2007). Guest satisfaction and restaurant performance. *Cornell Hotel and Restaurant Administration Quarterly*, 48(2): 284–298.

Ha, J., & Jang, S. (2009). Perceived justice in service recovery and behavioral intentions: The role of relationship quality. *International Journal of Hospitality Management*, 28(3): 319–327.

Hoffman, K. D., & Chung, B. G. (1999). Hospitality recovery strategies: Customer preference versus firm use. *Journal of Hospitality and Tourism Research*, 23: 71–84.

Hoffman, K. D., Kelley, S. W., & Rotalsky, H. M. (1995). Tracking service failures and employee recovery efforts. *Journal of Services Marketing*, 9: 49–61.

Kim, C., Kim, S., Im, S., & Shin, C. (2003). The effect of attitude and perception on consumer complaint intentions. *Journal of Consumer Marketing*, 20: 352–371.

Kim, W. G., Leong, J. K., & Lee, Y. (2005). Effect of service orientation on job satisfaction, organizational commitment, and intention of leaving in a casual dining restaurant. *International Journal of Hospitality Management*, 24: 171–193.

Lewis, B. R., & McCann, P. (2004). Service failure and recovery: Evidence from the hotel industry. *International Journal of Contemporary Hospitality Management*, 16(1): 6–17.

Liao, H. (2007). Do it right this time: The role of employee service recovery performance in customer-perceived justice and customer loyalty after service failures. *Journal of Applied Psychology*, 92(2): 475–489.

Mattila, A. S. (2004). The impact of service failures on customer loyalty: The moderating role of affective commitment. *International Journal of Service Industry Management*, 15(2): 134–149.

Maxham. J. G. III (2001). Service recovery's influence on consumer satisfaction, positive word-of-mouth, and purchase intentions. *Journal of Business Research*, 54: 11–24.

Richins, M. L. (1983). Negative word-of-mouth by dissatisfied consumers: A pilot study. *Journal of Marketing*, 47: 68–78.

Smith, A. K., Bolton, R. N., & Wagner, J. (1999). A model of customer satisfaction with service encounters involving failure and recovery. *Journal of Marketing Research*, 36: 356–372.

Spreng, R. A., Harrell, G. D., & Mackoy, R. D. (1995). Service recovery: Impact on satisfaction and intentions. *Journal of Services Marketing*, 9: 15–23.

Sundaram, D. S., Jurowski, C., & Webster, C. (1997). Service failure and recovery efforts in restaurant dining: The role of criticality of service consumption. *Hospitality Research Journal*, 20: 137–149.

Susskind, A. M. (2000). Efficacy and outcome expectations related to guest complaints about service experiences. *Communication Research*, 27(3): 353–378.

Susskind, A. M. (2002). I told you so! Restaurant consumers' word-of-mouth communication. *Cornell Hotel and Restaurant Administration Quarterly*, 43(2): 75–85.

Susskind, A. M. (2005). A content analysis of consumer complaints, remedies, and repatronage intentions regarding dissatisfying service experiences. *Journal of Hospitality and Tourism Research*, 2(2): 150–169.

Tax, S. S., Brown, S. W., & Chandrashekaran, M. (1998). Customer evaluation of service complaint experiences: Implications for relationship marketing. *Journal of Marketing*, 62: 60–76.

Wirtz, J., and Mattila, A. S. (2004). Consumer responses to compensation, speed of recovery and apology after a service failure. *International Journal of Service Industry Management*, 15(2): 150–166.

Yi, Y. (1990). Understanding the structure of consumers' satisfaction evaluations of service delivery. *Journal of the Academy of Marketing Science*, 19: 223–244.

5

Communication Richness

Why Some Guest Complaints Go Right to the Top—and Others Do Not

Alex M. Susskind

When a service encounter fails in some way, guests and service providers alike attempt to understand what went wrong, what can be done to fix it, and what could be done to prevent it from happening again. The starting point for this investigation is often a complaint lodged by the guest. Most restaurateurs (and operators of other service-based organizations) solicit guest comments and complaints as a means of ensuring customer satisfaction and a reduction of error. For the guest, a complaint is a way to inform the service provider of a problem. For operators, complaints act as a gauge of their performance and offer an avenue to improve their performance.

Despite the importance of guest complaints, we still do not have a firm indication of why guests choose a particular channel for their complaint. In this article, I examine guest complaints in connection with media richness theory to gain a greater understanding of guest preferences with regard to complaint channels. Based on the consumer-frustration hypothesis (Berkowitz, 1989; Susskind, 2004) and guests' perceptions of the complaint process (Day, 1984; Kowalski, 1996; Susskind, 2002, 2005), I present elements of media richness theory (Daft & Lengel, 1984, 1986) as a framework to demonstrate the objective decisions guests make when they make a complaint due to dissatisfaction with a service experience.

I will begin with a discussion of media richness theory and show how it relates to complaint communication. Next, I will describe complaints and complaint management in general, and outline three variables—propensity to complain, information inadequacy, and consumer frustration—that underlie how guests process service failures and their subsequent decisions to complain. Finally, I will present, test, and discuss the findings for three research questions in connection with those three variables.

Media Richness Theory

Media richness theory is a way to classify messages that vary in complexity and meaning, in this case, service-based complaints. The idea behind this theory is that individuals continually exchange information (Daft, Lengel, & Trevino, 1987; Robert & Dennis, 2005), but each exchange entails varying levels of certainty (lack of information) and equivocality (ambiguity). Uncertainty is normally reduced by receiving more data, while equivocality is normally reduced by discussion and debate. In general, to reduce equivocality, one uses richer communication channels, such as personal contact, while uncertainty, in contrast, can be reduced with less-rich communication channels, such as writing (Daft, Lengel, & Trevino, 1987). Richer communication channels have been shown to facilitate social perceptions of others and enhance the ability to evaluate interpersonal communication elements such as expertise, deception, agreement, acceptance, and persuasion. Leaner communication channels, on the other hand, have been shown to facilitate communication clarity when task-relevant knowledge is low (Kahai & Cooper, 2003). In addition, with richer communication channels, the sender must have the receiver's attention to effectively deliver the message (Robert & Dennis, 2005). This is based on the premise that richer communication will require more effort but will then hopefully lead to a more desirable result and facilitate better understanding on the part of both the sender and receiver (Robert & Dennis, 2005).

Media richness has been studied in several domains, notably in the use and adoption of technology, computer-mediated communication (Daft, Lengel, & Trevino, 1987; Dennis & Kinney, 1998; Kahai & Cooper, 1999, 2003; Schmitz & Fulk, 1991), and task performance and decision making (Dennis, Kinney, & Hung, 1999; Kahai & Cooper, 1999, 2003; Robert & Dennis, 2005). These studies have demonstrated the contrasting value of leaner and richer communication channels. Richer communication channels, for instance, result in better decision making, greater socioemotional communication, and greater task-oriented communication (Kahai & Cooper, 2003). In addition, the use of richer communication leads to greater agreement with and acceptance of decisions (Kahai & Cooper, 1999). On the other hand, Dennis, Kinney, and Hung (1999) found that the use of leaner communication channels resulted in lower performance because it took more time to reach a decision, but leaner communication channels did not affect decision quality or performance itself.

The richness of each communication channel is characterized by four qualities of information-carrying ability and exchange: (1) the capability to provide direct, rapid feedback to the receiver of the message (synchronous vs. asynchronous); (2) the number of communication channels and cues utilized to convey the message (such as verbal communication and nonverbal communication); (3) the use of natural language to convey the message; and (4) the source or focus of the communication (Daft & Lengel, 1984, 1986). Based on these four qualities, face-to-face interactions have been classified as the "richest" communication channel, and consequently, that channel is the benchmark to which emerging communication forms have been compared (Daft & Lengel, 1984, 1986; Trevino, Lengel, & Daft, 1987).

Communication channel richness also suggests that richer communication channels are more capable of conveying multiple cues beyond words, thereby enabling rapid, synchronous feedback and facilitating efficient information seeking and communication. Although guests do not expressly consider media richness theory when they need to communicate a complaint, they do examine the elements of the service failure, consider the different communication channels available to complain, and then choose the communication channel (or the combination of channels) that will get their message across regarding the unsatisfactory service experience (and its potential remedy).

In that context, the channels available to complaining guests would be (in descending order of richness) face-to-face communication with a manager, face-to-face communication with an employee, written communication directed to management (via letter, e-mail, or the internet), and (least rich) a comment card. Face-to-face communication with a manager or supervisor is richest because (in addition to using multiple cues) the manager has more control and authority to provide direct and immediate feedback and a solution to address the guest's concerns and can quickly react to issues that surface. Although face-to-face communication with an employee has almost as much richness as communication with a manager, the employee is not always capable of or empowered to offer a direct, agreeable solution to guests. So, even if the feedback can be immediate and synchronous, there may be limits on how the solution is derived and executed. Written communication (regardless of channel) is less rich because it offers neither multiple cues nor a direct mechanism for immediate feedback. Although the sender may expect a response in kind, not all hospitality organizations respond to internet comments, even though they monitor them (see, for example, Park & Allen, 2013). Comment cards are the least rich form of communication because they also fail to offer multiple cues. Moreover, in most cases, the comment cards are completed anonymously so there is little or no expectation of direct feedback from the operator. Beyond that, comment cards are not always completed with a particular receiver in mind (or, more on point, the guest does not know who will read them).

The guest's choice of a specific communication channel to lodge a complaint is based on the belief that the communication will have the intended effect on the person who receives the complaint. As noted by Robert and Dennis (2005), communication is first designed to get the attention of the receiver. For example, if you had a hard time getting your server to refill your beverage at the table (and wanted the problem solved during your meal), you would most likely directly ask your server to fill the glass. If that request was still not successful, however, you might flag down another server or a manager to resolve the service failure, or in media-richness terms, use richer, face-to-face contact to get the attention of the server or manager. For a potentially less critical or urgent matter (e.g., not liking the music or artwork), you might complete a low-richness comment card to complain rather than engaging a person directly.

Complaint Behavior

At root, for a complaint to take place, a guest must first identify an element of the service process that was not to his or her liking, determine that it should be corrected, determine who can or will correct it, and then select an approach to deliver the complaint. The media-richness framework suggests that the guest will choose the richest possible channel for a complaint because it involves a socioemotional communication, and communication of this type best suited for richer communication channels (Kahai & Cooper, 2003).

Particularly, if it involves a rich, face-to-face channel, a complaint constitutes a social confrontation. As a consequence, an individual's desire to complain about a dissatisfying service experience is based on his or her self-efficacy, which in turn involves the individual's estimate of whether she is able to make a complaint that successfully redresses a dissatisfying experience. For the individual, self-efficacy regarding a particular complaint then leads to outcome expectancy, which is the perception that the effort expended in voicing the complaint will lead to a desired resolution. Due to self-regulation, individuals vary in how they respond to dissatisfying experiences (Bagozzi, 1992; Maddux, Norton, & Stoltenberg, 1986; Singh & Wilkes, 1996), based on their gauge of self-efficacy (Makoul & Roloff, 1998; Susskind, 2000).

Taking this mechanism one step further, self-efficacy theory is a subset of expectancy-valence theories, where the propensity to engage in a specific behavior (such as communicating a complaint) is the product of the reinforcement value of an expected outcome and the expectation that specific behaviors will lead to that outcome (Bagozzi, 1992; Maddux, Norton, & Stoltenberg, 1986; Singh & Wilkes, 1996). In general, investigations addressing self-efficacy have shown that efficacy expectations to perform a specific behavior (like a complaint) lead to specific outcome expectations for that behavior (the desired remedy). More formally, efficacy expectations spawn intentions to perform a specific behavior and, further, the specific performance of behaviors (Susskind, 2000, 2005). At a practical level, guests will not initiate a social confrontation if they do not believe from the start that they have a chance at being successful. This is one explanation for the phenomenon that not all consumers will complain when dissatisfied. Noncomplainers either make an assessment that the situation is not within their control, deny that the problem exists, or avoid the situation by exiting and not lodging a complaint (Singh, 1988; Stephens & Gwinner, 1998).

Recently, hospitality researchers have done a thorough job of exploring the socioemotional antecedents and outcomes related to complaints in service episodes that are germane to this study. Mattila and Ro (2008), for example, found that anger that emerged from a service failure was directly connected to guests' desire to complain face-to-face to the service provider. This demonstrates that angry guests prefer richer communication channels. Sparks and Fredline (2007) have identified the role that mitigating information plays in service recovery, finding that referential explanations (information about the service failure, rather than justifications) by service providers were connected to higher levels of satisfaction and loyalty among guests. While many dimensions of the service process have been examined with regard to guest satisfaction, the connection between the communication channel selected for a complaint and how guests process complaints remains less than clear in service-based settings.

In this paper, I attempt to further our understanding of how guests process complaints by examining the relationship between the channel of communication guests select to complain about service failures and the following underlying factors: (1) their propensity to complain when dissatisfied, (2) their perceptions of information inadequacy about service experiences, and (3) their frustration with service experiences.

Propensity to Complain

There are a number of factors that drive guests' motivation to complain about service experiences. The decision process for the guest typically involves (1) a cognitive evaluation of the relevance of the service failure, (2) the guests' knowledge and experience with similar service-based failures, (3) the specific limitations of complaining in the particular instance, and (4) the likelihood of success in complaining (Day, 1984). Based on these elements, guests consider the extent to which they believe that they (1) are able to effectively complain about the dissatisfying situation and (2) believe that their complaint will lead to a desired remedy or expectancy (Singh, 1988; Singh & Wilkes, 1996; Susskind, 2000). This outline of the complaint process highlights in general how guests form specific attitudes and beliefs toward the act of complaining and how they assign value to it. This process could be defined as a global attitude toward complaining that is based on a collection of many experiences, not one alone (Susskind, 2002, 2005; Susskind & Viccari, 2011). When a guest experiences a service failure and determines that a remedy might be required, the particular service failure will prompt the guest to determine whether a complaint should be lodged in that instance and the appropriate communication channel for lodging the complaint. The guest also gauges the probability that a desired outcome will emerge from making a complaint (Kowalski, 1996; Sparks & Fredline, 2007; Susskind, 2000). Those who are predisposed to complain when dissatisfied are more likely to voice their concerns directly to the seller (Huppertz, Mower, & Associates, 2003). This has implications regarding the richness of the communication channel selected for the complaint, because a propensity to complain could be framed as a socioemotional characteristic, associated with the desire to use a richer communication channel (Kahai & Cooper, 2003).[1]

Guest Frustration

For the purposes of this study, guest frustration is defined as a negative emotional reaction to particular elements of a service experience (Susskind, 2004). In service experiences, guests become frustrated when the attainment of a specific desired outcome is blocked. Triggers of frustration in restaurants include waiting for food or a table, receiving incomplete or incorrect food and beverage orders, poor food or service quality, and discordant elements of the décor and atmosphere. Frustration also emerges in all hospitality organizations when you feel you have not been treated properly.

Service failure fits into the frustration-aggression hypothesis (Berkowitz, 1989; Dollard et al., 1939), which presented an early example of how the blocking of the attainment of expected outcomes likely leads to increased perceptions of frustration.[2] This phenomenon was tested by Harris (1974), when he had his research assistants cut in front of guests who were waiting in line for retail services. He found that guests became more frustrated with the "line cutting" as the size of the line increased. This suggests that guest frustration emerges when guests see an object blocking their receiving a product or service for which they are waiting. The potential for frustration in service experiences starts with the fact that consumers must give up direct control of the service experience to receive the products and services they expect (Guchait & Namasivayam, 2012). If factors beyond their control interfere with a service experience, frustration is a likely outcome (Susskind, 2004).

Frustration is an important foundation of the complaint process that is related not only to a failed outcome but also to a lack of information. This was the source of frustration in one study I conducted (Susskind, 2004), which found that retail consumers' frustration was related to their need for information, such that shoppers who felt they needed more information regarding their shopping experience reported higher levels of frustration.

Information Inadequacy

This issue of information inadequacy is related to consumers' need for control in the service experience (Guchait & Namasivayam, 2012). As guests evaluate the conditions surrounding a service failure, they will likely seek information regarding that failure. This information helps guests process and put closure on the failure and its surrounding circumstances as they attempt to regain a sense of control of the service experience. With mitigating information, the guest is able to make attributions about the service failure that affected them, determine how serious the service failure is, and decide what should be done about it. Guests also require information about service failures to help them better understand the technical or hidden aspects of the service delivery processes (Mittal, Huppertz, & Khare, 2008). In this regard, better informed customers make better decisions about how to proceed following service failures (Hui & Tse, 1996). For example, a guest who is told they will have to wait one hour for a table in a restaurant, yet sees an entire section of the dining room apparently available, would appreciate knowing why the restaurant is not seating people in that section.

If insufficient or inaccurate information is provided to the guest following a service failure, it adds uncertainty to the service experience, limits the guests' ability to evaluate the cause and effect of the service failure, and likely leads to frustration (Fornell & Westbrook, 1979; Susskind, 2004). Furthermore, guests who cannot attribute the cause of a service failure to either internal or external causes are more likely to create a negative image of the event (Mattila & Ro, 2008; Sparks & Fredline, 2007).

Guests who experience information inadequacy as a result of a service failure will likely seek a richer form of communication to deliver their complaint. This proposed relationship is based on the premise of information control, where more informed guests are likely to share their views about the service failure to restore balance in the service exchange with the service provider (Mittal, Huppertz, & Khare, 2008; Susskind, 2004), as opposed to defecting, switching, or engaging in negative word-of-mouth communication (Mattila & Ro, 2008).

Based on the above discussion, I examine guests' reactions to service failures and remedies by looking at several personal factors that influence their desire to complain and the way in which they choose to complain, as stated in the following four research questions:

> Research Question 1: What is the relationship between the communication channels guests choose to express their dissatisfaction with a service experience and their propensity to complain?
> Research Question 2: What is the relationship between the communication channels guests choose to lodge a complaint about a service experience and their need for information regarding service failures?
> Research Question 3: What is the relationship between the communication channels guests choose to lodge a complaint about a service experience and their level of guest frustration?
> Research Question 4: What is the relationship between the communication channels guests choose to lodge a complaint about a service experience and their sociodemographic characteristics?

Method

Participants and Procedure

To test these proposed relationships, we surveyed 513 mall patrons whom we solicited while they were shopping in three US cities adjacent to college campuses located in the Northeast, Southeast, and Midwest. Over the course of six months, we set up tables in front of the malls' food court between the hours of noon and 3:00 p.m. and from 6:00 to 8:00 p.m. on both weekdays and weekends. The participants in this convenience sample were asked to fill out the survey if they met the following three criteria: (1) they had eaten a meal in a table-service restaurant in the prior three months, (2) they had experienced some type of a service failure during their meal, and (3) they had lodged a complaint during or following that meal. Participants were given a lottery ticket costing $1.00 in exchange for their completed survey. We asked a total of 900 shoppers to participate, yielding the 513 participants who both qualified and agreed to participate in the study (a response rate of 57%).

The average age of the study participants was 32.10 years, ranging from 18 to 73; 59% of the study participants were women; 15.2% reported they held only a high school diploma, 7% had graduated from an associate's degree program or technical program, 42% indicated they hold a bachelor's degree or were currently earning one, and 36% reported they hold a graduate level degree or were currently earning one. On average, the participants reported they eat about three lunches and not quite three dinners a week in a restaurant, ranging from never to every day (lunch, M = 3.12; dinner, M = 2.53). See table 5.1 for a summary of the participants' sociodemographic characteristics that were measured categorically.

TABLE 5.1. Communication channel preferences to complain and the categorical sociodemographic variables

	N	%
Preferred communication channel		
Face-to-face with manager	246	48
Face-to-face with employee	140	27
Written (letter, e-mail, web)	84	17
Comment card	42	8
Education level		
High school graduate	78	15.2
Associates/technical	36	7.0
Bachelor's	215	41.9
Graduate	184	35.9
Income level		
$19,999 or less	17	3.3
$20,000 to $49,999	148	28.8
$50,000 to $99,999	217	42.3
$100,000 plus	131	25.5
Sex		
Female	303	59.06
Male	211	40.94

Measurement   The participants were also asked to select the channel of communication they prefer to use for restaurant service complaints from the list we discussed above: (1) face-to-face with a manager, (2) face-to-face with an employee, (3) written (either letter, e-mail, or the web), or (4) the organization's comment cards. These preference data are also summarized in table 5.1.

The participants' frustration level was measured using three items, and perceived information inadequacy was measured using five items, all of which I developed for an earlier study (Susskind, 2004). Attitudes toward complaining were measured using four items developed by Day (1984), which I also adjusted for service encounters. The respondents were asked to indicate their level of agreement with each statement using a five-point Likert-type scale (anchored by strongly agree = 5 and strongly disagree = 1). The survey items are presented below.

Survey item 1: Consumer frustration (adapted from Susskind, 2004)

1. I often get upset when I don't get what I expect in service experiences.
2. Customer service employees who don't care about me make me mad.
3. When service is not right in some way, it's not the mistakes that bother me it's how the employees handle them with me.

Survey item 2: Information inadequacy (adapted from Susskind, 2004)

1. When service is not right in some way, it frustrates me when I don't get accurate information from the service providers.
2. I wish service providers would be more honest with me when problems occur with service.
3. I wish service providers would inform me when they know a problem has occurred with their ability to serve me.
4. I feel like service providers rarely give me enough information when service problems occur (like airline flight delays).
5. At times I feel I would be less irritated when service problems occur if I received more information about what went wrong.

Survey item 3: Customers' attitude toward complaining (adapted from Day, 1984; Susskind, 2004)

1. Complaining is a consumers' right not an obligation.
2. I always complain when I am dissatisfied because I feel it my duty.
3. Complaining isn't always easy, but it should be done when "things" are not right.
4. I always feel better once I voice my dissatisfactions through a complaint.

All of the scales used in this study were content validated using Hinkin and Tracey's (1999) approach (cf. Susskind, 2004). To ensure that the scale items in this setting maintained the specified factor structure, the items were also subjected to a principal components analysis using a covariance matrix as input with a Varimax rotation. Results of the factor analyses (see table 5.2) support the factor structure I found in my earlier study (Susskind, 2004), as all of the items loaded on their a priori specified factors with no notable cross loadings and acceptable levels of measurement reliability (Cronbach's a values are reported in the diagonal of the correlation matrix presented as table 5.3).

TABLE 5.2. Principal components analysis of survey items

	1	2	3
Complaint 1	.314	−.075	.744
Complaint 2	−.173	.131	.745
Complaint 3	.200	−.096	.754
Complaint 4	.092	.228	.754
Frustration 1	.214	.866	.083
Frustration 2	.262	.871	.036
Frustration 3	.195	.840	.041
Info. deficiency 1	.665	.284	.100
Info. deficiency 2	.709	.177	.183
Info. deficiency 3	.735	.173	.164
Info. deficiency 4	.693	.131	−.096
Info. deficiency 5	.731	.102	.111

TABLE 5.3. Means, standard deviations, and correlations among the variables

	M	SD	(1)	(2)	(3)	(4)	(5)	(6)	(7)	(8)	(9)
(1) Sex	—	—	[—]								
(1) Age	32.10	14.58	.09*	[—]							
(2) Education†	3.99	1.01	-.02	.03	[—]						
(3) Income†	2.58	1.24	-.23**	.11*	.28**	[—]					
(4) Weekly lunch frequency	3.12	2.15	-.08	-.39**	-.17**	-.12**	[—]				
(5) Weekly dinner frequency	2.53	1.96	-.16**	-.38**	-.10	-.05	.57**	[—]			
(6) Propensity to complain	3.69	0.80	.01	.11*	.10*	.07	.01	-.06	[.87]		
(7) Information adequacy	4.05	0.67	.12**	.12**	.20*	.03	-.12**	-.10*	.36**	[.79]	
(8) Consumer frustration	3.59	0.98	.08	.00	.00	-.08	.00	-.04	.32**	.52**	[.76]

Note: Listwise N = 511; Cronbach's α is reported along the diagonal in brackets for the three scale variables.

†Education and income were measured using an ordinal/categorical format where lower-category numbers represent lower levels of the variable. Sex was measured categorically.

*p < .05. **p < .01.

Analyses To answer the research questions, I applied multi-variate analysis (MANOVA) to test the mean values of guests' propensity to complain, perceptions of information adequacy, and perceived frustration (as the dependent variables) compared with the channel of communication guests prefer to use when lodging complaints. I also entered the sociodemographic variables of age, sex, education level, income level, and dining frequency into the equation as covariates. Following the multivariate analyses, one-way analysis of variance (ANOVA) with a post hoc Duncan's multiple range test was used to test the magnitude and significance of the differences noted in the dependent variables across the four channels of complaint communication, and the categorical and ordinal sociodemographic variables. In addition to the MANOVA and one-way ANOVA analyses, I assessed the correlations among the continuous variables age and dining frequency, examined the effect of sex using an independent sample *t* test, and also analyzed the correlations among the ordinal variables of education and income.

Results

Multivariate Analysis

In general, the media richness theory did not entirely describe this sample's complaint communication preferences, although elements of the theory are applicable, as I will explain. That said, the multivariate model fit the data quite well, indicating that the channel of communication used by restaurant guests to report a service failure was associated with varying levels of their propensity to complain, their reported level of information adequacy, and their frustration with service failures. The Hotelling Trace Statistic was significant (.40, p < .001) with an F statistic of $F(9,1493) = 22.01$, p < .001, $\eta2 = .12$. Propensity to complain explained the largest amount of variance in the model ($\eta2 = .25$), followed by information inadequacy ($\eta2 = .16$) and consumer frustration ($\eta2 = .10$), confirming the multivariate model's sound fit to the data. The multivariate analyses also revealed that the participants' sex and education level were significant in the model. The Hotelling Trace Statistic was significant for respondent sex (.02, p = .03) with an F statistic of $F(3,499) = 2.91$, p = .04, $\eta2 = .02$, and for level of education (.06, p < .001) with an F statistic of $F(3,497) = 9.81$, p < .001, $\eta2 = .06$. I discuss the significant effects and further describe them through one-way ANOVA, t-tests, and correlations.

One-Way ANOVA

While several variables tested in the multivariate model and the between-subjects model were identified as significant, the one-way ANOVAs revealed mixed support for the application of a media-richness complaint framework. Several interesting relationships emerged from the data, as follows (see figure 5.1).

Propensity to Complain   In the test of Research Question 1, the one-way ANOVA results revealed significant differences among the means across the four communication modes, $F(3,509) = 53.12$, p < .000. Results from Duncan's multiple range tests indicated that face-to-face communication with a manager and a written letter to management were statistically different from both face-to-face communication with an employee and an

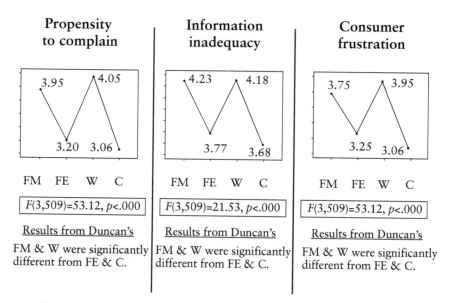

Figure 5.1. Results from the one-way analysis of variance. *Note:* Numbers on the charts are the mean responses for each dependent variable by communication mode. FM = face-to-face with a manger; FE = face-to-face with an employee; W = written letter, e-mail, or web; C = organizationally provided comment card.

organizationally provided comment card at the p < .001 level. This shows that guests who reported a higher propensity to complain about dissatisfying experiences indicated that complaining directly to a manager or drafting a letter to the company was their preferred choice of communication channel for lodging a complaint about their service experience as opposed to directing complaints to line-level employees or using an organization-provided comment card.

Information Adequacy Through the test of Research Question 2, the one-way ANOVA results revealed significant differences among the means across the four communication modes, $F(3,509) = 21.53$, p < .001. Results from Duncan's multiple range tests indicated that face-to-face communication with a manager and a written letter to management were statistically different from both face-to-face communication with an employee and an organizationally provided comment card at the p < .001 level. This shows that guests who reported a lower level of information adequacy reported that organization-provided comment cards and face-to-face communication with employees were their preferred complaint channels. Likewise, guests who reported higher levels of information inadequacy preferred to complain to a manager or draft a written complaint.

Consumer Frustration   The test of Research Question 3 produced a pattern of results similar to those of the previous two research questions. The one-way ANOVA results revealed significant differences among the means across the four communication modes, $F(3,509) = 17.66$, $p < .001$. Results from Duncan's multiple range tests indicated that face-to-face communication with a manager and a written letter to management were statistically different from both face-to-face communication with an employee and an organizationally provided comment card at the $p < .001$ level. These results show that individuals reporting lower levels of guest frustration reported the use of organization-provided comment cards, but contrary to the proposed media richness framework, guests who reported lower levels of frustration also indicated that they also preferred direct complaints to line-level employees. Respondents reporting higher levels of frustration regarding their service failure, however, preferred to make complaints to managers personally and complain in writing.

Sociodemographics

Turning to Research Question 4, of the sociodemographic variables included in the model, only respondent sex and education level were significant in the multivariate model, while income level and dining frequency during the lunch meal period each showed significant correlations with some the dependent variables.

Education   Education level was significantly and positively correlated with propensity to complain ($r = .10$, $p = .02$) and with perceptions of information inadequacy ($r = .20$, $p < .001$). Although significant, education level was negatively related to dining out for the lunchtime meal ($r = -.17$, $p < .001$). This shows that, generally, more educated people were more likely to complain when dissatisfied and reported a higher need for information during service failures, but were less likely to eat lunch at a full-service restaurant. The one-way ANOVA analyses revealed a significant effect for both propensity to complain, F (3,509) = 9.28, p < .001, and perceptions of information inadequacy, F (3,509) = 41.88, p < .001. Examining the degree levels, Duncan's multiple range tests indicated that those holding an associate's or technical degree reported a statistically lower propensity to complain along with lower information needs than those with high school diplomas, bachelor's degrees, or graduate degrees.

Education by Communication Channel   Because education was significant in the multivariate model, I conducted an additional $\chi 2$ test, which indicated that the respondents' education level was related to their preferred complaint channel. The $\chi 2$ test results, $\chi 2$ (9) = 47.82, p < .001, showed that those with graduate degrees preferred to complain via written communication, while no differences emerged for the other educational levels regarding this form of communication. Furthermore, there were no differences in the preference for face-to-face communication with line-level employees or the use of organizationally provided comment cards across all four educational levels measured. Last, regarding a preference for face-to-face communication with a manager, those holding associate's or technical degrees did not differ significantly from those with high school degrees or bachelor's and graduate degrees, but those holding bachelor's degrees and graduate degrees had a stronger, statistically significant preference for face-to-face communication with management compared with those holding only high school diplomas. One other difference by education level was that those holding associate's or technical degrees reported a lower propensity to complain and a lower need for information during service failures compared with the three other educational levels. This finding may have something to do with the work experiences associated with their educational background. Seventy percent of line-level food-service workers hold less than a high school diploma, while food-service managers typically hold at a minimum a high school diploma, and some have attended college (Bureau of Labor Statistics, US Department of Labor, 2014).[3] Therefore, those with technical degrees are likely to have more direct experience with line-level employees and consumer complaints in their workplaces. I infer that this would make them less sensitive to the nuances of the complaint process as consumers.

I believe that the finding that respondents with graduate degrees were more inclined to write a letter to management (compared with the other three educational levels) reflects on their belief that they can communicate more effectively through this channel (based on efficacy and outcome expectations; Susskind, 2000). While there were no differences across the four educational levels for the use of face-to-face communication with line-level employees and comment cards, those with bachelor's and graduate degrees showed a stronger preference for face-to-face communication with a manager, as compared with those with high school diplomas. As with the finding for written communication above, it appears that those holding college degrees prefer to bypass interaction with line-level staff when complaining and deal directly with management.

Sex   The analysis indicated that women desired more information in the midst of a service failure, as indicated by the finding that only information inadequacy was significant, with females reporting a higher need than males, M = 4.11 for women and M = 3.95 for men; t (509) = –2.03, p = .04. This finding is consistent with research that shows men place more importance on instrumental facets of a service experience, while women focus more on the relational facets, which involve information exchange (Sanchez-Hernandez et al., 2010; Susskind, 2004) and use both verbal and nonverbal cues in their communication. T tests revealed that the women in this survey were 2.5 years older on average, t (509) = –2.03, p = .04, and dined out for dinner less frequently, t (509) = 3.64, p < .001, than their male counterparts.

Sex by Communication Channel   Because sex was significant in the multivariate model (as was education), I conducted an additional $\chi 2$ test, which found that the respondents' sex was not associated with a single preferred communication channel to complain, $\chi 2$ (3) = 2.07, p = .56.

Income   While income was not significantly related to the dependent variables, those earning higher salaries were older and more educated but ate their lunchtime meal out less frequently than others, as indicated by significant correlations with increased age (r = .11, p = .01), reduced frequency of dining out for lunch (r = –.12, p = .006), and greater education (r = .28, p < .001). This also shows that those making less money ate lunch out more often. Despite the lack of significance for income in the multivariate model, I ran an additional $\chi 2$ test on communication channels, which found that income level was not associated with a preferred communication channel to complain, $\chi2$ (9) = 13.57, p = .14.

Age   Older respondents reported a significantly lower level of frequency for dining out for both the lunchtime meal (r = −.39, p < .001) and dinnertime meal (r = −.38, p < .001), had higher incomes (r = .11, p = .01), and reported a higher level of information inadequacy during service failures (r = .12, p < .001).

Discussion

I mentioned above that a pure media richness approach did not completely apply in this case. I say this because face-to-face communication—the richest form of communication—was not uniformly preferred by guests to address complaints, as the theory proposes. The results do show that guests prefer to use different communication channels to lodge complaints depending upon their perception of service experiences and their specific perceptions of complaints and the complaint process.

While those who favored richer communication channels reported higher levels of frustration, a propensity to complain, and information inadequacy (which the theory suggests means richer communication channels), these respondents viewed complaining directly to a manager as being essentially similar to writing a letter to someone high in the organization. Conversely, complaining to a line-level employee (which the theory views as a rich channel) was viewed similarly to using a comment card, which is the least rich channel of the four I measured here. These findings suggest that guests view complaints delivered at the line level differently than complaints delivered directly to management.

Managerial Implications

As a starting point, guests who are not satisfied with a service experience may not complain, depending upon the circumstances of the service failure and their own evaluation and processing of the service failure (Singh, 1988; Sparks & Fredline, 2007; Susskind, 2000). This is a dynamic of the customer-server exchange that remains a challenge for operators to manage effectively. Managers generally want guests to complain when they are not fully satisfied with the service they receive, but encouraging complaints involves considerable uncertainty. When guests do decide that they are going to complain, this study shows that they take different approaches regarding to whom and how they complain based in part on their personal characteristics.

Complaints, just like compliments, are direct feedback from guests. Complaint management is an unavoidable part of the customer-server exchange and is a key to building long-term relationships between guests and operators. When a complaint is lodged, the service provider has a limited window of time to effectively address the complaint. As managers and employees gain a better understanding of how to react and respond to guest complaints, it (theoretically) becomes easier to remedy existing complaints and prevent similar problems that led to the complaint in the first place. The question is whether theory can become reality.

This study revealed that guests who were more likely complain, who have a higher need for information about a service failure, and who report a higher level of frustration prefer to complain directly to managers face-to-face or via written communication. These guests are not interested in generic comment cards, nor are they likely to complain directly to employees. This shows in this case that restaurant guests—based on their perceptions of the complaint process—categorized complaints in two main ways: those directed toward management and those directed to the line-level employees.

As I said, this finding differs from a strict media richness framework, but media richness theory does shed some new light on how restaurant consumers view and process complaints. A main tenet of this theory is that the person initiating the communication needs sufficient motivation to complain and needs to engage in such a way to attract the attention of the receiver (Robert & Dennis, 2005). This aspect of media richness theory does help explain the findings. As a complaint involves a social confrontation (Susskind, 2000, 2004), dealing directly with management requires more effort and, by implication, more motivation on the part of the guest. In addition, a complaint lodged directly to management reflects the premise that the guest is frustrated by a lack of control of the circumstances or a lack of adequate information (Guchait & Namasivayam, 2012; Mittal, Huppertz, & Khare, 2008; Susskind, 2004). The logical conclusion here is that a sense of control emerges from interaction with management (Mittal, Huppertz, & Khare, 2008), regardless of the richness of the communication channel used. In sum, I conclude that the distinctive nature of service experiences in a restaurant means that this deviation from a strict media richness theory framework makes sense for restaurants, particularly since restaurant service is notably different from the context of other media richness studies.

Managers should realize that the guests who have chosen to complain to management, either face-to-face or via written communication, require some kind of response that is greater than what they perceive is available from their server or through a comment card. The roots of such complaints to management begin with the guests' belief that they should make such a complaint, in particular due to their frustration, and they likely require a substantial response that includes information about what went wrong and why. In addition to expressing appreciation for the feedback, managers should provide these complaining guests with a swift, factual accounting of the problem, the proposed remedy, and how that would solve the problem now and prevent it from repeating in the future. This type of response acknowledges these guests' higher need for information regarding service failures and mitigates any looming frustration by ensuring that the problem is resolved to their satisfaction.

All of the above is (or should be) a fairly standard procedure for responding to complaints, but the point here is that these steps are supported by the theory and the findings of this study. Managers should, of course, also follow up with guests after the service failure is corrected or send written correspondence to show guests that you (as the manager) took ownership of the failure, truly valued their feedback, and sincerely wanted to correct the problem for them. As a reminder, this study indicates that it is important to ensure that you offer enough information about the failure and recovery to satisfy this subgroup's need for information.

None of the above is to say that complaints lodged via comment cards or directly to service staff members are not important or do not merit a response. All complaints and comments should be taken seriously and resolved as quickly and completely as possible. For direct complaints to line-level service staff, the problem often can be resolved while the service experience is still in process. In such a situation, if the service failure is not complex and can easily be identified and addressed, it should be handled quickly at the line level, and a system should be in place to do so. This speaks to the issue of complaint severity, which was not addressed in this study but which may be connected to a guest's choice of a particular complaint channel.

Study Limitations

A chief limitation of this research is that it was a field-based survey project that did not take place in a restaurant. We collected our data at shopping malls to gain a large, diverse group of consumers who had been recent guests of full-service restaurants. While this was a convenience sample, the sample accurately captured participants from the desired population. In addition, because data were collected from three disparate locations and at various times, the participants represented a decent cross-section of age, sex, and education. The screening process meant that sampling was not truly random, but it was essential that the participants meet the three qualifications for inclusion in the study. In addition, it should be noted that all three malls where the data were collected were located in communities supported by large research-based universities; therefore, the sample included a higher proportion of those holding (or working toward) bachelor's degrees and graduate degrees.

This study did not explore the use of social media to complain about service issues. Given the prevalence of social media in today's marketplace, future studies of complaint management and media richness should include measures of social media to complement existing research and examine the influences from this relatively new communication channel. Including social media as a communication channel may provide additional insight into complaint management.

Finally, I want to point out three pieces of data that were not collected in this investigation that would have added depth to the analysis and interpretation. These are the nature of the service failures guests reported, the severity of the service failures, and whether their complaint was fully redressed to their satisfaction. I have included these variables in past studies (see, for example, Susskind, 2005; Susskind & Viccari, 2011), and they may very well have an effect on the guests' choices of the richness of a complaint channel.

The perishable nature of food service, the hospitality business, at large has a substantial effect on complaint dimensions. While this study only focused on consumers' complaints relative to restaurant experiences, it is possible that this study can inform managers of other hospitality and service-related businesses too. Understanding why and how your guests or customers complain are the first steps to being able to offer consistent, timely, and appropriate service recovery.

Notes

Original citation: Susskind, A. M. (2014). Communication richness: Why some guest complaints go right to the top—and others do not. *Cornell Hospitality Quarterly 56*(3): 320–331.

1. Third-party complaints—complaints addressed to a third party, not the seller—through social media sites have grown exponentially over the past several years. It is also important to note that when posting a third-party complaint through social media, there is no guarantee or expectation that redress will occur, as the service provider may never get wind of the complaint. Singh (1988) also notes that customers can also address third-party complaints to agencies or organizations designed to manage consumer complaint to get redress, such as the Better Business Bureau and other consumer advocacy groups. In these cases, consumers have a heightened expectation of some sort of resolution through these third parties. Therefore, guests who want a complaint resolved (opposed to just venting) would most likely complain directly to the seller.

2. It is important to note that frustration and aggression are two related, but separate, constructs (Neuman & Baron, 1998). Psychologically speaking, aggression is a consequent of frustration, meaning that not all frustration leads to aggression.

3. Bureau of Labor Statistics Handbook (Bureau of Labor Statistics, US Department of Labor, 2014) reported that 30% of restaurant managers did not hold a high school diploma.

References

Bagozzi, R. P. (1992). The self-regulation of attitudes, intentions, and behavior. *Social Psychology Quarterly, 55*: 178–204.

Berkowitz, L. (1989). Frustration-aggression hypothesis: Examination and reformulation. *Psychological Bulletin 106*(1): 59–73.

Bureau of Labor Statistics, US Department of Labor. (2014). Occupational outlook handbook, 2014–15 edition, food and beverage serving and related workers. http://www.bls.gov/ooh/food-preparation-and-serving/food-and-beverage-serv-ing-and-related-workers.htm.

Daft, R. L., & Lengel, R. H. (1984). Information richness: A new approach to managerial information processing and organizational design. *Research in Organizational Behavior, 6*: 191–233.

Daft, R. L., & Lengel, R. H. (1986). Organizational information requirements, richness, and structural design. *Management Science, 32*: 554–571.

Daft, R. L., Lengel, R. H., & Trevino, L. K. (1987). Message equivocality, media selection, and manager performance: Implications for information systems. *MIS Quarterly*, 11: 355–366.

Day, R. L. (1984). Modeling choices among alternative responses to dissatisfaction. *Advances in Consumer Research*, 11: 496–499.

Dennis, A. R., & Kinney, S. T. (1998). Testing media richness theory in the new media: The effects of cues, feedback, and task equivocality. *Information Systems Research*, 9(3): 256–274.

Dennis, A. R., Kinney, S. T., & Hung, Y. C. (1999). Gender differences in the effects of media richness. *Small Group Research*, 30(4): 405–437.

Dollard, J., Doob, L., Miller, N., Mowrer, O., & Sears, R. (1939). *Frustration and aggression*. New Haven, CT: Yale University Press.

Fornell, C., & Westbrook, R. A. (1979). An exploratory study of assertiveness, aggressiveness, and consumer complaining behavior. *Advances in Consumer Research*, 6: 105–110.

Guchait, P., & Namasivayam, K. (2012). Customer creation of products: Role of frustration in customer evaluations. *Journal of Services Marketing*, 26: 216–224.

Harris, M. B. (1974). Mediators between frustration and aggression in a field experiment. *Journal of Experimental Social Psychology*, 10(5): 561–571.

Hinkin, T. R., & Tracey, J. B. (1999). An analysis of variance approach to content validation. *Organizational Research Methods*, 2: 175–186.

Hui, M. K., & Tse, D. K. (1996). What to tell customers in waits of different lengths: An integrative model of service evaluation. *Journal of Marketing*, 60(2): 81–90.

Huppertz, J. W., Mower, E., and Associates. (2003). An effort model of first stage complaining behavior. *Journal of Consumer Satisfaction, Dissatisfaction, and Complaining Behavior*, 16: 132–144.

Kahai, S. S., & Cooper, R. B. (1999). The effect of computer-mediated communication on agreement and acceptance. *Journal of Management Information Systems*, 16 (Summer): 263–299.

Kahai, S. S., & Cooper, R. B. (2003). Exploring the core concepts of media richness theory: The impact of cue multiplicity and feedback immediacy on decision quality. *Journal of Management Information Systems*, 19 (Summer): 165–188.

Kowalski, R. M. (1996). Complaints and complaining: Functions, antecedents, and consequences. *Psychological Bulletin*, 119(2): 179–196.

Maddux, J. E., Norton, L. W., & Stoltenberg, C. D. (1986). Self-efficacy expectancy, outcome expectancy, and outcome value: Relative effects on behavioral intentions. *Journal of Personality and Social Psychology*, 51: 783–789.

Makoul, G., & Roloff, M. E. (1998). The role of efficacy and outcome expectations in the decision withhold relational complaints. *Communication Research*, 25: 5–29.

Mattila, A. S., & Ro, H. (2008). Discrete negative emotions and customer dissatisfaction responses in a casual restaurant setting. *Journal of Hospitality & Tourism Research*, 32(1): 89–107.

Mittal, V., Huppertz, J. W., & Khare, A. (2008). Customer complaining: The role of tie strength and information control. *Journal of Retailing*, 84(2): 195–204.

Neuman, J. H., & Baron, R. A. (1998). Workplace violence and workplace aggression: Evidence concerning specific forms, potential causes, and preferred target. *Journal of Management, 24*(3): 391–419.

Park, S., & Allen, J. P. (2013). Responding to online reviews problem solving and engagement in hotels. *Cornell Hospitality Quarterly, 54*(1): 64–73.

Robert, L. P., & Dennis, A. R. (2005). Paradox of richness: A cognitive model of media choice. *IEEE Transactions on Professional Communication, 48*(1): 10–21.

Sanchez-Hernandez, R. M., Martinez-Tur, V., Peiro, J. M., & Moliner, C. (2010). Linking functional and relational service quality to consumer satisfaction and loyalty: Differences between men and women. *Psychological Reports, 106*(2): 598–610.

Schmitz, J., & Fulk, J. (1991). Organizational colleagues, media richness, and electronic mail. *Communication Research, 18*(4): 487–523.

Singh, J. (1988). Consumer complaint intentions and behavior: Definitional and taxonomical issues. *Journal of Marketing, 52*(1): 93–107.

Singh, J., & Wilkes, R. E. (1996). When consumers complain: A path analysis of the key antecedents of consumer complaint response estimates. *Journal of the Academy of Marketing Science, 24*(4): 350–365.

Sparks, B., & Fredline, L. (2007). Providing and explanation for service failure: Context, content, and customer responses. *Journal of Hospitality & Tourism Research, 31*(2): 241–260.

Stephens, N., & Gwinner, K. P. (1998). Why some people complain? A cognitive-emotive process model of consumer complaint behavior. *Journal of the Academy of Marketing Science, 26*: 172–189.

Susskind, A. M. (2000). Efficacy and outcome expectations related to guest complaints about service experiences. *Communication Research, 27*(3): 353–378.

Susskind, A. M. (2002). I told you so! Restaurant consumers' word-of-mouth communication. *Cornell Hotel and Restaurant Administration Quarterly, 43*(2): 75–85.

Susskind, A. M. (2004). Consumer frustration in the guest-server exchange: The role of attitudes toward complaining and information inadequacy related to service failures. *Journal of Hospitality & Tourism Research, 28*(1): 200–223.

Susskind, A. M. (2005). A content analysis of consumer complaints, remedies, and repatronage intentions regarding dissatisfying service experiences. *Journal of Hospitality & Tourism Research, 29*(2): 150–169.

Susskind, A. M., & Viccari, A. E. (2011). A look at the relationship between service failures, guest satisfaction, and repeat-patronage intentions of casual dining guests. *Cornell Hospitality Quarterly, 52*(4): 360–367.

Trevino, L. K., Lengel, R. H., & Daft, R. L. (1987). Media symbolism, media richness, and media choice in organizations. *Communication Research, 14*: 553–574.

Part III

AMBIANCE AND DESIGN

The Understated Elements of Excellence

ALEX M. SUSSKIND AND MARK MAYNARD

Alex: While we have spent considerable time so far talking about the nuances of creating and delivering service experiences, we have focused mainly on service process management and creating an understanding of how the "big three" (food, service, and ambiance) relate to service excellence.

This section gives us a chance to further address the importance of design and the more tangible parts of a service experience. Before I dive into talking about the two articles by Robson and Kimes (2007, 2009), it is safe to say that very little academic research has been conducted in this domain. In speaking with Robson directly for this part, she said there are plenty of talented restaurateurs and, more formally, restaurant designers out there conceptualizing and designing restaurants, but very few take an academic approach to their work and publish their findings. This is not a criticism, per se; it is identifying a noticeable gap.

Conceptualizing a restaurant is no small undertaking. After developing an initial idea, the concept needs to be translated into the big three so that it is clear and understandable for guests. Menus are developed taking into account the market—that is, who the guests are, why they will be interested in the business, and where the business will be located. Food and beverage offerings will be the foundation of the business, or the "What." Service processes will be "How," and the physical space will be "Where." The physical space is the stage.

That being said, the stage has to be the right size and contain the needed functionality and layout, such as entrances and spaces for guests, employees, and managers and supplies, utilities, equipment and utensils, storage, furniture, fixtures, art, and décor, including lighting. These elements need to be assembled in such a way that food and beverage products can be procured, secured, prepared, served, sold, and consumed in line with the vision for the concept. Each of the elements of functionality and layout need to be part of a comprehensive plan to ensure that the stage has been set meaningfully and properly. All of this has to occur through known and realistic limits to available space and resources. Very few restaurateurs have blank checks to set their stage, and they must consider all of these elements carefully. Each decision is interconnected with the overall design intent, and the results of these decisions will live on for a very long time: you will see them every day.

In the articles selected for this part, Robson and Kimes write about two very important design considerations: (1) lighting, in "Examining the Effects of Full-Spectrum Lighting in a Restaurant" (2007), and (2) table spacing and configurations in dining rooms, in "Don't Sit So Close to Me: Restaurant Table Characteristics and Guest Satisfaction" (2009).

Lighting is an important part of the restaurant experience. From a practical perspective, lighting needs to be sufficient in work spaces for staff members to do their jobs safely. In guest-related areas, lighting takes on a dual role of allowing guests to properly see what they are doing (reading, eating, and interacting) and to be a part of the ambiance and décor. Neither role is necessarily more important than the other. Consider the lighting design employed at Hillstone Restaurant Group as an example. Lighting is carefully located and directed on the tables and bar spaces to ensure that spaces occupied by guests have sufficient lighting to read and to see the food and beverage and fellow guests. Likewise, surrounding the tables and other parts of the guest-centric spaces, the lighting is more subdued and helps create a visual separation between the tables and the rest of the public spaces. This design concept is consistently executed in all of their restaurants. They are not the only restaurant group to do this with lighting, but they do it very well.

Robson and Kimes, in "Examining the Effects of Full-Spectrum Lighting in a Restaurant," describe how lighting is used in restaurant spaces to create and affect atmosphere. In their study, Robson and Kimes were interested in testing the effect of full-spectrum lighting (which mimics natural daylight) on guests' dining behavior—that is, does full-spectrum lighting affect guests' spending levels or meal duration in a restaurant when compared to incandescent lighting? This study was conducted to investigate lighting manufacturers' claims that full-spectrum lighting stimulates sales. They conducted a field experiment and set up two different dining spaces in a restaurant to test their hypotheses that full-spectrum incandescent lighting would lead to higher sales and shorter dining duration compared to regular incandescent lighting. They used point-of-sales data to examine spending and meal duration and did not ask guests questions about lighting to avoid priming the subjects to the issues under study. Their results showed that there were no notable increases in spending or decreases in meal duration that they could confidently say resulted directly from the full-spectrum incandescent lighting, hence showing that manufacturers' claims do not apply in this case. This study highlights a couple of very important outcomes: first, selection of décor and lighting needs to convey the intended feel and ambiance. In their article, Robson and Kimes identify many ways that lighting can be configured and designed and the effects it can bring to the dining experience. Second, tracking revenue, table turns, and other dining room productivity metrics is very important. Available data should be used to inform decisions and make sure that design decisions take into account the goals of creating and managing a successful operation for guests, employees, and other stakeholders. It's also worth noting that the data may change. In addition to hard sales data, it is helpful (and smart) to collect feedback from guests and other users of the space to gauge their reactions. Based on feedback and data, lighting configurations can be changed to better support the concept. Finally, it's helpful to remember that lighting is but one variable in a restaurant design.

Mark: Lighting is one of the most important elements to get right to create a great dining/drinking experience. Along with noise levels, lighting sets the mood and lets your guests know what's important to you while giving them cues for how to interact with the space. I was fortunate to work with the same great lighting designer for the last three places I helped design: Jazz Standard, Blue Smoke Battery Park City, and Porchlight. All three concepts have lighting that improves the overall interior design of the architect while amplifying the concept of the business. While none of these places are self-consciously "design-y," there are certain elements in each space that benefit from very thoughtful lighting. Most of us are not lighting experts, and we may be inclined to blindly trust the architect or lighting designer to accentuate what she thinks is important. That could be a mistake, because the designers could miss an opportunity to hear your philosophy and intent on specific aspects of the guest experience. During the course of planning my most recent projects, the architect, lighting designer, and I sat down to discuss every fixture that would be used in the space, regardless of whether that fixture would be visible to the guest. I asked them the design intent of each piece, and they explained to me, in layman's terms, how each light would affect the mood of that certain area or element. It was an incredibly fun exercise, but also incredibly important to the success of the spaces. It was one more way for us to make sure we were on the same page, long before we started running wires and hammering nails. For example, when discussing Porchlight, it was important for the designer to understand that alcohol would represent 75% of sales and that the most important aspect of the experience would be human interaction. Unlike some bars, Porchlight would not be a temple to a chef or bartender. It would be a place for people to connect and get to know one another, with our cocktails and food as the vehicles to help make that happen. We discussed that we wanted different zones, to facilitate different experiences, from a group of friends playing darts to colleagues discussing business to couples looking for a romantic escape. The designers then worked together to make those zones happen, and the result was very successful.

With regard to the research, I would have personally hypothesized that lower lighting would be the thing to improve sales. The lighting at Porchlight is all LED, which generally has a cooler tone than incandescent, but the designer specified warm filters to make the room much more welcoming and to bathe guests in a warm glow. As one guest said to me several months after Porchlight opened, "I love coming here because the lighting makes me look so good!" When I heard this, I remembered that schematic plan and was grateful that at least one guest appreciated her design intent.

In your design, don't forget to consider how to light back-of-house spaces. I have experienced places where the designers seem to have forgotten that lights from kitchen doors and work stations can kill the mood of the dining room. Restaurants with open kitchens need to nail this conundrum so that everything happening in the kitchen looks more, not less, appetizing. This is challenging, because we rely on bright lights in the kitchen to see the food and notice anything wrong with the plate (fingerprints, for example) before the service team delivers the food to the guest. Working in low light can make this more challenging for the cooks. Porchlight has a unique challenge, because there is a pass-through window between the bar and kitchen. So, while most of the kitchen lighting is not directly visible from the public areas, some of it is. Our lighting designer specified kitchen lights that can be dimmed in the evening, and she also included under-shelf lighting to illuminate the cooks' work surface without being visible to the guests at the bar.

One final lighting consideration is what the space looks like from the outside. An effective lighting scheme can make your guests salivate before they even walk through the door. We chose the name "Porchlight" because we felt it conveyed a feeling of warmth. Located in an industrial neighborhood along the windy Hudson River, it was especially important for the lighting to reinforce our intent. From over 100 feet away, the space seems to glow, long before someone walking down the street can see what is happening inside. The light that bathes the sidewalk conjures up the feeling that everything is going to be all right. On a cold night, it is almost impossible to pass by without wanting to walk in.

Alex: In the second article, "Don't Sit So Close to Me: Restaurant Table Characteristics and Guest Satisfaction," Robson and Kimes examine the connection between table characteristics (spacing distance and size), meal duration, spending, and guest satisfaction in a full-service restaurant. Their study was conducted in New York City, where space considerations in restaurants are an important design element and often limit or constrain a restaurant's capacity. The idea is that more space at a table and between tables for guests should make them more comfortable and invite them to spend more, but also may encourage them to stay longer. The footprint of the dining room determines how many tables can fit, but many factors determine how large a table should be. From a revenue management perspective, tables should be as small and close together as practical, but there are many aesthetic elements to consider beyond revenue management efficiency or optimization. For example, the china, glassware, and silverware can influence the need for space at a table. Larger plates or food served family-style will require more space per table for the service to work well. Similarly, tapas or mezze, where guests share multiple items throughout the meal, may require more space at the table to facilitate sharing. If the concept encourages guests to order bottles of wine as opposed to single-service beverages, more space may be required; and in luxury restaurants, guests will expect more space, regardless of the china or glassware used. The choice of china, glass, and silver should be carefully matched to the menu, how guests consume food and beverages, and how the food is delivered and served to the tables. Yes, table size matters for all the functional reasons listed above, and, in addition, table selection, configuration, size, and spacing can influence the appeal and feel of the dining room for guests. Another factor regarding table selection is spacing. There are several theories that address the importance of regulating personal space, the need for distance based on interpersonal closeness (friends vs. acquaintances vs. strangers), and the need or the perceived need for control over personal space. Personal space, therefore, is a factor that can help people feel comfortable when deemed sufficient or uncomfortable when perceived as too tight or close.

In examining these factors, Robson and Kimes, in "Don't Sit So Close to Me," found that guests who were seated at tables larger than needed for the party size (that is, seating two guests at a four-top), reported higher levels of satisfaction with the food, service, timing of the meal, overall satisfaction, and comfort compared to those guests seated at a "right-sized" table (that is, seating two guests at a two-top). The study also found that guests at larger-than-needed tables, compared to those at right-sized tables, reported they felt less crowded by adjacent tables, spent more on average, and had a longer meal duration. Larger-than-needed tables were not, however, associated with significantly higher reports of repeat-patronage intentions or willingness to recommend the restaurant to others.

Regarding the distance between tables, Robson and Kimes found that guests seated at tables that were the closest together reported the lowest levels of satisfaction and were, hence, the least likely to return. In this case, the size of the table was clearly an important factor that guests positively reacted to, but table spacing seems to be the factor most strongly leading to dissatisfaction. This finding is similar to studies about how bathroom cleanliness is typically viewed by guests: very few guests will report that the cleanliness of the bathroom added satisfaction to their consumption of the dining experience; they will, however, notice when the bathroom is not clean, which will drive dissatisfaction with the experience. So it can be argued that, much like bathroom cleanliness, proper table spacing (distance) is a dissatisfier when not managed properly to guests' needs, while table size (comfort) is a satisfier.

Mark: As with offering guests a choice of table at the front door, sitting at a larger table can make people feel powerful. There is nothing quite like sitting with a guest at a four-top and spreading out. Seating guests at a "larger than needed" table is less about improving sales and more about recognizing special occasions or for engendering loyalty to those guests who have been there in good times and bad—especially those regular guests who show up at 9:00 p.m. on a snowy Tuesday in February. It's a small way we can show our loyal guests that we appreciate them, and I feel it's more genuine than simply comping an extra glass of wine (which is sometimes the right move, too). I saw this in action from my first day at Union Square Cafe. Lunchtime at USC was a bustling scene of writers, publishers, designers, and ad executives, most of whom were regular guests using the dining room as an extension of their office. It was a huge challenge to seat the room, and Danny taught me to always balance the needs of the guests (especially regulars) with the realities of the space. I learned to seat regulars (almost always parties of two) at four-tops whenever possible. These regulars were the lifeblood of our lunch business. They considered USC home, and they felt comfortable. We honored their incredible loyalty by booking last-minute reservations and seating them at larger tables. There was almost nothing more important than making them feel special. Since our regular guests knew that we always tried to seat them at larger tables, they were rarely disappointed when we would have to seat them at a banquette, surrounded by other guests, during a very busy lunch service. They wanted us to succeed as much as we tried to take care of them. It was the ultimate virtuous cycle.

With regard to the research about table size and return intentions, I am not surprised that people would be more satisfied but not necessarily more likely to return. As mentioned in chapter 2, repeat intentions stem mostly from the first impression at the door ("cheerful greeting," to use the researchers' terminology) and food presentation. But, what if the maître d' had done something special for a guest and thoughtfully seated them at a larger table in recognition of a special event or achievement? Would that have the same effect? I have a hard time believing that a couple celebrating an anniversary or a sales person closing a deal would not appreciate the larger table, but they would have to know that someone made the decision and that it didn't just happen by chance. While no one likes a smarmy maître d' at the front door, I feel great when I am a guest and the maître d' holds a special table for me. Talk about making someone feel important! Something as simple as, "I've saved you a choice of two tables to help you celebrate. Would you prefer a cozy corner table or a nice large table in the main dining room?" Without being explicit, the maître d' in this instance subtly tells the guest that the restaurant knows there is something special happening and that guest has been heard. Again, offering a choice gives the host of the party power, which can be incredibly impactful in front of a guest.

As Alex outlines above, it's important that table size is aligned with the concept of the business. A low-priced, quick-service establishment with smaller tables (and brighter lighting) makes more sense than a fine dining restaurant with the same configuration. I believe guests intuitively understand this. The challenge for me is when a restaurant that features a prix fixe tasting menu with wine pairings has tables that would be more appropriate in a burrito joint. This can definitely make guests feel that the business is not on their side, potentially engendering resentment. But from a practical angle, it can be incredibly annoying for both staff and guests if serviceware simply doesn't fit on the table. When planning our restaurants, we typically use plywood templates in various sizes to represent the table sizes we are considering, and we use those templates when we are choosing our china, glass, and silverware. When planning Blue Smoke, we realized that we needed to make our deuces slightly larger to accommodate the many side dishes we would be serving. We started by considering that each table would be pre-set with a sauce caddy and that servers would greet guests with a plate of homemade sliced bread and a jar of pickles. So, before guests even ordered, there was the potential of having a crowded table. Adding those extra few inches to the table made all the difference in the guest experience. Conversely, we decided to make the tables at Porchlight much smaller, given that food would represent only 25% of nighttime sales. Fewer plates means smaller tables. But, stemming from our fine dining roots, we chose to make our tables larger than our bar peers, ensuring that our guests would have ample room to enjoy the whole experience.

In terms of table spacing, it can be deeply frustrating to be closer to a neighboring guest than to your date across the table. I would also argue that, since it's less comfortable for guests and more challenging for the staff, tight table spacing could actually hurt, not help, revenue. If tables are too tight and uncomfortable, guests may be inclined to shorten the experience, opting to skip dessert or an after-dinner drink. Sure, this decreases table-turn times, but as we have seen in the data, the sale will be fleeting, with a lower likelihood for a repeat sale down the road. There could also be more mundane consequences, like increased breakage of glassware (ever try standing up from a tight table without bumping the guests next to you?). I would rather raise the price of every menu item by a dollar and give everyone (staff and guests) a more comfortable experience than cram tables together.

By now, it's clear that we believe table size needs to fit the concept (and the stuff that supports the concept) and that table spacing needs to give guests the personal space they want so they can relax. Giving your service staff the space they need to work will also improve the guest experience. Taken together, these considerations foster a virtuous cycle of service that will encourage people to return.

6

Examining the Effects of Full-Spectrum Lighting in a Restaurant

Stephani K. A. Robson and Sheryl E. Kimes

Lighting is a large contributor to diners' overall restaurants experience. A common belief among restaurateurs is that subtle environmental effects such as music or lighting influence guests' behavior, whether that means increased table turns or higher spending. Managers' beliefs about how atmospheric elements affect diners are based to some extent on conjecture and anecdotal information.[1] Moreover, any beliefs might be susceptible to manufacturers' claims about the effectiveness of particular lighting or sound systems. One such claim is that full-spectrum lighting—light that appears similar to natural daylight—increases sales. For this report, we investigated whether full-spectrum lighting actually influences diners in a full-service restaurant, whether by encouraging them to spend more or by speeding up their meal. We first discuss lighting, and provide a brief overview of what is known about lighting's effects on behavior. We then summarize the results of our research that tested full-spectrum lighting against regular incandescent lighting in an operating dining environment. We conclude by examining claims regarding full-spectrum lighting.

Restaurant designers often put considerable emphasis on lighting to create warm, inviting, or even dramatic effects. While a simple take-out operation might use only the familiar and utilitarian ceiling-mounted fluorescent fixtures because of their low cost, full-service restaurants often apply some combination of hanging fixtures (pendants), recessed down lights, small spotlights on tracks or cables, and table-top accent lights to create atmosphere in the dining room. The lighting budget can reach well into the tens of thousands of dollars for a high-end restaurant. A designer's lighting decisions are typically made according to the desired lighting effect, although a good designer will also take into account ongoing costs for energy and of replacing bulbs (called "lamps") over time.

Perceived brightness, color temperature, and light quality all combine in an effective lighting design, and any of these aspects might influence diners' behavior. Perceived brightness is largely a function of lamp wattage, but that is modified with shielding by means of lenses or shades. Color temperature expresses the apparent color of the light, whether bluish, reddish, or yellow, for instance. Color temperatures that have been measured relative to a standard using the Kelvin scale are usually termed "corrected" color temperatures.[2] Most lamps have a corrected color temperature rating listed on the packaging. As a comparison, everyday incandescent lamps have a corrected color temperature of around 2,500°K and appear warmer, or more yellow, than cool-appearing, fluorescent lights, which have a corrected color temperature of around 4,500°K and appear bluer to most people. A final light variable, light quality, which can be affected by the type of shade, light placement, and the type of lamp, relates to the way the light appears to a viewer. The intensity of an incandescent lamp filament stands in contrast to the more uniform, less intense fluorescent lamp. The attributes of fluorescent light, coupled with its longer lamp life and lower energy costs, make it a popular choice for back-of-house areas and some dining areas (particularly in quick-service or take-out operations), but it does not allow as much creative freedom to the designer as does incandescent light.

Most people prefer the warm, flattering light given off by incandescent lamps to that of fluorescents. Because incandescent lighting lends itself to being focused or directed, designers can use incandescent lamps of several types to define areas in the restaurant, highlight key functions (such as a food display or an open kitchen), emphasize textures on the walls or ceiling, and establish a mood. Pendants over individual dining tables can make each table feel intimate, while ceiling-mounted spotlights can be trained on menu boards, artwork, carving stations, or back bars to draw the guest's attention and add life to the dining room.

The availability of so-called full-spectrum light—intended to match daylight—has added another choice for restaurant designers. A popular choice for residential use, full-spectrum light is supposed to render colors so that they appear more natural and attractive, and some vendors assert that this form of light enhances people's mood, sharpens mental awareness, and even increases sales in retail environments, among other benefits.[3] Lamps with a corrected color temperature of greater than 5,000°K can be considered to be full-spectrum, although we know of no standard within the lighting industry for the color temperature of full-spectrum lamps. Full-spectrum lighting is available in both fluorescent and incandescent forms.

Most people recognize that fluorescent lights are more energy efficient than incandescent lamps.[4] Moreover, full-spectrum lighting tends to have a shorter life than lamps with cooler corrected temperatures, making the full-spectrum light a more costly investment for the operator. Nevertheless, restaurateurs and designers may be attracted to incandescent, full-spectrum lighting because of its ability to render colors well or because of its claimed effects on customers. We examine the accuracy of these claims of behavioral effects, particularly in view of the higher price of full-spectrum lighting.

Research on Lighting

Recently, researchers have examined how atmospheric elements in the service environment affect customers. Most of these studies have focused on manipulating music or scent, and sometimes music and scent in combination.[5] These two atmospheric elements are relatively easy to adjust. In most of these studies, modest but significant effects have been identified that appear to influence customer behavior.

Unlike music and scent, lighting in service environments has not been extensively studied despite being acknowledged as an important element of the consumer experience.[6] Manipulating lighting in a real environment is more challenging than manipulating music or scent, and therefore many of the studies that involve lighting rely on adjusting light levels using existing fixtures[7] or simply changing the brightness setting when showing videos of restaurants to participants.[8] Some studies have examined the apparent color temperature of the lighting, finding that warm light encourages feelings of comfort,[9] although this effect appears to vary by gender.[10]

Many studies have been done using daylight or natural light, determining that daylight appears to have significant effects on people, such as reduced agitation in Alzheimer's patients,[11] improved healing after surgery,[12] and increased purchasing in a discount store.[13] Studies have found that warm-color lighting influences mood[14] and is preferred for residential and other casual settings.[15] This appears to have some basis in human biology: humans have photoreceptors that are sensitive to the chromatic character of light, exhibiting increased arousal under bluish (or "cooler") light and reduced arousal in warmer (reddish) light.[16]

There have been many claims regarding the effects of full-spectrum fluorescent lighting in office settings, including improvements in task performance, visual acuity, and sense of well-being. However, independent research into the effects of full-spectrum lighting on health, mood, and productivity has found inconsistent results. Some studies indicate that full-spectrum light has such favorable effects,[17] while others found no significant evidence.[18] We could find only a single proprietary study performed by a consultant to a lighting system manufacturer that offered evidence of positive effects of a dynamic full-spectrum lighting system on duration, mood, and customer attitudes in a retail environment.[19]

We have found little published research examining the influence of lighting in restaurants. A few authors have made connections between lighting and food consumption habits, but there is little agreement in the few studies done of dining under different lighting conditions.[20] Only one study appears to present any evidence of changes in lighting's effect on diners. In that one, Sommer found that bar patrons had shorter lengths of stay and consumed fewer drinks in brightly lit environments.[21]

Certainly one goal of restaurant lighting is to create an attractive, pleasant setting for a meal. Pleasure has been linked with spending behavior and restaurant preference, which are mediated by emotions that can be influenced by lighting's character.[22] So it might be surmised that pleasing lighting may encourage higher spending that is motivated by people's favorable emotional response to the environment. Light—both in terms of its color and its brightness—has also been shown to influence arousal,[23] which in turn affects consumer behavior.[24] However, arousal in a restaurant setting must be considered carefully; diners have different preferred levels of arousal depending on the desired experience.[25] Environments that are too arousing can be overstimulating and unpleasant, whereas insufficient arousal can be perceived as dull and uninteresting.[26] A key factor, then, in determining the appropriate lighting for a restaurant would be adjusting the light to be sufficiently arousing but not excessively so. The literature, however, does not make clear what such a light level might be. With the dozens of lighting choices available to a restaurant operator, making an informed decision when planning a restaurant environment becomes more challenging without tests of different types of lighting in a real dining setting.

Testing Full-Spectrum Lighting

We developed four hypotheses about how full-spectrum lighting might influence dining patrons' behavior, based on findings from the lighting and consumer behavior literature. In general, we hypothesized that full-spectrum incandescent lighting (cooler light) would shorten dining duration, while regular incandescent lighting (warmer light) would lengthen it. This is consistent with research which suggests that more arousing environments result in faster dining speed.[27] We also hypothesized that a more arousing environment such as that generated by cooler light would increase spending, whereas warmer light would result in lower spending.

To base our study on objective observation, we purposely did not examine guests' preferences regarding lighting, nor did we ask for self-reports regarding responses to lighting conditions. We did not want the possibility of influencing diners' behavior by calling attention to the lighting with a questionnaire. Another reason for limiting the study to observed behavior was to align the study with actual actions rather than with perceptions. However, we were careful to keep the lighting we tested consistent with the concept of the restaurant and realistic for a dining operation.

For the test, we altered lighting conditions in a full-service, casual dining restaurant in upstate New York. The facility has two distinct dining environments: a 30-seat main dining room with windows on one side of the space, and a secondary 36-seat dining space with expansive windows on two sides. (The restaurant also has a separate bar area, which was not examined in our study.) Because the windows in the main dining room were flanked by heavy window treatments and only a small proportion of the wall space admitted natural light, we elected to change the lighting only in the main dining room. This allowed us to use the secondary dining room as a comparison for control purposes. We also collected data only during the evening, when lighting conditions in both dining rooms were least likely to be affected by daylight. Thus, we were able to control the light conditions relatively closely without disturbing patrons' typical dining experience.

Existing lighting in the main dining room consisted of three ceiling-mounted pendants, clustered in groups of three, mounted at between 79 and 81 inches above the floor. Each fixture held a single 25-watt amber-colored incandescent "chandelier-style" lamp, shielded by a handmade shade of wire and glass beads. In addition to the three pendant fixtures, the main dining room had five ceiling-mounted spotlights, each with a 75-watt halogen lamp mounted 89 inches above the floor. These fixtures were track-mounted and could be aimed in any direction, but were positioned to illuminate circulation routes and to provide focus lighting on wall-mounted menu blackboards. Finally, the space included four wall-mounted sconces, each with a 25-watt incandescent chandelier lamp similar to that used by the pendants, and shielded in the same manner. The sconces were wired to a single circuit with a simple on-off switch, while the pendants and ceiling-mounted fixtures were wired together on a single 40-amp circuit with a dimmer switch. A reflected ceiling plan of the main dining room is shown in figure 6.1.

The room had no other lighting, although some light from the service areas and the open kitchen at the rear of the room could be seen in the dining area. This light was not strong, and we didn't feel it would influence the dining experience in the main dining room. The light fixtures and their placement in the secondary dining room were similar, allowing it to serve as a good basis for comparison.

We conducted two light manipulations over a seven-week period, as described below. In each study period, measurements of light levels were taken with a photographer's light meter at the start of the study period

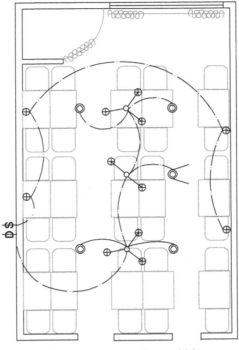

⊕   Beaded covers over 25w amber candelabra
      bulbs 79–81" AFF (varies) (sconces at 63–65" AFF)

◎   PAR 38 downlights (wattage to be determined)

◎   PAR 38 angled at menuboard

Figure 6.1. Reflected ceiling plan of experimental dining room

and on two other evening occasions during each phase of the study to
ensure consistency across lighting conditions. Tables throughout the restaurant were identified by number in the point-of-sale system, allowing
us to collect sales and duration data by date and table type. Thus, we
could compare each table with similar tables in the other dining room.
This allowed us to control for variations in customer behavior that may
have occurred due to day of the week, weather conditions, menu specials,
and other factors that would be consistent for all parts of the restaurant.
We also collected point-of-sale data for a representative four-week period

prior to the study period so that typical spending and duration behavior for each dining room could be assessed.

We studied the effects of three lighting conditions: existing lighting conditions (the "baseline"); a "pendants-only" condition, in which we installed full-spectrum chandelier lamps in the sconces and pendant lights only, but left the regular incandescent track lights untouched; and an "all lighting" condition in which we used full-spectrum lamps in all of the fixtures in the main dining room. Because of the limited availability of full-spectrum lamps that would fit the restaurant's existing fixtures, the experimental lamps burned at a slightly higher wattage than the baseline lamps did. To fix that, we adjusted the dimmer switch to compensate and conducted the periodic checks with the light meter to ensure that the light levels were consistent across the three lighting conditions. The shift manager was made aware of the importance of maintaining consistent light levels during data collection periods, but the restaurant's other employees were not informed that a study was taking place. In all other respects, the restaurant operated in its usual fashion.

Because the POS system's reporting functions were not able to provide party-size data for each transaction, we analyzed only two-top tables. This gave us a reliable calculation of party size (two), because this restaurant seated singletons in the bar area. Dining duration was measured as the elapsed time from the opening of a table's check to the closing of that check as recorded in the POS. This measure of duration, while imperfect, has proved to be a reliable method of collecting duration data for large sample sizes.[28] Spending was measured as the total value of each party's check divided by the number of seats at the table. Lastly, we created a composite variable—spending per minute (SPM)—by dividing the average check by the duration to get a simple measure of each table's performance.[29]

Results

A total of 2,888 transactions for two-top tables were recorded during the experimental period across the two dining environments. Further analysis revealed that for some of these transactions, tables had been combined to accommodate larger parties, so those observations were deleted from the analysis, as were any tables with a dining duration that was unusually short (under 10 minutes) or long (over 3 hours). Table 6.1 summarizes the resulting sample.

TABLE 6.1. Sample sizes by lighting condition and dining area

Lighting condition	Main dining room (experimental space)	Secondary dining room (control)	Total observations
Baseline	250	419	669
Pendants only	250	412	662
All fixtures	162	274	436
Total	662	1,105	1,767

The differences in the sample sizes were largely a function of the number of tables for two in each dining space; the control room had six deuces, while the main dining room had only three. In addition, the all-fixtures data-collection period was nine days shorter than the other data-collection periods, a fact that largely accounts for the smaller samples for that treatment in both dining spaces. We shortened the all-fixtures data collection period because of a seasonal slowdown that takes place near the December holidays; we wanted to ensure that all of our data was collected on typical days for the restaurant. However, even with unequal groups to compare, the relatively high number of observations in each condition reflects favorably on the study's validity.

As an initial measure of the influence of full-spectrum lighting on guest behavior, we computed and compared the means and standard deviations for average check and duration for each dining area for each lighting condition (table 6.2).

Spending and duration in the two dining spaces showed consistent significant differences, regardless of the lighting condition. Diners both stayed longer and spent more money in the secondary dining room than they did in the main dining room. (For confirmation, POS data from this restaurant collected for an earlier study was evaluated, and this pattern of duration and spending across the two dining areas was found in that study as well.) We could not determine why this might be the case. The dining rooms have identical menus and operating hours, as well as similar décor, table spacing, and layout. The chief difference is that the secondary dining room has many more windows than the main dining room has. We believe that this factor deserves further study, but we cannot see how this affects our study because light from the exterior was kept to a minimum by collecting data only at night. Despite the stronger performance in the

TABLE 6.2. Average check and dining duration by dining area and lighting condition

	No manipulation	Pendant fixtures only	All fixtures
Main dining room		Mean (standard deviation)	
Average check	$27.41 ($10.98)	$26.05 ($10.39)	$25.32 ($9.15)*
Duration	59 minutes (:24)	57.8 minutes (:24)	59.4 minutes (:24)
Spend per minute (SPM)	$0.99 ($.37)	$0.95 ($.36)	$0.93 ($.37)
Secondary dining room		Mean (standard deviation)	
Average check	$32.86 ($17.27)	$33.30 ($16.33)	$31.22 ($16.51)
Duration	61.2 minutes (:18)	62.5 minutes (:24)	66 minutes (:24)
Spend per minute (SPM)	$1.11 ($.51)	$1.11 ($.48)	$1.00 ($.49)

*Significant difference from baseline, $p < .05$.

secondary dining room in all conditions, this room still serves as a useful control, as the degree of variation for each lighting condition can still be compared between the two dining rooms.

The average check in the main dining room was significantly lower in the all-fixtures lighting condition than it was in the baseline condition, but in all other cases, there was no significant difference in spending, duration, or spending per minute in the three different lighting conditions in the main dining room.

In fact, we recorded declines in spending per minute across all three lighting conditions in both dining areas (see figure 6.2). Controlling for server, day of the week, and table location within each dining room did not change our results.

It was possible that normal variations in spending and duration behavior from day to day masked any modest effects of lighting condition. So, we prepared an additional analysis of average check and duration in each dining room for each day of our study. For this analysis, the data collection period ran from September 23, 2006, to December 18, 2006, resulting in 87 days of observations. Although the restaurant operated every day during the study period, special dates such as Halloween and Thanksgiving had distinctive customer profiles. Moreover, on a few days,

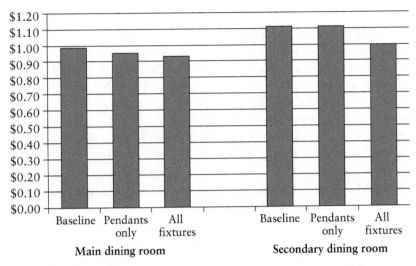

Figure 6.2. Spending per minute by dining area and lighting condition

private parties had exclusive use of the secondary dining room, and so we removed these dates from the analysis. Statistical analysis that compared the differences in average check and duration between each dining area for each day of the study once again indicated that there was no significant difference across the different lighting conditions.

Discussion

These analyses together appear to indicate that the provision of full-spectrum lighting in the main dining room had no significant effect on check averages or meal duration. There was one small but significant reduction in mean average check between normal conditions and the all-full-spectrum lighting condition in the dining room we tested, but this was the only significant effect observed. Duration remained statistically consistent across all three lighting conditions in this space, as did spending per minute.

While it may be tempting to attribute the decrease in average check to the switch to full-spectrum lighting, a closer look at the data shows that there was a modest reduction in average check in both the main dining room and secondary dining room as the experiment went on. The fact that this change occurred in the dining room in which the lights were not manipulated as well as in the one where we changed the lighting indicates that some factor or factors other than the full-spectrum lighting are influencing spending. It is possible that the change in the seasons may be affecting average check, given the approaching December holidays. Also, students make up a significant portion of this restaurant's clientele, and student bank balances are quite possibly depleted at the end of the term. Whatever the explanation for this small decline in guest spending, it cannot be attributed to the provision of full-spectrum lighting.

Duration stayed roughly the same in the main dining room, while it increased slightly in the secondary dining room over the course of the study. Again, this is unlikely to be a function of the lighting, as the change occurred in the room where the lighting was not manipulated. It is difficult to pinpoint what might be causing this longer duration in one part of the restaurant but not another, but it is possible that the restaurant's practice of seating larger parties in the secondary dining room might have affected service to other tables in that dining room, including the two-tops we studied. Large parties become more common in December, and therefore the variations in service speed would be more marked during this period.

Other controllable aspects of the dining experience that can influence diners' purchasing and table duration are differences between servers, days of the week, and the location of the table.[30] We tested for the effects of these three factors, but we found no statistical support for any of them as contributing to the spending and duration variation we observed in the two rooms. Clearly, more study is needed.

Our finding that full-spectrum lighting had no effect on diners' behavior is consistent with studies of full-spectrum fluorescent lighting performed in office environments. Not-withstanding manufacturers' claims, several researchers have been unable to identify a significant effect of full-spectrum lighting on performance, mood, or health. We note that none of these studies was performed in a service setting.[31]

Even though our experiment examined full-spectrum incandescent light rather than full-spectrum fluorescent lighting, the fact that a significant effect on users could not be identified strengthens the literature regarding the inability of full-spectrum lighting to influence behavior significantly in everyday settings.

Implications for Managers

This study fails to support the claims of some lighting manufacturers that full-spectrum lighting can influence consumers' behavior. Equipping a restaurant dining room with full-spectrum lighting resulted in neither an increase in spending nor a change in the length of the meal. Although we did see some variation in spending and dining duration in the two dining rooms we tested for this study, it seems clear to us that these variations are due to effects other than the full-spectrum lighting.

Managers who are looking for ways to increase revenue by manipulating the dining environment often look to products like full-spectrum lighting which are promoted as being "better" for customers than regular lights. We see no such advantage, especially given that full-spectrum lighting is more costly to purchase, needs to be replaced more frequently, and is less efficient in terms of light output than regular incandescent light. Based on this study we must suggest that restaurant managers save their funds and stick to the familiar incandescent lamps when choosing or replacing bulbs in dining room fixtures.

It should be noted that we only tested incandescent lights in this study. Compact fluorescent light is a much more economical form of lighting and has attracted a great deal of attention because of its reduced energy costs compared to incandescent light. Governments are even exploring ways to legislate the use of compact fluorescent light as a way to combat global warming by cutting back on energy demands.[32] The availability of compact fluorescent lamps that can fit in many common light fixtures has made them an appealing choice financially, although many people are unhappy with the relatively flat light these lamps provide. High-corrected color temperature options (over 5,000°K) are available in compact fluorescent form, but they are often marketed under different proprietary brand names rather than as "full-spectrum."

We did not examine compact fluorescent lighting in our study due to the limitations of the existing fixtures in the restaurant. Even though compact fluorescents are sold in a variety of shapes and sizes, they still have a comparatively massive base that does not fit every fixture. We could not find full-spectrum compact fluorescent lamps that would fit many of the fixtures in the dining room. But the fact that full-spectrum lighting did not appear to have any influence on dining duration or spending suggests that restaurant operators may want to choose the least expensive lamp option if moving, choosing compact fluorescent lighting. In any event, we suggest being wary of claims that full-spectrum choices will be better for the operation. Of course, if the cooler light given off by full-spectrum lamps is preferred for aesthetic reasons, an operator might be able to justify their higher life cycle cost as a cost of the design. However, the visual effects of these lamps cannot be said to improve the restaurant's bottom line in any significant way.

Limitations and Conclusion

Although this experiment examined consumers' behavior in a field setting rather than in a laboratory, its real-world setting raises some important limitations. The concerns of the restaurant operator limited the study's lighting manipulations to ones that would not substantially compromise the design intent of the restaurant. When seen side by side with normal incandescent light, most people see full-spectrum light as markedly different, but without such a reference, it may be that the dimmed full-spectrum incandescent light was too similar to regular incandescent light to have an effect on guests. Testing a variety of lighting types (e.g., full-spectrum and regular fluorescent; natural daylight) in a laboratory setting where conditions can be carefully controlled may result in a more significant finding regarding light's effects.

Light levels, or brightness, also influence how people perceive lighting. In keeping with the restaurant operator's wishes, we did not test different light levels in this study, even though earlier research in other types of environments suggests that brighter lighting may have a significant effect on arousal and, thus, duration and spending. Further studies should be performed in a restaurant setting where brightness can be tested.

We made every attempt to control external factors in the study, but it remains only a quasi-experiment due to the lack of random assignment of patrons to lighting conditions. We were also unable to control patrons' demographics. Thus, lighting might have had a significant effect on a small subset of customers, but that may have been masked in the larger sample. Although the restaurant where the study took place is popular with a wide range of people, it seems not to appeal to old customers. Those people might be more sensitive to lighting than are young people, whether because of the physical changes in vision or long-established preferences.[33] While lighting has been studied in nursing homes and other institutional settings with old individuals, it does not appear that any studies have looked at lighting in restaurants or other service environments in relation to customers' age.

Last, the findings here represent results from a single restaurant operation. As with all research, replication in comparable settings may give us a better understanding of what influence, if any, that lighting has on restaurant patron spending and length of stay.

In summary, there appears to be little evidence that full-spectrum lighting makes any difference to diners' purchases in a full-service restaurant. While much more needs to be done to determine what types of lighting are the best choice for a restaurant operator, this study suggests removing one family of options from consideration. The extra purchase cost and ongoing operational costs of full-spectrum lighting do not appear to be offset by any benefit in customer spending or duration.

Notes

Original citation: Robson, S. K. A., & Kimes, S. E. (2007). Examining the effects of full-spectrum lighting in a restaurant. *Cornell Hospitality Report*, 7(12): 6–15.

1. C. S. Areni (2003), Exploring managers' implicit theories of atmospheric music: Comparing academic analysis to industry insight, *Journal of Services Marketing*, 17(2): 161–184.

2. M. Rea, L. Deng, & R. Wolsey (2003), Full-spectrum light sources, *Lighting Answers*, 7(5) (National Lighting Product Information Program, Rensselaer Polytechnic Institute, Troy, NY).

3. Ibid.

4. Ibid.

5. See A. C. North, A. Shilcock, & D. J. Hargreaves (2003), The effect of music style on restaurant customers' spending, *Environment and Behavior*, 35(5): 712–718; J-C. Chebat & R. Michon (2003), The impact of ambient odors on mall shoppers' emotions, cognition, and spending: A test of competitive causal theories, *Journal of Business Research*, 56(7): 529–539; and A. S. Mattila & J. Wirtz (2001), Congruency of scent and music as a driver of in-store evaluations and behavior," *Journal of Retailing*, 77: 273–289.

6. R. J. Donovan & J. R. Rossiter (1992), Store atmosphere: An environmental psychology approach, *Journal of Retailing*, 58 (Spring): 34–57.

7. C. S. Areni & D. Kim (1994), The influence of in-store lighting on consumers' examination of merchandise in a wine-store, *International Journal of Research in Marketing*, 11: 117–125.

8. J. Baker, M. Levy, & D. Grewal (1992), An experimental approach to making retail store environmental decisions, *Journal of Retailing*, 68(4): 445–460.

9. B. Lyman (1989), *A psychology of food: More than a matter of taste* (New York: Van Nostrand Reinhold).

10. I. Knez (1995), Effects of indoor lighting on mood and cognition, *Journal of Environmental Psychology*, 15: 39–51.

11. M. LaGarce (2002), Lighting affects behavior of Alzheimer's patients, *Journal of Interior Design*, 28(2): 15–25.

12. R. S. Ulrich (1991), Effects of health facility interior design on wellness: Theory and scientific research, *Journal of Health Care Design*, 3: 97–109.

13. L. Heschong, R. L. Wright, & S. Okura (2002), Daylighting impacts on retail sales performance, *Journal of the Illuminating Engineering Society of North America*, 31(2): 21–25.

14. I. Knez & C. Kers (2000), Effects of indoor lighting, gender and age on mood and cognitive performance, *Environment and Behavior*, 32(6): 817–831.

15. J. E. Flynn (1977), A study of subjective responses to low energy and non-uniform lighting systems, *Lighting Design and Application*, 7: 6–15.

16. D. M. Berson, F. A. Dunn, & T. Motoharu (2002), Phototransduction by retinal ganglion cells that set the circadian clock, *Science*, 295 (February 8): 1070.

17. W. P. London (1987), Full-spectrum classroom light and sickness in pupils, *The Lancet*, 330(8569): 1205–1206.

18. J. A. Veitch & S. L. McColl (2001), Full-spectrum lighting: A review of its effects on physiology and health, *Psychological Medicine*, 31: 949–964.

19. M. L. Tullman (2000), *Dynamic full spectrum digital lighting of retail displays positively affects consumer behavior* (Boston, MA: Color Kinetics Incorporated).

20. Lyman, *Psychology of food*, and N. Stroebele & J. M. De Castro (2004), Effect of ambience on food intake and food choice, *Nutrition*, 20(9): 821–838.

21. R. Sommer (1969), *Personal space: The behavioral basis of design* (Englewood Cliffs, NJ: Prentice-Hall).

22. E. Sherman, A. Mathur, & R. B. Smith (1997), Store environment and consumer purchase behavior: Mediating role of consumer emotions, *Psychology and Marketing*, 14(4): 361–378.

23. D. L. Butler & P. M. Biner (1987), Preferred lighting levels: Variability among settings, behaviors and individuals, *Environment and Behavior*, 19: 695.

24. M. P. Gardner (1985), Mood states and consumer behavior: A critical review, *Journal of Consumer Research*, 12: 281–300.

25. J. Wirtz, A. S. Mattila, & R. L. P. Tan (2000), The moderating role of target-arousal on the impact of affect on satisfaction: An examination in the context of service experiences, *Journal of Retailing*, 76(3): 347–365.

26. A. Mehrabian & J. Russell (1974), *An approach to environmental psychology* (Cambridge MA: MIT Press).

27. R. E. Milliman (1986), The influence of background music on the behavior of restaurant patrons, *Journal of Consumer Research*, 13(2): 286–289.

28. S. E. Kimes, R. B. Chase, S. Choi, P. Y. Lee, & E. N. Ngonzi (1998), Restaurant revenue management: Applying yield management to the restaurant industry, *Cornell Hotel and Restaurant Administration Quarterly*, 39(3): 32–39.

29. See S. E. Kimes & S. K. A. Robson (2004), The impact of table characteristics on dining duration and spending, *Cornell Hotel and Restaurant Administration Quarterly, 45*(4): 333–346.

30. Ibid.

31. J. A. Veitch (1997), Revisiting the performance and mood effects of information about lighting and fluorescent lamp type, *Journal of Environmental Psychology, 17*: 253–262.

32. W. L. Hamilton (2007), Ideas and trends: Illuminating; incandescence, yes. Fluorescence, we'll see, *New York Times*, January 7.

33. M. LaGarce, Lighting affects behavior of Alzheimer's patients.

7

Don't Sit So Close to Me

Restaurant Table Characteristics and Guest Satisfaction

Stephani K. A. Robson and Sheryl E. Kimes

Most restaurant operators will agree that it makes good sense from a revenue management standpoint to match party sizes to table sizes, particularly during busy meal periods. Moreover, most restaurateurs arrange their dining rooms to have the greatest possible number of tables (or seats) on the floor without inappropriately crowding guests. The question we examine here is what effect table size and proximity have on guests' spending, or, to put it more precisely, to determine whether tightly spaced tables interfere with restaurant patrons' satisfaction or affect their patronage behavior.

Our study is motivated by the realization that even the most rigorous application of revenue management practices won't result in greater profits if customers are dissatisfied with their dining experience. Diners are offended, for example, when they notice that operators are using RM strategies that seem unfair or uncomfortable.[1] One complaint that guests often make on dining websites is their discomfort with tables that are closely spaced. From a revenue management perspective, tight table spacing might be viewed as the most efficient use of dining room square footage, but it is unclear whether such an approach is actually doing more harm than good if being too close to neighboring tables is perceived negatively. If we agree that guests want to feel uncrowded when they dine, one question to ask is whether that means a larger table than their party size needs or whether the issue is more one of proximity to adjoining tables. In our earlier work, we have seen indications that some table arrangements generate higher spending per minute than others (based on their design characteristics),[2] but in that study we were not able to find out whether guests were more satisfied at one particular kind of table, all else being equal, nor could we connect satisfaction to spending or length of time at the table. In this report, we attempt to explore connections between the guest's personal space, satisfaction, and behavior. We do this via an observational study that tests whether providing diners with more space—by seating smaller parties at tables that are larger than necessary or by leaving more room between tables—results in more positive outcomes for the operators compared with more traditional RM strategies such as right-size seating and maximizing dining room capacity by spacing tables tightly together.

Personal Space and Guest Satisfaction

We all recognize a need for room around our bodies that is free from encroachment by others, particularly strangers. The study of human spatial behavior—how we position ourselves relative to one another—has come to be known as proxemics. Edward Hall coined this term, which he defined as the study of "the interrelated observations and theories of man's use of space as a specialized elaboration of culture."[3] Proxemic behavior relates to how people create personal space for themselves in social and transitory public settings. Its basic premises are by now familiar.[4] We need little personal space with people we know well, but we prefer to keep those we don't know at a reasonable distance (reasonable being defined differently in various cultures). We feel real discomfort if someone violates that space without good reason. In restaurant settings where we are often surrounded by parties of strangers, we prefer to sit at tables where we can have the most control over our personal space, either by having ample space to work with or by having some kind of physical feature separating us from nearby diners.[5] This desire for more personal space may explain the popularity of booths, with their tangible physical boundaries.

Here are three theories that attempt to explain why we use space the way we do. The first, affiliative conflict theory, suggests that interpersonal distance is a function of two competing needs: to affiliate with others and to protect one's personal space.[6] The spacing we choose in a given circumstance is at a point of equilibrium between these two needs, which may vary as an interaction continues. Another theoretical view argues that interpersonal distance serves as a social regulator.[7] Friends will adopt closer distances than will acquaintances, and in turn acquaintances will be approached more closely than total strangers might be.[8] A third perspective is that our spatial behavior is a response to the stress of having less control over an environment or a situation than one desires. In this view, stress abates when one regains an appropriate level of control either through one's own action or through a change in circumstance.[9] One area where we seek control is in creating and maintaining privacy. If we feel that we have a lack of privacy in a public situation, our stress level goes up,[10] and it is likely that our satisfaction with our experience will decrease. Close proximity, defined in most western cultures as being within 18 inches (45 cm) of someone else,[11] can be overstimulating and stressful if the person nearby is not an intimate of ours, and we will seek ways to reduce our discomfort by either increasing our personal space when conditions allow or by leaving the environment as soon as possible.

Despite our desire to avoid stress and maintain privacy, we still need some degree of stimulation to make experiences interesting and engaging. The key for restaurateurs is to provide just the right amount of stimulation to attract and sustain guests' interest without going overboard. An appropriately stimulating environment encourages what Mehrabian and Russell call "approach behaviors,"[12] which include entering an environment, spending time there, and making purchases.[13] The link between stimulation and approach behaviors can be seen when we consider a bland restaurant design. Unless there is an exceptional reason to stay, patrons are likely to dine elsewhere.

Researchers have identified direct links between stimulation, approach behavior, and satisfaction.[14] If an environment offers the appropriate amount of stimulation for its customers, users are more likely to be satisfied as well as demonstrate approach behaviors that increase profits, such as patronizing the restaurant in the first place or increasing their spending once they are there.[15] Earlier work has shown that the optimal supply of dining seats not only mirrors the party sizes that patronize the restaurant but also offers guests' psychological comfort.[16] Making guests comfortable includes giving them appropriate amounts of personal space so that they can feel adequately separated from strangers at other tables.

Another way of offering comfort is to make it easier for diners to achieve their goals, which in the course of a meal typically involves interaction with dining companions. Proxemic studies show that most people prefer to sit at right angles to their partners in conversation.[17] Compare that finding to the arrangement most restaurants offer parties of two. Only in slow times would couples be seated at a four-top that would allow them to sit at an angle. Instead, most parties of two are seated at the typical face-to-face deuces. Proxemics suggests that this arrangement can be viewed as confrontational. Certainly it's hard for two people to have an intimate discussion with a table between them. Fine dining restaurants recognize this and may offer side-by-side seating for parties of two, especially couples. This kind of seating is more efficient from a revenue management standpoint than placing a couple at a table for four, but is likely to be viewed as too intimate for business dining.

The issue of balancing personal space, stimulation, and guest satisfaction raises the question of whether guests seated at a table that offers more personal space would exhibit increased approach behaviors and be more satisfied with their dining experience than would guests seated at tables that offered less personal space. In this regard we speak of two different kinds of personal space: namely, space between tables and tables meant for larger parties. This leads to the following three questions, which we tested in this study.

(1) Do parties of two express higher levels of satisfaction when seated at four-top tables than they do when they are seated at tables for two?;

(2) Do parties seated at tables that are farther away from adjacent tables express higher levels of satisfaction than parties seated at tables that are closer together?; and

(3) Do the size and spacing of tables influence how much guests spend or how long they stay?

This last research question relates to the standard RM practice of controlling how long a patron uses a table as a way of managing capacity.

As discussed elsewhere, meals of shorter duration allow the restaurateur to process more guests in a particular period of time.[18] We have seen that certain table types appear to reduce duration, particularly those that offer guests reduced psychological comfort.[19] If having less personal space reduces the ability to control privacy and therefore increases stress, then it is possible that diners will adopt "avoidance" behaviors, which are the opposite of the approach behaviors described above. One avoidance behavior is to leave the environment, so we might expect to see shorter stays when guests are uncomfortable, and another is reduced spending. Effective revenue management strategies are those that result in long-term benefits to the operator. Therefore, understanding how personal space influences approach and avoidance behaviors in a restaurant as well as guest satisfaction is important to making successful RM decisions both during the design stage and once the restaurant is up and running.

Methodology

To test whether guests are more satisfied or behave differently when they have extra personal space, we extracted POS data and surveyed guests at an 80-seat, full-service restaurant in the Soho neighborhood of New York City. This restaurant was selected for the study because it offered the following three distinct advantages for our research: (1) its seating arrangements included both standard face-to-face deuces and rectangular four-tops; (2) because the restaurant welcomed a high volume of parties of two, it periodically was required to seat these parties at the four-tops ; and (3) it used a point-of-sale system for recording all meal transactions, thus facilitating the collection of spending and dining duration data for each party. The dining room offered a variety of table spacings. Some tables for two were closely spaced, but others were relatively far apart. In addition, the restaurant featured a prix fixe menu. This allowed us greater control in our spending analysis, because we could assess the effects of personal space on spending for extras, such as drinks and surcharge entrées. Last, the restaurant's management was also eager to obtain general satisfaction data from its guests, so we were able to dovetail our study with the restaurant's own satisfaction survey program.

Our data collection process was relatively straightforward. During two month-long periods, we collected point-of-sale data and surveyed the restaurant's dinner guests. Each party's check was identified in the POS system by a transaction number and a table number. Using those numbers we could match transactions to specific groups of diners, determine what was purchased, and record how long the check was open (an imperfect but reasonable proxy for meal duration[20]). To address outliers, we eliminated checks that showed spending of less than $10 or more than $200 per person, as well as those that were open for less than ten minutes or more than three hours. We also eliminated split checks and other anomalies.

To collect satisfaction data, servers presented guests with a short questionnaire along with the check (see figure 7.1).

The questionnaire solicited feedback on the food, service, table characteristics, overall guest experience, and likelihood of return, as well as simple demographic information such as age and gender. The survey included specific questions regarding whether (1) guests felt that they had enough room at their table, (2) they felt their table was adequately spaced relative to others, and (3) they felt uncomfortable at their table. These questions were included so that we could be sure we were measuring seating satisfaction as distinct from satisfaction with the food, the service, or other aspects of the restaurant. Guests were asked to rate each aspect of their dining experience on a seven-level Likert scale, and reverse scaling was used on four of the questions to help control for response error. The server collected completed questionnaires and stapled them to the merchant's copy of that particular guest's check. In turn, the cashier recorded the transaction number and the table number from the check on the survey so that we could accurately match up the POS data with the survey responses.

Once all the data were collected, we combined data from the restaurant's POS system with the completed surveys for analysis. To keep the analysis straightforward, we used only the data from parties of two, especially given the evidence that larger party sizes have both higher spending and longer durations than smaller parties.[21] Specifically, we tried to isolate parties of two that had completed the questionnaire in full and that were seated at either a typical deuce or a table for four, which would allow us to accurately compare satisfaction and behavior data for these two table sizes at various table locations. The POS data also allowed us to control for any influence from the server or day of the week.

This restaurant and Cornell University are working together to study how to create better dining experiences. You can help by taking a moment to complete the following short survey. Please leave your completed survey in the check folder, or you may give it to the host as you depart. Thank you for your feedback!

1. Please indicate your agreement with each of the following questions about your dining experience today.

(1 = Strongly Disagree, 7 = Strongly Agree)

I was pleased with my dining experience
1   2   3   4   5   6   7

I had enough room at my table
1   2   3   4   5   6   7

I was happy with my food
1   2   3   4   5   6   7

This restaurant was a wise choice
1   2   3   4   5   6   7

I felt rushed during my dining experience
1   2   3   4   5   6   7

The servers did a good job for me
1   2   3   4   5   6   7

I was uncomfortable in my seat
1   2   3   4   5   6   7

The staff was friendly and hospitable
1   2   3   4   5   6   7

My table was too close to other tables
1   2   3   4   5   6   7

I was very dissatisfied by my experience
1   2   3   4   5   6   7

2. Is this your first visit to this restaurant?
Yes   No
If yes, how did you find out about this restaurant?
_____

3. How likely are you to return to this restaurant?
(1= Very Unlikely, 7 = Very Likely)
1   2   3   4   5   6   7

4. How likely are you to recommend this restaurant to others?
(1= Very Unlikely, 7 = Very Likely)
1   2   3   4   5   6   7

5. Please tell us a little about yourself (to be completed by only one member of your party):
You are: Male ____ Female ____
Your age is: Under 25 ____   26-49 ____   50+ ____

6. How often do you eat out at a restaurant for dinner?
(please choose one)
More than twice a week ____
1-2 times a week   ____
2-3 times a month   ____
Once a month   ____
Less than once a month ____

7. If you were the manager of this restaurant, what would you change about the experience?
_____

THANK YOU FOR PARTICIPATING AND FOR DINING WITH US TODAY.

Figure 7.1. Personal space questionnaire

Findings

After excluding transactions that did not qualify and eliminating incomplete surveys, we had a total of 285 valid records, which were well distributed across the different table locations in the dining room. However, not as many parties of two were seated at four-tops as we had originally hoped; only 22 of these 285 observations were for parties seated at larger tables. (This restaurant clearly was largely successful in meeting the revenue management goal of matching parties and table sizes.) This imbalance raises questions of validity for our statistical analysis, but there are nevertheless interesting findings that should be valuable to restaurateurs.

Table Size

In most cases, mean satisfaction ratings were slightly higher when guests were seated at larger tables than their party required (see figure 7.2).

Diners seated at larger tables gave a higher rating to the food (6.73), the service (6.73), the timing of the meal (6.13), and their overall experience

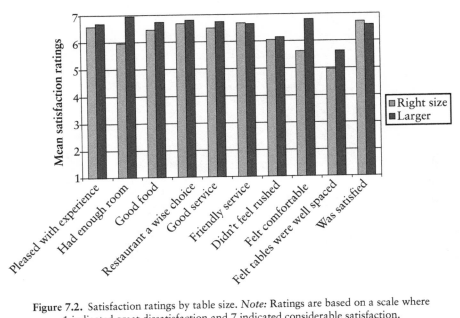

Figure 7.2. Satisfaction ratings by table size. *Note:* Ratings are based on a scale where 1 indicated great dissatisfaction and 7 indicated considerable satisfaction.

(6.73) than did those guests who were seated at a right-size table, although none of these differences were statistically significant. Both sets of diners had similar ratings of whether they felt the restaurant was a wise choice for their dining occasion (6.80 for diners at larger tables and 6.70 for diners at right-size tables). Only two of our satisfaction measures showed statistically significant differences for the two table types when the unequal sample sizes were taken into account.[22] Those were whether guests felt they had enough room at their table and whether guests felt comfortable. In both cases, guests seated at larger tables indicated that they felt they had more room at their table (6.93, compared to 5.97 for those at right-size tables) and were much more likely to feel comfortable than diners at right-size tables did (6.80 versus 5.62). We obtained similar results when we asked guests whether they felt the spacing between tables was appropriate. Guests at larger tables were less likely to feel crowded by adjacent tables than were guests at right-size tables. Parties seated at the four-tops rated the quality of the table spacing higher (5.60) than did those at the deuces (4.96). This difference was not statistically significant, but we note that this was the lowest of any of the satisfaction ratings we measured. Having said that, we found no noticeable difference by table size regarding whether our respondents would return to the restaurant or be willing to recommend it to others (figure 7.3).

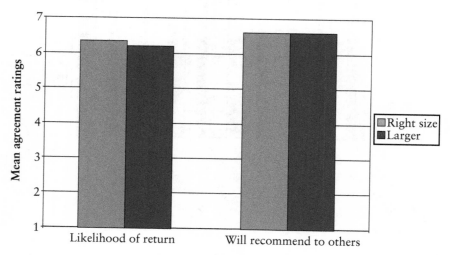

Figure 7.3. Future behavior by table size. *Note:* Ratings are based on a scale where 1 indicated low agreement and 7 indicated considerable agreement.

On the other hand, we did see a noticeable difference in spending behavior between the two table sizes, although it was not statistically significant (figure 7.4). Parties at the right-size table spent less per person ($58.35) than did those seated at a larger table ($67.98).

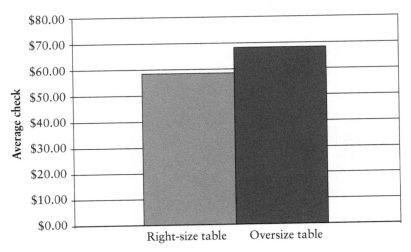

Figure 7.4. Spending by table size

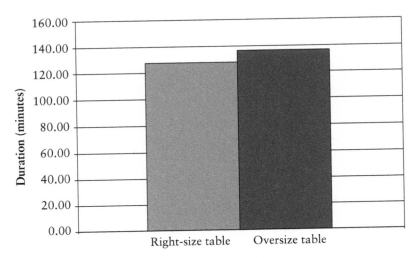

Figure 7.5. Duration by table size

Our last test, whether parties of two seated at larger tables had a longer duration than those seated at deuces, showed that those at the four-top tables stayed 6.7% longer than those at the deuces (134.13 minutes at the four-tops versus 125.65 minutes at the smaller tables; see figure 7.5).

This difference was not statistically significant. When we combined average check and duration into a single measure of spending per minute, or SPM, we only noticed a small difference for the two groups ($.477 per minute for right-size tables and $.507 per minute at larger tables) that was again not statistically significant.

Table Spacing

Regardless of table size, the guests gave the lowest satisfaction ratings of all to the issue of table spacing (overall mean: 4.99) This finding prompted us to look more closely at the effect that the distance between tables might have had on satisfaction ratings, spending, and meal duration. The spacing between tables at this restaurant varied considerably. Some two-tops along a banquette were spaced only 17 inches apart (less than half a meter), while other two-tops along the window were as much as 65 inches away from the nearest table. We categorized tables that were 20 inches or less from an adjacent table as being "near," more than 20 inches but less than 36 inches away as "moderate," and 36 inches or more (essentially, a minimum of a meter) away from the next closest table as "far." This restaurant had parallel two-top seating in two contrasting locations in the dining room—along an exterior wall and along an interior railing—which allowed us to also compare similar tables in two distinctive locations to see whether table location was a factor in satisfaction or behavior, as we had seen in earlier studies.[23]

We did see significant differences in the satisfaction ratings for different levels of table spacing (figure 7.6). Diners at closely spaced tables rated the appropriateness of the spacing much lower (4.27) than did guests at widely spaced tables (6.41). Even moderately spaced tables left guests less happy. Diners at the moderately spaced tables rated their table spacing almost as low as did those at the closest tables (4.38).

Comparing satisfaction ratings for other components of the dining experience, we saw that diners seated at tables that were tightly spaced generally expressed lower satisfaction in almost every category. Compared

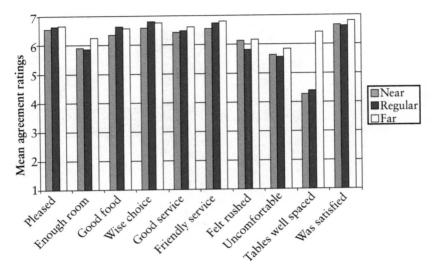

Figure 7.6. Satisfaction ratings by table spacing. *Note:* Ratings are based on a scale where 1 indicated great dissatisfaction and 7 indicated considerable satisfaction.

to those at the widely spaced tables, guests seated at deuces near to each other were less happy with the food (5.92 vs. 6.25), the friendliness of the service (6.55 vs. 6.80), and the wisdom of this choice of restaurant (6.59 vs. 6.78). All of these differences were statistically significant.

By the same token, parties that indicated greater satisfaction with table spacing also gave higher ratings to all other parts of their dining experience as compared to those who were dissatisfied with the distance between tables. The average of all satisfaction scores for diners seated at tables that were far apart (6.49) was significantly higher than the overall satisfaction rating for those at tables that were moderately spaced tables (6.11) and those at closely spaced tables (6.10). Even when we removed the ratings directly related to table spacing from the overall satisfaction average, this pattern still held. The revised mean satisfaction ratings were 6.50 for well-spaced tables, 6.35 for moderately spaced tables, and 6.31 for tables that were close together. Clearly, the spacing between tables had a substantial effect on guest satisfaction. In that regard, guests seated close to other tables expressed a significantly lower likelihood of returning (6.16) than those at well-spaced tables (6.51), whereas willingness to

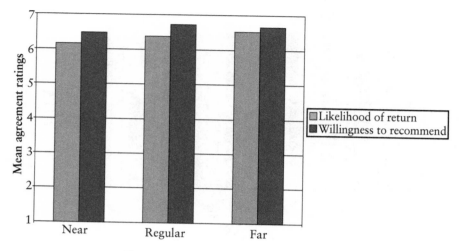

Figure 7.7. Future behavior by table spacing

recommend the restaurant to others was statistically the same regardless of table spacing (figure 7.7).

Spending Levels

It wasn't just satisfaction that was influenced by the proximity of neighboring tables. We also found that spending and duration varied with table spacing (table 7.1).

Parties seated near to other tables had a significantly higher rate of spending ($0.493 per minute) than did tables that were far apart ($0.462). This was largely due to a longer meal duration at tables that were well spaced (128 minutes vs. 122 minutes at tightly spaced tables). However,

TABLE 7.1. Diner spending and duration behaviors by table spacing

	Near spacing (n = 122)	Moderate spacing (n = 71)	Far spacing (n = 92)
Average check	$59.09	$62.02	$56.80
Duration	122 minutes	130 minutes	128 minutes
Spending per minute (SPM)	$ .493	$ .484	$ .462

this difference in duration was not itself statistically significant, nor were any other differences in diner behavior that we noted.

Spacing, Not Size

Our findings seem to support the argument that restaurant goers appreciate at least a modicum of privacy. While our respondents appreciated generous personal space, these findings indicate that table size in and of itself seems not to invoke personal space issues (based on the satisfaction and behavior data), but table positioning does do so.

To confirm that table spacing rather than table location was responsible for our results, we compared the duration, satisfaction, and spending results for the closely spaced two-top tables along the window wall banquette with those of the closely spaced tables on the interior railing. As shown in figure 7.8 and table 7.2, we saw no difference in results between these two table locations. Patrons had the same satisfaction ratings and dining behaviors in both locations, suggesting that the close spacing mattered more to guests than table location.

Clearly, closely spaced tables diminished the guests' experience at this particular restaurant, which in turn translated into a reduced likelihood of

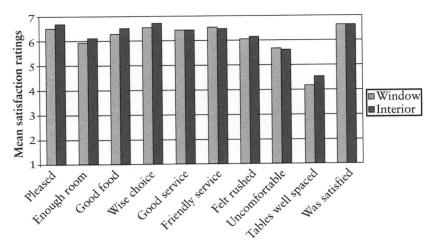

Figure 7.8. Satisfaction ratings of closely spaced tables by location

TABLE 7.2. Spending and duration behaviors by table location for closely spaced tables

	Window (n = 85)	Interior railing (n =58)
Average check	$58.81	$57.89
Duration	125 minutes	123 minutes
Spending per minute (SPM)	$ .487	$ .480

return. Although diners at closely spaced tables exhibited a slightly higher level of spending per minute, the reduced satisfaction with these tables should be cause for concern.

Implications for Restaurateurs

We must caution that our study occurred at only one restaurant, during one meal period. Thus, the implications below would apply most directly to dinner at a full-service, upscale restaurant. It's possible that we would see different outcomes during lunch at the same restaurant. Moreover, our results regarding oversize tables are colored somewhat by the small number of couples seated at four-tops.

Given what is known about proxemics and psychological comfort, it is not surprising that guests seated at tables that afforded them more personal space would feel more comfortable. However, this greater psychological comfort from having a larger-than-necessary table did not appear to influence the ratings of other components of the dining experience, nor did it affect guests' ratings of overall satisfaction. We did see some indication of an effect on spending. Guests at tables larger than required had a higher check average than those at tables matched to their party size, although this effect was not statistically significant. Comfort levels in general did not appear to result in greater spending, so we can tentatively say that the provision of extra room at the table was an influential factor in spending behavior.

Slightly higher check averages, however, should not deter restaurateurs from seating parties at right-size tables. Although there are modest increases in some satisfaction measures when guests are seated at tables that are larger than necessary, these don't appear to translate into dramatically improved satisfaction, and there is no real difference in spending or duration across table sizes. Any slight increase in spending associated with seating guests at larger tables doesn't appear to be enough to offset the lost revenue from inefficient seat utilization (and the lower spending per minute that we recorded at the large tables). Diners at oversize tables are no more likely to return or recommend the restaurant to others than are those seated at a correctly sized table, and both are equally likely to be satisfied customers. The most effective revenue management approach remains monitoring party sizes and ensuring that all parties are seated at tables of appropriate size.

Restaurateurs may want to consider reasonably wide spacing between tables, based on this study. Diners at closely spaced tables were significantly more dissatisfied with almost every dimension of their dining experience than were those at tables that are far apart. Spending per minute was affected not because those at closely spaced tables spent more but because they recorded shorter meal duration. While revenue management principles suggest that shorter durations are not always undesirable—particularly when they are accompanied by higher check averages and quicker table turns—the apparent reduction in guest satisfaction by having tables too close together that we observed in this study should not be taken lightly. Although we did not see a relationship between satisfaction and likelihood of return or willingness to recommend this restaurant, other studies have repeatedly shown the negative effects of customer dissatisfaction.[24] Clearly, further research is needed to see just how influential the distance between tables might be in terms of guest satisfaction and behavior and to identify the optimal table spacing for generating revenues, maximizing the use of dining space, and creating satisfied guests.

Notes

Original citation: Robson, S. K. A., & Kimes, S. E. (2009). Don't sit so close to me: Restaurant table characteristics and guest satisfaction. *Cornell Hospitality Report, 9*(2): 6–16.

The authors would like to thank Fred Eydt and the Center for Hospitality Research for the funding that supported this research. The authors also wish to thank undergraduate student Steve Byung Hwang Huang for his invaluable assistance in preparing the data and extend sincere appreciation to Alexis Kahn and her team for making their guests and their POS data available.

1. S. E. Kimes & J. Wirtz (2002), Perceived fairness of demand-based pricing for restaurants, *Cornell Hotel and Restaurant Administration Quarterly, 43*(1) (February), 31–38; and

S. E. Kimes & J. Wirtz (2003), When does revenue management become acceptable?, *Journal of Service Research*, 7(2), 125–135.

2. S. E. Kimes & S. K. A. Robson (2004), The impact of table characteristics on dining duration and spending, *Cornell Hotel and Restaurant Administration Quarterly*, 45(4) (October): 333–346.

3. E. T. Hall, *The hidden dimension* (New York: Doubleday, 1966), 1.

4. P. Underhill (1999), *Why we buy: The science of shopping* (New York: Simon & Schuster).

5. S. K. A. Robson (2008), Scenes from a restaurant: Privacy regulation in stressful situations, *Journal of Environmental Psychology*, 28(4): 373–378.

6. M. Argyle & J. Dean (1965), Eye contact, distance, and affiliation, *Sociometry*, 28(3): 289–304.

7. I. Altman (1975), *The environment and social behavior* (Monterey, CA: Brooks/Cole).

8. E. Sundstrom & I. Altman (1976), Interpersonal relationships and personal space: Research review and theoretical model, *Human Ecology*, 4(1): 47–67.

9. G. W. Evans & R. B. Howard (1973), Personal space, *Psychological Bulletin*, 80(4): 334–344.

10. Ibid.

11. Hall, *Hidden dimension*.

12. A. Mehrabian & J. A. Russell (1974), *An approach to environmental psychology* (Cambridge, MA: MIT Press).

13. R. J. Donovan, J. R. Rossiter, G. Marcoolyn, & A. Nesdale (1994), Store atmosphere and purchasing behavior, *Journal of Retailing*, 70(3): 283–294.

14. J. Wirtz, A. S. Mattila, & R. L. P. Tan (2000), The moderating role of target-arousal on the impact of affect on satisfaction: An examination in the context of service experiences, *Journal of Retailing*, 76(3): 347–365.

15. A. S. Mattila & J. Wirtz (2006), Arousal expectations and service evaluations, *International Journal of Service Industry Management*, 17(3): 229–244.

16. S. E. Kimes & G. M. Thompson (2004), Restaurant revenue management at Chevys: Determining the best table mix, *Decision Sciences Journal*, 35(3): 371–391.

17. A. Mehrabian & S. G. Diamond (1971), Seating arrangement and conversation, *Sociometry*, 34(2): 281–289.

18. S. E. Kimes, J. Wirtz, & B. M. Noone (2002), How long should dinner take? Measuring expected meal duration for restaurant revenue management, *Journal of Revenue and Pricing Management*, 1(3): 220–233; and B. M. Noone, S. E. Kimes, A. Mattila, & J. Wirtz (2007), The effect of meal pace on customer satisfaction, *Cornell Hotel and Restaurant Administration Quarterly*, 48(3) (August): 231–245.

19. Kimes & Robson, Impact of table characteristics.

20. S. E. Kimes et al. (1998), Restaurant revenue management: Applying yield management to the restaurant industry, *Cornell Hotel and Restaurant Administration Quarterly*, 39(3): 32–39.

21. Kimes & Thompson, Restaurant revenue management at Chevys.

22. Levene's Test was used to determine whether the variances of the unbalanced samples were significantly different, and the appropriate t-test was performed based on the results.

23. Kimes & Robson, Impact of table characteristics.

24. Noone et al., Effect of meal pace on customer satisfaction.

Part IV

TECHNOLOGY

The Next Frontier

ALEX M. SUSSKIND AND MARK MAYNARD

Alex: Technology is an ever-present part of our lives. Wherever we are—home, school, work, traveling—we use technology or are connected to technology. Before I move into the summary of the articles selected for this part, I want to reflect a bit on the importance of technology and how we deal with advances in technology all the time.

The first restaurant I worked in starting in 1980 was a pub-style independent restaurant on Long Island, NY, right around the time that "fern bars" and the casual dining segment as we know it was making its mark in the history books of the restaurant business. The three guys I worked for had all just left the chain Victoria's Station to go out on their own. In their new restaurant, the Rose and Thistle, they had order technology in place that was used by the service staff to take and record orders and by the kitchen staff to receive and prepare orders and acted as a control mechanism for management to ensure that orders that were placed and served were connected to revenue and that revenue was collected. Sounds like a point-of-sales system (POS), right? It was—the POS technology we used was called "numbered duplicate checks." That's right, the use of duplicate checks was the prevalent form of POS technology at the time. Servers were issued numbered checks at the start of their shifts, and they took orders on the checks, which produced carbon copies to be distributed to the various stations that prepared the orders (the bottom part was for appetizers, the middle part was for main courses, the top part was for desserts, and beverages were added on the back of the check). If guests at a table asked for single/separate checks, servers would have to use multiple checks and would enter the information for each guest on her own check and let the kitchen know the people were together (or, by hand, you simply separated each guest's part of the meal off the larger check for payment). At the end of the meal, servers would present the base hardcopy of the check with the food and beverage total plus sales tax to each table (or guest) for payment. Servers would reconcile their sales for the day, return the used and unused checks to their manager, and cash out/check out. At the end of the night, the closing manager would take the hardcopies, the duplicate checks (dupes) off the "spindle," and reconcile them to make sure everything matched up. That was the POS technology at the time. We made math mistakes, forgot to add things to checks, wrote down the wrong things, and had a hard time reading other peoples' handwriting or notes about special requests. But the system seemed to work pretty well (or better than what we did before, or we simply did not know any better). Not long after that, maybe in 1983, we got our first MICROS system, which automated the entire process with terminals, printers, the capacity to print summary reports, and many other features—all things that we readily did by hand for years (or decades). Next came supply and inventory management systems, recipe systems, reservation systems, and labor management and payroll systems, and the list goes on. I mention this first because technology is constantly evolving and changing, and in the process it is supposed to make us better, stronger, and faster. To some extent I agree: advances in technology we have seen over the past century or so (not just in restaurants) have made our lives, and hence our work, easier in many ways. Fast forward to today: few operators use the dupe system I described above; but guests still ask for separate checks (despite the statement at the bottom of the menu "no separate checks, please"), servers (and cooks) still make mistakes, and we still have to reconcile our banks each and every shift. What is new (or newer) is that we now have technology in restaurants that our guests use as part of the service experience. Rather than continue with a retrospective journey describing the evolution of technology in restaurants over the last century (the conveyor belt for plating in Marriott banquet kitchens I worked in being my personal favorite), I will shift to talking about guest-facing technology.

Ever since the airline industry introduced self-check-in, in the mid-1990s, there has been a gradual but consistent adoption of self-service technology (SST). In 2004, it was estimated that roughly 80% of airline travelers checked in for their flights at counters using humans; in 2017 only 20% opted for the human option, while 80% used some form of SST to check in.[1] This trend has emerged and moved into almost all elements of the retail business, with grocery store self-checkout being one of the fastest-growing segments using SST.

The use of self-service technology affects both operators and guests in restaurants. The first article in this part, "Customer-Facing Payment Technology in the US Restaurant Industry" (Kimes & Collier, 2014), looks at how restaurant operators react to and make decisions about SST adoption, and the last two articles, "Guests' Reactions to Tabletop Technology in Full-Service Restaurants" (Susskind, Awan, Parikh, & Suri, 2015), and "The Influence of Tabletop Technology in Full-Service Restaurants" (Susskind & Curry, 2016), look at how guests react to the use of tabletop technology in restaurants and how tabletop technology can influence sales and labor, respectively.

From a restaurant operator's perspective, the use and adoption of SST comes with advantages and disadvantages. Restaurant operators do not take these decisions lightly, and many have cautiously added technology as a part of the guest experience. For advantages, both independent and chain operators, ranging from quick service through fine dining, reported several interrelated outcomes that can be associated with SST. First, SST can speed up check processing time when customers settle their bill and complete the payment. This also has the potential to reduce the amount of time a guest needs to wait to settle her bill and can in turn reduce table turn times and potentially reduce service labor costs. It was also reported that operators believed SST would lead to higher levels of guest satisfaction, higher guest spending, and better payment security. Along with the advantages come some disadvantages. Operators noted concerns that SST can be expensive to purchase and implement, may not integrate well with existing technologies, and can pose a security risk if data becomes compromised. Kimes and Collier, in "Customer-Facing Payment Technology in the US Restaurant Industry," laid out well the elements that operators should consider as they make decisions about SST adoption and use. To date, SST is seen in all types of restaurants in the form of web ordering, kiosks, mobile apps, tabletop apps, and the like. It is increasing in prevalence every day, and operators' reactions to the advantages and disadvantages are very important to ensure that the industry understands what it is doing and where it is headed. Operators need a clear strategy to guide their choices as they move into adopting new technologies.

After seeing the research done by Kimes and Collier, I was very curious to get a better understanding of how guests react to SST in restaurants and if notable benefits or problems could be captured by examining guests' behavior and attitudes toward SST. In my coauthored article "Guests' Reactions to Tabletop Technology in Full-Service Restaurants," by Susskind, Awan, Parikh, and Suri, we looked at how guests reacted to the use of tabletop devices in full-service casual dining restaurants and tried to draw a connection between the use of the device, the likability of device, their desire to return to the restaurant, and whether the use of the device helped or hindered servers' tips. With the help of a tabletop device company and one of their clients we were able to dig deep into guests' reactions to the technology.

To begin, we asked over 20,000 guests who used the tabletop devices in a casual dining chain what they thought about the technology. Five general sets of responses emerged, ranging from very negative to very positive. Those who responded negatively (about 20% of the guests) reported that they did not like the device and noted that it takes away from human interaction in the restaurant and/or that it was difficult to use or malfunctioned in some way. The guests who reported positive or neutral reactions stated that the devices added convenience, were fun to use, added a sense of payment security, and enhanced the experience overall. Additionally, the guests reported that they would return to the restaurant because of the device. There was no significant impact on servers' tips as a result of guests using the tabletop devices. From this study my coauthors and I concluded that overall the technology was viewed overwhelmingly as a benefit to guests (and operators) and when used well served as an added benefit to the service experience ("an added layer of service"). Our research also highlighted that you cannot ignore the 20% of the guests who did not enjoy using the technology. Service providers need to be prepared to ensure that guests who are not comfortable using the technology are not left behind, period. Taking a parallel from the airline industry, despite all the options you have to check in for a flight with technology, you can still go to the counter and have a human help you; Peterson's 2017 study cited above noted that 20% of airline customers still prefer to use human check-in, much as 20% of the restaurant guests we surveyed did not like using the tabletop technology as they dined.

Knowing that tabletop technology is viewed very favorably by the guests in the study described above, I wanted to dig a little deeper and see if I could quantify any benefits that operators could gain from the use of the technology. In "The Influence of Tabletop Technology in Full-Service Restaurants," by Susskind and Curry, we did just that: we looked at how guests' use of tabletop can influence sales and labor, respectively. I note here that while Kimes and Collier gathered operators' opinions and perceptions of benefits and concerns over SST, they did not specifically quantify those benefits or differences. To fill that gap, my coauthor, Benjamin Curry, and I looked at a casual dining restaurant chain before and after they implemented tabletop devices in their restaurants. From the study, comparing the restaurant before and after the implementation of the technology, we found three very interesting things: first, when guests used the tabletop devices to order their food and beverages and to settle their bill, the restaurant needed 31% less service labor to attend to the guests; second, meal duration was shorter by 15.5%; and third, guests spent on average $3.61 more. These findings identify tangible benefits for operators that can emerge from the use and implementation of tabletop devices in full-service restaurants. With the potential labor savings restaurant operators need to determine how to use them—they can cut the number of staff in the dining room or they can have servers offer service enhancements (that is, more service contact) to their guests with their newfound time. It is also important for operators to continue to track and measure improvements to average check and table turns and make sure these gains can be permanent. As always, operators need to make sure their guests are happy with the big three they deliver (food, service, and atmosphere) with the added layer of technology and build return patronage intentions.

Mark: I love reading about Alex's experience, because it reminds me how far we have come to integrate technology into our businesses, especially in the last five years. In my commentary, I'll address the articles while delving into other tech-related subjects, from choosing a technology partner to sharing my hopes for the future of hospitality tech.

Tabletop technology makes perfect sense in certain segments of our industry. As the research we cite illustrates, it has the potential to make a significant impact in increasing check average, reducing meal duration, and improving labor costs. It has transformed quick-service restaurants and airport operations, for example, and these changes have come at the perfect time, when severe staffing shortages have gripped our industry. In the world of fine dining, however, I do not see tabletop tech taking hold in the foreseeable future, even though some upscale operators have started to put their wine lists on tablets. The premise of tabletop tech is that people dine out to eat and drink. However, I would argue that food and drink are merely tools that help build relationships among the people sharing them. In thirty years of serving and observing millions of guests, I see a direct correlation between engagement with the staff and a positive guest experience. While people's social media posts may center around what's on the table, it's what happens *around* the table that creates meaningful outcomes. If technology can somehow enhance those outcomes, then I am in full support. However, if tech becomes intrusive or an impediment to personal interactions, then I would argue that most people will opt for human interaction, as noted by 20% of the guests surveyed in Alex's first study discussed above.

I am eager to see expanded use of handheld tablets by servers in fine dining establishments, as I believe this is precisely the type of tech that can enhance connection. In this hybrid model (using tech but preserving human interaction), the server and the guest still make eye contact and have a conversation. I sincerely hope that this basic human interaction never goes away from what we do, as it is the core of our existence. But I believe technology can actively facilitate more meaningful interactions while eliminating unnecessary "utilitarian" interactions, to borrow Kimes and Collier's language. Consistent with the research in the Kimes and Collier report, I have found that one of the most frustrating roadblocks to a positive guest experience is entering an order in the POS system. Let's suppose a server takes an order for a group of six guests. The server speaks to each guest at the table, answers any questions, makes suggestions, and, ultimately, writes down their order and seat number on a paper pad. That server then walks across the dining room to a POS terminal, where he may need to wait for another server entering an order. He gets to the terminal, enters his password, opens the table, and starts to enter the order. Upon pressing "send," the ticket prints in the kitchen and service bar, and those people begin to organize and prepare the items. In even the quickest scenario, it will take two to four minutes from the time the guest decides what she wants to the time the service bartender begins to make the cocktail. And that is if the bartender doesn't already have a pile of tickets in front of the order. Now imagine that the server has a tablet in hand at the table, thereby saving the step of writing anything down. Once reviewing the order with the guests, the server presses "send" while still tableside, obviating the need to walk anywhere. Instead, he can walk to another table to greet new guests, take another order, check in with guests who are already dining, and, importantly, not leave the sight of his guests.

This is my dream scenario for fine dining. It's the best of both worlds. So why don't more businesses use this system? They have been used effectively in Darden's Seasons 52 restaurants since 2004 and can certainly be adopted and implemented by other full-service restaurants elsewhere. As Alex has mentioned, up-front costs are a major issue. A supercharged handheld terminal can cost considerably more than a traditional wall-mounted unit. In addition, tablets are fragile, can be prone to glitches, and need to be regularly charged, repaired, updated, and replaced. Most wall-mounted POS systems are designed to be bulletproof, while a durable tablet tends to be very heavy. A light tablet (think iPad mini) is fragile, and dropping one can cost thousands of dollars and ruin a busy service. Since tablet technology operates over Wi-Fi, the tablets can be slower and less reliable than a hard-cabled machine. Also, there has yet to be a system that makes technology, legal, and compliance officers comfortable in safeguarding the business's data and the guests' privacy while still functioning as well as a hard-cabled system. Given the prevalence of hacking and identity theft, it is understandable that operators have been reluctant to expose their business and guests to unnecessary risks. One bright spot has been America's late adoption of EMV, or chip, technology for credit card payments. This advance has made it possible for companies such as Square to develop an integrated suite of hardware and software to improve both speed and security for payments. The issue at the moment is that the ordering and inventory capabilities of these systems have not caught up to the payment technology.

The stigma of technology in a dining room should also not be underestimated. Given that many people who frequent high-end fine dining establishments are over 50 years old, and that many of these guests have not fully integrated tech into their day-to-day lives, seeing a tablet in a luxury restaurant with a tasting menu may seem less personal and professional to the over-50 crowd. Finally, there is not a tablet on the market at the moment that emits a warm light. So, if a dining room or bar has low light levels, the blue light emitted by a handheld tablet could ruin the mood of the room.

But times are thankfully changing, and millennials' demand for speed, efficiency, and elegant design has prompted tech companies and restaurant operators to innovate to satisfy a growing number of guests. Maureen Cushing, USHG's vice president of technology and cofounder of Tech-Table, explores the intersection of hospitality and technology for a living. In fact, the slogan of TechTable is "High Tech for High Touch," optimistically implying that tech has the power to improve, not impede, hospitality. Maureen dreams of a world in which mobile and contactless payments are the norm, skipping chip technology altogether. Adoption of this technology is quickly on the rise in much of Europe and Asia, especially in less complex businesses, like small retail shops and small restaurants. Case in point: in Disney theme parks, they now use radio frequency identification tech for those guests who stay on property to allow guests to automatically, without going through a transaction, charge their room for purchases made throughout the park. Though it has yet to take hold in multi-unit restaurant groups in the United States, its use is slowly rising every month. I share Maureen's dream, and I believe it is only a matter of time before we stop using physical credit cards entirely.

In addition to helping the guest-staff relationship, an integrated POS system can provide real-time data about how the business is performing at any moment. From hourly revenue and labor reports to daily item sales reports, having the ability to leverage real-time data can be the difference between success and failure. As we discussed in chapter 4, many guests are reluctant to provide feedback, so knowing buying patterns is crucial when launching a new menu or trying to determine which menu items to eliminate. Here's an anecdote to help illustrate this point: on the same day, two of our bar-centered businesses (Porchlight and GreenRiver) launched brand-new cocktail menus. Every morning for the first week, the general managers of each business received an item sales report to see which cocktails guests were trying and which were getting reordered. The data tells a tale of two very different guests. At GreenRiver, the top-selling cocktail was strong, stirred, and bourbon-based, far eclipsing the next three most popular drinks. At Porchlight, a new stirred bourbon drink was in the lowest quintile, while sales of the light, shaken tequila cocktail were off the charts. Having this information helps us decide how we will purchase spirits for the duration of the menu and helps us chart an overall direction for the list. For example, after the success of the stirred cocktail, the GreenRiver team launched a series of barrel-aged boozy cocktails. Those, too, sold incredibly well, confirming that the GreenRiver guest likes a strong drink. Having this data at our disposal every morning has been crucial to the success of the program. Moving forward, it is clear that we will probably focus more on stirred drinks at GreenRiver and shaken drinks at Porchlight. This data, coupled with informally collected feedback from guests and staff, will help us steer the ship. As more data rolls in over a period of weeks after a menu change, it becomes more reliable, and it is easier to make informed decisions.

When we were planning Porchlight's 2015 launch, I wanted to be at the leading edge of technology integration. I worked with our IT team to explore the many options on the market at the time. After months of research, we landed on an old-fashioned POS system. I was disappointed that there was not a product that could satisfy our demand for a portable, secure, and easy-to-use POS system with a substantial back-office component.

Fortunately, marketplace competition has spurred innovation in the POS space, resulting in more options. Unfortunately, there is still not a holy grail POS system that can be used for reservations, guest orders, mobile payments, labor scheduling, sales reporting, and inventory management while remaining PCI-compliant and secure. As a result, software companies such as Avero and Omnivore have begun to fill the gap between what operators want and what POS platforms can deliver. Avero provides reporting software that promises to improve profitability and productivity. Daily sales and labor data are collected, parsed, and presented in user-friendly reports that can be easily interpreted by operators. But the reports are only as helpful as the operator's ability to execute on the information provided. Omnivore's mission is to integrate restaurant POS systems with apps in the realms of reservations, loyalty, delivery, and payment, aiming to solve the problem that most POS systems don't elegantly communicate between and among other technology platforms. Omnivore is a layer that sits on a restaurant POS that lets it integrate with these other systems securely and seamlessly in real time. It's too early to tell if a solution like this is here to stay or if POS companies will work to provide the same integration. An obvious concern with any third-party solution is that success requires integration among companies, so the end user can be left in the lurch if there is a disconnect between two of the providers.

As you explore tech partners and consider how to integrate technology into your business, it's important to be honest with yourself and your team about your philosophy on tech. Are you well-informed? Do you tend to be an early adopter? Or are you a Luddite who protests the encroachment of technology into your lo-tech existence? While you may think about technology 10–20% of the time, there are people who live and breathe tech. It's likely that you will collaborate with a technology partner at some point. With this in mind, it would be helpful to avoid some of the common mistakes of entering into a relationship while setting your organization up for success. With the help of Lauren Hobbs, cofounder of TechTable, I have compiled some recommendations and questions to tackle when looking to expand your technology footprint.

1. Make sure you understand who has the final say. Who are the ultimate decision makers? Are they on board?
2. Identify one champion of the new technology. This person will need to be there in good times and bad, must be a master communicator, and must have the ability to unify disparate teams to ensure success of the project.
3. Ensure that the team understands the budget and financial implications of the agreement. What are up-front costs, monthly expenses, time lost during the ramp-up, and potential time saved once the system is up and running?
4. Write clear standard operating procedures and stick to them. If they need to be changed, be sure to over-communicate any changes to the entire team
5. Include line employees/end users in the exploration process. Is there a respected member of the team who understands tech and can be an advocate? Success will be fleeting if the people using the tech do not support it.

6. Create a realistic rollout timeline. Once a decision has been made, don't rush the launch. Yes, there will be pressure to meet deadlines, but pull the trigger only when enough people are ready and when there's a good chance that the guests will not be adversely affected.
7. Invest in staff education. There is no one more important in improving the guest experience than the line employees using the tech, and if it feels clunky to the line staff, it will feel clunky to guests.
8. Have a Plan B. What happens when the power goes down?

So where are we headed?

While I don't have a crystal ball, I see some very promising things emerging that could make an impact in the future. Customization and recognition are two of the strongest trends I see gaining some traction.

POS and software companies are learning that they can create a common framework and allow their customers to customize their system. At the moment, these tech providers don't necessarily advertise that their tech can be customized, but just as you would customize your phone, it is possible to tailor some of the POS functions to reflect the guest experience you are trying to convey. Fifteen years ago, websites were either fully customized or had to adhere to strict frameworks. Then, companies such as Square Space and BentoBox emerged with a third way, creating inexpensive frameworks that can be elegantly adapted. My hope is that a similar evolution will occur in point-of-sale systems.

The term "recognition" can be interpreted in many ways. In the traditional sense, a host greets you by name when you walk through the door. You have been recognized, and many surveys have found and confirmed that one of the top reasons people return to an establishment is being recognized and welcomed by name. In a more contemporary sense, Amazon recognizes customers' buying patterns and suggests items that "you may also like." Like Amazon, other online companies remember previous orders, making it easier for customers to reorder their favorites. These forms of recognition help the consumer save time while increasing revenue for the company. Now imagine if you could do that at your favorite restaurant. Regular guests may already have a close relationship with their favorite bartender ("The usual?"), but what about if that bartender isn't there, or if you're not yet a regular? Any good maître d' will research guests to learn about their background, but, until that guest has visited an establishment many times, the server or bartender may not know that a particular guest likes his ice on the side or extra candied pecans on her ice cream sundae. One potential option is to use technology to communicate with each guest's social media footprint to learn about each guest in advance of her visit, facilitating an opportunity to create meaningful experiences that are truly customized to the individual without wreaking havoc on the restaurant during service due to "special" requests. What the guest loses in terms of privacy is outweighed by a unique experience that is sure to exceed expectations and improve guests' intention to return. While this concept may seem far-fetched at the moment, I don't think it is that far away.

In fact, I feel we are very close to achieving a scenario that harnesses new technology to elegantly build on the tradition of the highest level of guest service. Returning to the example of a server using a tablet to place an order, now imagine that all of the restaurant's recipes, menu descriptions, and wine descriptions were linked to the POS software that the server is using. Upon the completion of the meal, the server thanks the guest and handwrites a note on the tablet to the guest. Along with the guest check, the note is emailed to the guest (or added to her cloud account). Attached to the note is a list of everything that was ordered during the meal, complete with recipes for every menu item, side dish, and garnish. Each wine ordered is listed, with a description from the sommelier from the restaurant's database and a photo of the label. In addition, there is a list of wine stores within a 50-mile radius of where the person lives that carry each wine. The famed restaurant Cellar in the Sky would present guests with a book of wine labels at the end of the meal to serve as a keepsake for the experience. I see this scenario as the twenty-first-century version of that sort of high-touch gesture. All of the puzzle pieces are there, and it is only a matter of time before the pieces are combined to create a beautiful picture.

Note

1. L. Peterson (2017), The adaption problem: Airline self-check-in, *Wayfind*, http://wdwayfind.com/research/the-adaption-problem/ on September 17, 2017.

8

Customer-Facing Payment Technology in the US Restaurant Industry

Sheryl E. Kimes and Joel E. Collier

Customer-facing payment technology (CFPT), which uses such equipment as smartphones, tablets, and RFIDs, is gradually growing in popularity among both consumers and restaurants. Implementation of this technology can benefit all concerned, yet restaurant operators have been slow to adopt these technologies for check settlement. The National Restaurant Association reports that over half of full-service restaurant customers would use CFPT if it were available, but that less than 5% of restaurants have installed such technology.[1] Consumers like CFPT because of its ease, speed, security, and control,[2] while restaurants see the potential for reduced labor costs, increased revenue, and improved customer satisfaction. CFPT has been particularly successful for quick-service and fast-casual restaurants. For example, Starbucks launched its mobile payment service in 2011, and by 2013, 20% of its transactions were made using a mobile payment app.[3] Juniper Research estimates that the global mobile payment market will grow from US$170 billion in 2010 to US$630 billion in 2014,[4] while Gartner Research estimates that by 2016 the global mobile payment market will encompass 448 million users with a transaction value of US$617 billion.[5]

In consideration of this growing trend, this report reviews the role of payment processes in restaurants, the types of CFPT available, and the potential advantages and disadvantages of using CFPT. Then we consider customer adoption and reaction to payment via CFPT, followed by the results of a study on CFPT usage and attitudes among US restaurant operators. Although a relatively small percentage of restaurants have implemented CFPT, it's clear that this is about to change, and CFPT is set to explode.

The Role of Payment Processes in Restaurants

Before discussing CFPT, it might be useful to revisit the world of restaurant payment. The full-service restaurant payment process has been addressed in previous research,[6] but it might be helpful to view the payment process in the context of the customer dining experience.[7] The customer dining experience consists of the following six main components (figure 8.1):

- Pre-Arrival: from when customers decide they want to go to the restaurant until they arrive at the restaurant,
- Post-Arrival: from when customers arrive at the restaurant to when they are seated,
- Pre-Process: from when customers are seated at the restaurant until they receive their first food order,
- In-Process: from when they receive their order until they request payment,
- Post Process: from when they request payment until they leave the restaurant, and
- Table Turnover: from when customers leave until the table is reseated.

For most customers, the most pleasurable part of their dining experience is the in-process stage when they are enjoying their meal. The other stages of the meal are more utilitarian in nature. The payment process typically occurs during the post-process, but with some online and mobile ordering systems, payment may even occur during the pre-arrival stage.

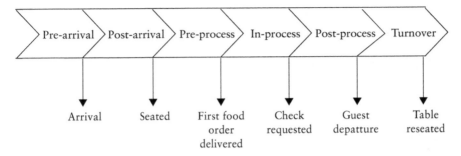

Figure 8.1. Stages of dining experience

Payment technology can have a strong influence on meal pacing, particularly for the post-process steps. Studies have been conducted on how long customers think dinner should last[8] and on the impact of pace on customer satisfaction.[9] The effect of pace varies depending upon the stage of the meal and the type of restaurant. In casual and upscale casual restaurants, customers prefer a faster pace during the pre-process and post-process stages but a slower pace during the in-process stage. This implies that faster payment processes should lead to improved customer satisfaction. In addition to the potential for improved customer satisfaction, the shorter meal duration from speeding up the payment process can also allow additional guests to be seated in busy periods.[10]

European full-service restaurants have used handheld credit card machines for a number of years, but US restaurant operators have been slow to adopt the technology. The transaction with the handheld machine is faster since the server does not have to leave the table, find the POS terminal, wait for other servers to use the terminal, wait for authorization, and then return to the table in the midst of other duties. It also allows the server to spend more time concentrating on guests rather than going off the floor to use a POS terminal.

Types of Customer-Facing Payment Technology

There are three basic types of CFPTs: mobile wallets, table-based tablets, and mobile remote payment. At the moment, it appears that the majority of payments made via CFPT will be on-site, using wallets or tablets.[11]

With mobile wallets, such as the approach used by Starbucks, customers have the option of linking their credit or debit card to a smartphone-based app and then using their smartphone to pay for their transaction. The use of near field communications (NFC) means that the smartphone or mobile device never leaves the customers' hands when they scan their payment. Some mobile wallet apps (e.g., Google Wallet, SquareWallet, Isis) require the customer to tap their smart-phone against a specialized reader while others (e.g., MCX, TabbedOut) automatically detect where the customer is and do not require a specialized reader. The National Restaurant Association estimates that about 10% of limited-service restaurants offer mobile wallet payment, but that about 30% of customers would pay via a mobile wallet if it were available.[12]

Tabletop tablets, which are most commonly seen in family or casual restaurants, are placed where customers are seated and have been quite successful. The tablets provide a variety of services including credit or debit card payment, ordering, entertainment, and information. Some of the major players in this market include Ziosk, E la Carte and eTab. The National Restaurant Association reports that fewer than 5% of full-service restaurants offer tablets. However, 52% of customers would use this technology if it were available.[13]

Mobile remote payments allow customers the chance to purchase their meal without being physically present at the restaurant. Mobile remote payments frequently occur in conjunction with online and mobile food ordering. Many online and mobile ordering systems allow customers to save their payment information so that they can quickly submit payment once they have verified the accuracy of their order.

Potential Benefits and Concerns about CFPT

While most restaurants have not yet adopted CFPT, restaurateurs believe that such technology will become more prevalent in the future because of the associated speed and enhanced customer satisfaction.[14] As we indicated above, most of the benefits associated with CFPT stem from increased transaction speed. CFPT can reduce the payment transaction time in both limited-service restaurants and in full-service restaurants. American Express has found that contactless payment is 63% faster than cash payment and 53% faster than the typical credit card payment.[15]

Speed is not the only consideration, however. By allowing operators to reduce the number of steps in the payment process, CFPT offers the opportunity to improve customer satisfaction, reduce labor costs, increase revenue, and provide better customer data, as well as offer entertainment options to guests, as we outline here.

1. Improved customer satisfaction. As discussed above, faster payment time can improve customer satisfaction, particularly in quick-service and fast-casual restaurants and in casual sit-down restaurants. Approximately two-thirds of restaurant operators believe that CFPT will lead to an improvement in customer satisfaction, a perception that is supported by the research we mentioned earlier, which found that a faster post-process experience in casual and upscale casual restaurants leads to improved customer satisfaction.[16] Speed of transaction is also a key driver of customer satisfaction in limited service restaurants.

2. Labor scheduling. CFPT has the potential to reduce labor costs because faster payment times also result in less employee time involved with processing payments. This is particularly relevant for casual and upscale casual restaurants in which the multiple steps required for payment can absorb well over ten minutes of a server's time. Alternatively, operators may decide to maintain the same level of labor, but instead have servers focus on providing better customer service and on doing a more effective job with suggestive selling and upselling. This has the potential to lead to increased restaurant revenue and server tips.

3. Increased revenue. At certain times of the day, faster transaction time may help restaurant operators increase revenue, particularly those in the quick-service and fast-casual segments, since they will be able to serve more customers during peak demand times. The Hospitality Technology study found that 73.4% of respondents believed that CFPT allowed them to serve guests more quickly.[17] For example, MasterCard has found that CFPT is particularly effective in restaurants that offer drive-through service, and that it reduces the transaction time by 12 to 18 seconds.[18] This may not seem like a significant drop, but in many QSRs, this time reduction could allow the restaurant to be able to serve 20 to 25% more customers in the same amount of time—particularly critical when

the drive-through lines are long. The potential revenue impact in full-service restaurants will likely be lower because of the longer meal duration, but depending upon the speed improvement, restaurants with high demand would be able to serve more customers in the same amount of time and as a result would be able to increase revenue.

4. Better customer data. Some types of CFPT provide improved information regarding customer preferences and buying patterns by integrating with the point-of-sale (POS) system. Some even offer customer satisfaction survey capabilities that tie satisfaction ratings to menu items purchased or to the server. By developing better information on individual customer buying behavior, restaurants can provide more customized service, develop more targeted promotions, and create better customer profiles.

5. Provide entertainment. Some of the table-based and tablet systems also provide entertainment options for guests. This is particularly appealing for families with small children and potentially provides another revenue source.

Potential Barriers to CFPT

Potential barriers to CFPT adoption include infrastructure issues, the cost of CFPT devices, the cost of integrating CFPT with existing POS and payment systems, security concerns, and the impact of reduced customer contact. In addition, the CFPT industry is still fragmented, and many restaurateurs are unsure of which vendor or technology to select. Let's look at these potential barriers.

1. Infrastructure issues. Credit card companies and banks may be resistant to CFPTs for a variety of reasons. For example, credit card companies may be concerned about reductions in transaction fees that may result from widespread adoption of CFPT. Similarly, banks that issue credit cards may be reluctant to absorb the expense of offering chip-enabled credit cards to their customers. This is particularly an issue in the US, where chip-enabled credit cards are not yet widely used.

2. Cost of CFPT. While CFPT can reduce transaction time and improve customer satisfaction, it still requires investment in hardware and system integration. When using customer-supplied CFPT, restaurants would not have to invest as much in hardware, but would still need to invest in POS integration. If operators decide to offer the hardware, they will need to invest in both the hardware and the POS integration. Operators will need to balance whether the benefits outweigh the costs.

3. System integration. Operators would also need to ensure that their CFPT devices are seamlessly integrated with their POS and other payment systems. The integration would likely involve some cost.

4. Security concerns. Some restaurants have expressed concern with the security of CFPT information, but CFPT enhances at least one key security issue, since the credit card or smartphone does not leave the customer's hands. Evidence of this is provided by the Hospitality Technology survey. Only 18.6% of respondents believed that a mobile POS was not a secure payment system, while over half (57.8%) believed that mobile payment would reduce credit card skimming.[19]

5. Reduced interaction with guests. While some operators may be concerned that CFPT may reduce the amount of time that their employees have direct guest contact, this is probably not an issue, except perhaps for fine-dining restaurants. Most customers in other types of restaurant prefer a relatively fast post-process experience when they are ready to leave. That said, some fine-dining guests also may appreciate the option of using a CFPT as an alternative to traditional payment methods.

6. Aesthetics. Some operators, particularly those in the fine-dining segment, may think that the look and feel of some of the CFPTs, particularly the table-based ones, are inconsistent with the décor and ambience of their restaurant.

7. Disjointed CFPT industry. As discussed above, the CFPT industry has yet to consolidate, and no dominant players have yet emerged. Because of this, some operators may be reluctant to try CFPT because they are unsure of which vendors will survive and do not want to forge an agreement with a CFPT provider that may cease to exist after a few years.

8. Customer acceptance. Another possible concern may be related to customer acceptance of CFPT. Other than for fine-dining restaurants, this concern is likely unwarranted, since customers are well acquainted with electronic processes in many areas of their lives. Most like the improved speed, security, and control resulting from mobile payment, and as I discuss next, they would support tableside payment.

Customer Adoption of CFPT

The National Restaurant Association survey that we cited above found that over half of US customers state that they would use a tableside payment option.[20] In that context, let's examine the potential benefits to consumers, which include enhanced speed, improved convenience, additional control, and increased security.

1. Speed. CFPTs provide a faster post-process experience for customers, and in the case of QSRs, help facilitate a faster service experience. The speed of a self-service transaction has been mentioned numerous times as an important influence on satisfaction, attitudes, and intentions.[21] Pujari, for instance, found that the number one contributor to self-service satisfaction was improved speed.[22] That finding aligns with other studies which showed that customers prefer to have the post-process be as fast as possible in casual and upscale restaurants.[23] Once customers ask for their bill, they are ready to end their service experience and depart.

2. Convenience. Related to increased speed, improved convenience is also associated with an increase in satisfaction.[24] Some CFPTs, particularly mobile wallets, are much more convenient for customers since they do not have to worry about finding their credit card or making sure they have enough cash. The associated ease reduces the effort that customers have to exert to complete the payment process. The importance of convenience in a self-service setting, such as technology-based payment, cannot be understated, with research finding that convenience has a strong influence on the evaluation of a self-service experience.[25]

3. Increased control. When customers perceive that they have more control over a service encounter, they are more likely to be satisfied with that encounter.[26] Payment by CFPT gives customers more control over how their time is spent and also gives them more control over their credit or debit card. As one operator stated: "Our guests want to be able to have control over their payment method and when they want to leave the restaurant without having to hunt down the server."[27]

4. Security. Credit card security has become a major issue as incidents of credit card fraud have increased.[28] As mentioned above, CFPT means that customers retain control of their credit card and payment information during the entire payment process. They do not have to worry about credit card theft or someone putting unauthorized charges on their credit card.

The Restaurant Experience

To find out what restaurant operators think about customer-facing payment technology, we worked with *Nation's Restaurant News* and *Restaurant Hospitality* to distribute an online survey in August 2013 to a sample of their subscribers. A total of 385 restaurateurs participated to tell us about their current payment processes, their awareness of various CFPTs, and the experience of the respondents who have adopted some sort of CFPT.

Restaurant Profile

The sample was divided as follows: 21.9% of respondents were from upscale-casual restaurants, 19.1% from casual restaurants, 16.6% from family restaurants, 12.7% from fast-casual restaurants, and 6.8% from quick-service restaurants. Just over two-thirds (68.1%) of respondents were from independent restaurants, and the remainder operated chain restaurants (see table 8.1).

About half of the independent restaurants had annual sales of from $1 million to under $5 million. The majority (70.3%) had average checks

TABLE 8.1. Demographic profile ($n = 385$)

Segment		Independent or chain?	
Quick-service or fast-food	9.1%	Independent	68.1%
Fast-casual	10.4%	Chain	31.9%
Casual-dining or theme	19.8%		
Family	16.8%	**Chain profile**	
Upscale casual-dining	24.2%	Sales volume	
Fine-dining	9.3%	Less than $1 million	6.3%
Hotel foodservice	3.3%	$1 million to under $5 million	42.0%
Cafeteria or buffet	1.4%	$5 million to under $10 million	4.5%
Other	5.8%	$10 million to under $50 million	18.8%
		$50 million to under $100 million	7.1%
Independent profile		$100 million to under $200 million	4.5%
Sales volume		$200 million or more	17.0%
Less than $500,000	13.8%		
$500,000 to under $1 million	26.9%	**Number of units**	
$1 million to under $5 million	49.8%	2–5	19.6%
$5 million to under $10 million	7.5%	6–10	12.5%
$10 million or more	2.0%	11–20	12.5%
		21–50	14.3%
Average check per person		51–100	13.4%
Under $10	7.9%	101–300	5.4%
$10–$19.99	37.2%	301–600	5.4%
$20–$34.99	34.8%	601–1000	5.4%
$35–$49.99	11.9%	More than 1000	11.6%
Over $50	8.3%		
		Department	
Position		Marketing	4.9%
General manager	24.9%	Operations	34.4%
Assistant manager	3.6%	IT	3.3%
Chef	7.5%	Menu development/culinary	1.6%
Kitchen	0.4%	Store development	3.3%
Server	0.4%	Company officer	36.1%
Owner	51.8%	Purchasing	0.0%
Other	11.5%	Human resources	3.3%
		Finance	8.2%
Location		Other	4.9%
Urban area	31.2%		
Suburban area	28.5%		
Small town	31.6%		
Rural	8.7%		

per person between $10 and $35 ($10–$20, 36.1%; $20–$35, 34.2%). About a third (31.2%) of respondents were located in urban areas and another third (31.6%) were located in small towns. About half (50.4%) of the respondents owned their restaurant and another 24.8% were general managers.

Of the chain restaurant respondents, 44.8% were at corporate or franchisor headquarters, 37.6% were at the restaurant itself, and 9.6% held a regional position. The number of restaurants operated by respondents ranged from two to over 10,000. About a quarter (25.6%) had over 100 restaurants in their chain or franchise organization, while 47.2% had fewer than twenty-one units. About half (53.3%) of the respondents had annual revenue of less than $10 million per year, while 16.7% had revenue of over $200 million per year. About a third (32.4%) of respondents were company officers and another 33.8% were involved in operations.

Current Payment Approaches

The large majority (86.5%) of restaurants had a POS system. Overall, the respondents reported that over half (53.8%) of payments were made by credit card, followed by 29.6% cash and 12.9% debit card (figure 8.2). By restaurant category, over half of QSR payments were made with cash (53.5%), and buffet restaurants were 60% cash.

In terms of timing and location of settlement processes, most respondents from limited service restaurants indicated that their customers paid upon ordering their meal (67.0%). Another 16.5% stated that payment was made on receipt of the meal and 15.4% upon completion of the meal. The majority (81.8%) of limited-service restaurants accepted payment at a cashier, while the remainder did so at the table.

The payment process at limited-service restaurants was relatively fast: 67.4% of respondents stated that on average, their payment process took less than one minute. The large majority (81.9%) of respondents from limited-service restaurants indicated that they require a signature for all credit card transactions, while 15.7% said that they require a signature only if the transaction was above a certain amount, and 2.3% indicated that they did not require a signature.

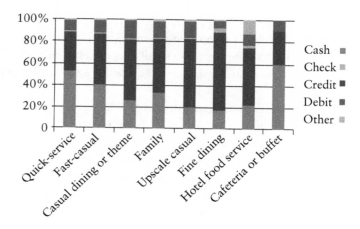

Figure 8.2. Payment type by restaurant segment

The majority (76.9%) of respondents from full-service restaurants indicated that their customers paid at the table, but this percentage varied by type of full-service restaurant. Almost all customers (98.9%) in upscale-casual restaurants paid at the table, but that figure fell below half (48.3%) in family restaurants. Not surprisingly, the payment process took longer at full-service restaurants. About half (48.8%) of respondents stated that it took between 1 and 3 minutes for customers to pay their bill, while another 34.9% stated that it took between 4 and 6 minutes.

Payment Technology Awareness, Current Use, and Intent to Use

We wanted to ascertain respondents' awareness and use of different CFPTs. Almost all (97.9%) respondents had heard of at least one CFPT. Smartphones (74.3%), tablets (63.4%), and portable credit card readers (61.6%) led the list, but respondents also had some familiarity with on-table self-payment devices (48.3%), mobile wallets (43.9%), and NFC devices (41.3%), as shown in figure 8.3.

Respondents from limited-service restaurants were significantly more likely to be familiar with NFC devices, while respondents from chain restaurants were significantly more likely to be familiar with on-table self-payment devices.

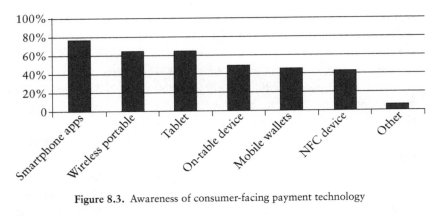

Figure 8.3. Awareness of consumer-facing payment technology

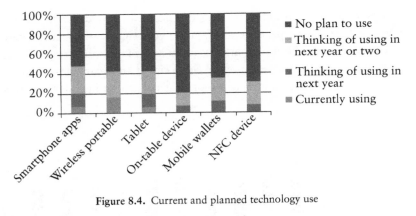

Figure 8.4. Current and planned technology use

We asked respondents who were aware of CFPTs whether they were actually using the technology or were thinking of adopting it in the next few years. Only one-eighth (12.2% of respondents) were using some sort of CFPT, but another 47.3% were thinking of implementing the technology in the next two years.

As shown in figure 8.4, smartphone payment was the most popular option (5.5% in current use; possible use in the next year, 9.9%; possible use in the next year or two, 21.0%). For wireless portable payment card readers, 3.6% of respondents said they were in current use, 8.1% were thinking of implementing these in the next year, and 14.3% in the next year or two. The figures for tablets were: 2.6% current use; 8.8% thinking of using in the next year; and 16.1% in the next year or two. On-table self-payment devices were the least used option (currently using, 0.3%; thinking of using in the next year, 3.6%; thinking of using in the next year or two, 6.5%). Responses did not vary by segment (limited service vs. full service), but respondents from chain restaurants were significantly more likely to be using or thinking of using on-table self-payment devices.

Respondents noted several anticipated advantages of CFPT, as shown in figure 8.5.

The most important among these are improved customer satisfaction (4.32 on a 5-point scale), lower transaction fees (4.26), and improved payment security (4.16). Shorter guest waiting time (4.00) and higher guest spending (4.02) were also considered to be important.

Respondents from different types of restaurant saw different advantages to CFPTs. Independent restaurants were significantly more likely to consider reduced transaction costs as an advantage, while respondents from chain restaurants were more likely to cite as an advantage the resulting higher guest spending because of targeted marketing. Respondents

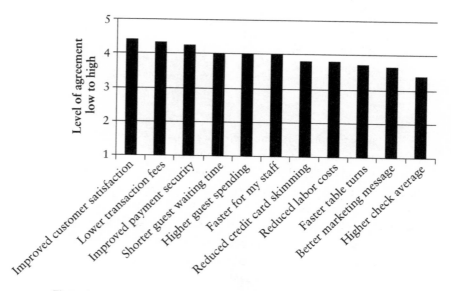

Figure 8.5. Perceived advantages of customer-facing payment technology

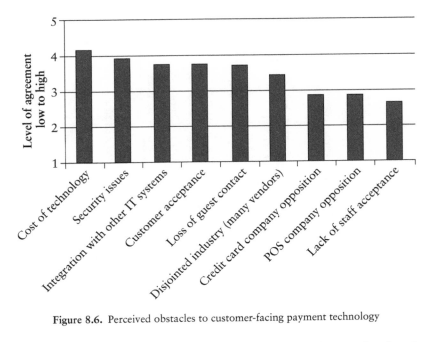

Figure 8.6. Perceived obstacles to customer-facing payment technology

from full-service restaurants were significantly more likely to rank reduced labor costs and more turns as advantages than respondents from limited-service restaurants.

The cost of technology ranked as the biggest obstacle to the adoption of CFPTs, scoring 4.14 on a five-point scale where 5 = strongly agree (figure 8.6).

Other obstacles included security issues (3.93) and integration with other IT systems (3.75). Responses did not vary by whether respondents were from a chain or were from an independent restaurant, but did vary by segment. Respondents from full-service restaurants were more likely to view the loss of guest contact, the lack of staff acceptance, and lack of customer acceptance as significant obstacles.

The User Experience

The relatively small group of respondents who had installed the technology were significantly more likely to be from limited service restaurants

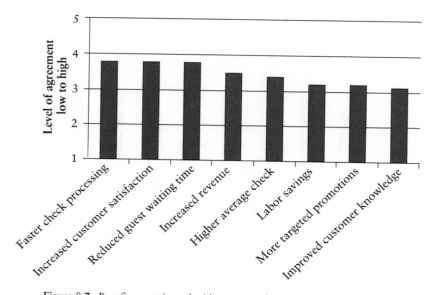

Figure 8.7. Benefits experienced with customer-facing payment technology

(19.3% of respondents from limited service restaurants were using some sort of payment technology) and from chain restaurants (16.3% of respondents from chain restaurants were using some sort of payment technology). One quarter (25.6%) had been using the technology for over two years and another 28.2% had been using the technology for one to two years.

As shown in figure 8.7, the top three benefits that these restaurateurs cited were faster check processing (3.78 of 5), increased customer satisfaction (3.75 of 5), and reduced customer-waiting time (3.75 of 5). As shown in figure 8.8, the top three obstacles mentioned were integration with other IT systems (56.3%), the cost of the technology (43.8%), and customer acceptance (37.5%).

Implications

Even though only 12.2% of respondents to this survey had adopted a CFPT, almost all respondents were aware of CFPTs, and half of them were

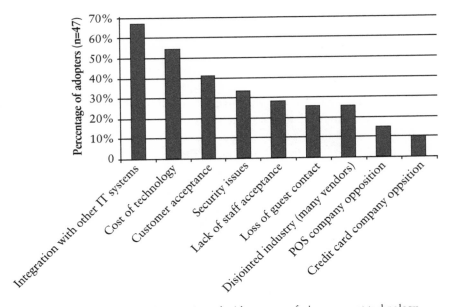

Figure 8.8. Obstacles experienced with customer-facing payment technology

thinking of adopting a CFPT in the next two years. This strongly suggests that restaurant adoption of CFPT will significantly increase in the near future. Given this fact, it may be useful to look at the experience of current users to see whether some insights can be gleaned from their experiences.

The top three benefits of CFPT, as perceived by both users and non-users, were improved customer satisfaction, lower transaction fees, and improved payment security. Even though about half of respondents were thinking of adopting a CFPT in the next few years, this may not have quite as much of an impact on limited-service restaurants because over half of QSR transactions are still made with cash. This high proportion of cash payments may indicate that mobile wallet approaches in particular may not have as much potential for QSRs and buffet restaurants unless they adopt some sort of pre-payment or debit payment approach.

Although the top three perceived obstacles to CFPT adoption were the cost of the technology, security issues, and integration with other IT systems, CFPT users were significantly less likely to consider the cost and security issues as obstacles than were non-users. This may indicate that the experience with a CFPT leads to the realization that some of the perceived barriers are not as much of an issue as had been anticipated.

System integration is a serious consideration. The importance of POS integration cannot be overstated, given that CFPT adopters indicated that integration with other IT systems was the most important issue that they had faced with CFPT. Presumably, integration will become less of a concern in the future, but still the fact that it was identified as the top problem reinforces the fact that operators should be sure that any type of CFPT under consideration is fully integrated with their other IT systems.

Surprisingly, CFPT adopters rated customer acceptance as one of the top three issues. This is puzzling, given that over half of US customers state that they would use a tableside payment option.[29] This finding may indicate a need to provide better customer and employee education on the use of the CFPT and to give guests the option to pay using traditional means if desired. In addition to offering alternative payment options, restaurants must ensure that the CFPT is intuitive and easy to use. In addition, depending on the goal of the CFPT adoption, it may be worthwhile to offer incentives to encourage guests to use the CFPT rather than traditional approaches.

Once employees are on board, they need to be able to clearly explain the technology to guests. At the same time, guests should always be offered more traditional payment options. Research has shown that forced use of a self-service technology such as CFPT leads to customer dissatisfaction with both the technology and with the service provider offering that technology.[30]

Limitations

As with all research, this study has certain limitations. First of all, the study was survey-based, and so it is possible that non-response bias exists, that respondents may not have answered the questions accurately, or that they might not have understood the intended meaning of the questions. In addition, the respondents were from a convenience sample, so they may not be representative of all US restaurant operators. Finally, the study was only conducted in the US, and it is possible that the results would have been different if conducted in other countries.

Future research

The intent of this study was to give a snapshot of current attitudes and usage of CFPT. Given that only one-eighth of respondents in this study had installed CFPT in their restaurants, it would be interesting to do a more in-depth study with CFPT users. This sort of study could provide deeper insights into restaurants' experiences with CFPT, how they use the CFPT, and how they have integrated it into their business. In addition, it would be interesting to obtain a more detailed insight into the percentage of customers who use CFPT and to compare their average checks and tips with those who use traditional payment methods.

While this report has focused on restaurant operators, it would also be interesting to study consumers' use of and attitudes towards CFPT in other businesses. Such a study could provide additional understanding of the perceived benefits of CFPT as well as gain insight into the drivers of satisfaction with CFPT. Finally, it would be interesting and valuable to extend this survey of both restaurant operators and restaurant consumers to other parts of the world.

Conclusion

Almost all of the responding restaurateurs were aware of consumer payment technologies, and about half were considering installing them in the next two years. At the moment a relatively small percentage of restaurants have done so, at least based on the responses to this survey. This strongly suggests that restaurant adoption of CFPT will significantly increase in the near future.

Based on the experience of those early adopters, before adopting a CFPT, restaurant operators should ensure that the technology will be fully integrated with their POS system. They need to dispel incorrect assumptions about the technology and train their employees both on how to use the system themselves and how to help solve any problems that guests may encounter. Any system should be easy for customers to understand and use. Finally, it is essential that a traditional payment option should be available for any customers who choose to use it.

Notes

Original citation: Kimes, S. E., & Collier, J. (2014). Customer-facing payment technology in the US restaurant industry. *Cornell Hospitality Report*, 14(12): 6–17.

The authors express their appreciation to Nation's Restaurant News and Restaurant Hospitality, two Penton divisions, for their assistance in gathering data for this study.

1. National Restaurant Association (2012), *2013 Restaurant industry forecast* (Chicago: National Restaurant Association).

2. Michael J. Dixon, Sheryl E. Kimes, & Rohit Verma (2009), Customer preferences and use of technology-based service innovations in restaurants, *Cornell Hospitality Report*, 9(7), Cornell University Center for Hospitality Research.

3. James Wester (2013), Starbucks still feeling a buzz from mobile payments, Fastcasual. com, http://www.fastcasual.com/article/207367/Starbucks-still-feel-ing-a-buzz-from-mobile-payments. Last viewed 11/19/2013.

4. Suzanne Cluckey, Mobile payments 101: Restaurant, mobilepaymentstoday.com (2011), http://www.mobilepaymentstoday.com/whitepapers/4216/Mobile-Payments-101-Restaurant.

5. Gartner Research (2013), Restaurant technology goes full apectrum, *Hospitality Technology Magazine*, http://www.hospitalitytechnology.edgl.com/reports/2013-Restaurant-Technology-Study85036.

6. Sheryl E. Kimes & Stephen A. Mutkoski (1989), The express guest check: Saving steps with process design, *Cornell Hotel and Restaurant Administration Quarterly*, 30(2): 21–25.

7. Sheryl E. Kimes (2008), The role of technology in restaurant revenue management, *Cornell Hospitality Quarterly*, 49(3): 297–309.

8. Sheryl E. Kimes, Jochen Wirtz, & Breffni M. Noone (2002), How long should dinner take? Measuring expected meal duration for restaurant revenue management, *Journal of Revenue and Pricing Management*, 1(3): 220–233.

9. Breffni M. Noone & Sheryl E. Kimes (2005), Dining duration and customer satisfaction, *Cornell Hospitality Report*, 5(9), Center for Hospitality Research; Breffni Noone, Sheryl E. Kimes, Anna Mattila, and Jochen Wirtz (2007), The effect of meal pace on customer satisfaction, *Cornell Hotel and Restaurant Administration Quarterly*, 48(3): 231–245.

10. Noone & Kimes, Dining duration and customer satisfaction; Noone et al., Effect of meal pace on customer satisfaction.

11. Cluckey, Mobile payments 101.

12. National Restaurant Association, *2013 restaurant industry forecast*.

13. Ibid.

14. Ibid.

15. Smart Card Alliance (2007), Contactless payments: Frequently asked questions, http://www.smartcardalliance.org/resources/pdf/Contact-less_Payments_FAQ.pdf.

16. Noone & Kimes, Dining duration and customer satisfaction; Noone et al., Effect of meal pace on customer satisfaction.

17. *Hospitality Technology*, Restaurant technology goes full spectrum.

18. MasterCard (2004), Frequently asked questions: MasterCard PayPass," MasterCard International, http://www.mastercard.com/us/company/en/docs/Paypass_FAQ.pdf.

19. *Hospitality Technology*, Restaurant technology goes full spectrum.

20. National Restaurant Association, *2013 restaurant industry forecast*.

21. Pratibha A. Dabholkar (1996), Consumer evaluations of new technology-based self-service options: An investigation of alternative models of service quality, *International Journal of Research in Marketing*, 13(1): 29–51; and Devashish Pujari (2004), Self-service with a

smile? Self-Service Technology (SST) encounters among Canadian business to business, *International Journal in Service Industry Management*, 15(2): 200–219.

22. Pujari, Self-service with a smile?

23. Noone & Kimes, Dining duration and customer satisfaction; Noone et al., Effect of meal pace on customer satisfaction.

24. Leonard L. Berry, Kathleen Seiders, & Dhruv Grewal (2002), Understanding service convenience, *Journal of Marketing*, 66(3): 1–17.

25. Joel E. Collier & Daniel L. Sherrell (2010), Examining the influence of control and convenience in a self-service setting, *Journal of the Academy of Marketing Science*, 38(4): 490–509; David Xin Ding, Paul Jen-Hwa Hu, Rohit Verma, & Don G Wardell (2010), The impact of service system design and flow experience on customer satisfaction in online financial services, *Journal of Service Research*, 13(1): 96–110.

26. James R. Averill (1973), Personal control over aversive stimuli and its relationship to stress, *Psychological Bulletin*, 80(4): 286–303; Michael K. Hui & David K. Tse (1996), What to tell consumers in waits of different lengths: An integrative model of service evaluation, *Journal of Marketing*, 60 (April): 81–90; Michael K. Hui & John E. G. Bateson (1991), Perceived control and the effects of crowding and consumer choice on the service experience, *Journal of Consumer Research*, 18 (September): 174–184; Ellen J. Langer (1983), *The psychology of control* (Beverly Hills, CA: Sage).

27. *Hospitality Technology*, Restaurant technology goes full spectrum.

28. M. P. McQueen (2007, March 15), How to protect your plastic; Recent thefts of credit- and debit-card information highlight need for consumer caution; Beware of unbranded ATMs, *Wall Street Journal*, D1; Robin Sidel (2007), In data leaks, culprits are often mom, pop; Credit-card industry tries to add safeguards; Honest errors occur, *Wall Street Journal*, September 22, B1.

29. National Restaurant Association, *2013 restaurant industry forecast*.

30. Machiel J. Reinders, Pratibha A. Dabholkar, & Ruud T. Frambach (2008), Consequences of forcing consumers to use technology-based self-service, *Journal of Service Research*, 11(2): 107–123.

Guests' Reactions to Tabletop Technology in Full-Service Restaurants

Alex M. Susskind, Saqib Awan, Ron Parikh, and Rajat Suri

The hospitality industry is gradually installing various types of technology to deliver or augment service processes, and such technology has in many cases altered the nature of the guest-employee service interaction. One model that is useful for examining the effects of technology on service is the Customer-Server Exchange (CSE), which is rooted in the Service-Profit Chain. The CSE details the interrelationship between service providers' reactions to organizational standards for service delivery and how these standards are related to staff perceptions of coworkers' and managers' support. With those models as the base, this paper considers two effects of the addition of customer-facing technology in restaurants: namely, the likelihood that a guest will return, and any changes in tip levels resulting from the technology. These two key outcomes are in question because technology adds or expands customer participation in the service experience and could lead to perceptions of less employee involvement.

This paper studied customers' reaction to implementation of tabletop technology in 21 restaurants in a single full-service casual-dining restaurant chain. Until recently, such technology has not typically been used in full-service restaurants, in part due to concerns about customers' reactions to the reduction of contact with and attention from servers. With regard to restaurants as a whole, there is a concern about customer acceptance. A study by the National Restaurant Association found that 37 percent of US consumers reported that technology makes restaurant visits and ordering more complicated. At the same time, technology is expanding into full-service casual-dining restaurant chains such as Applebee's, Chili's, Genghis Grill, and Olive Garden. It seems reasonable to project that guests will become more accepting of the technology as time goes on, particularly if they see a value to the revised service process.

So, What's in It for Me?

Customer-facing technology must operate in keeping with four principles.

- The technology must be consistent with the brand image;
- Marketing activities that reach customers prior to their experience with the technology must be congruent with their needs and expectations to ensure that the stage is set properly for the adoption and use of the new technology;
- The actual services that are offered via the technology need to be customer-focused; and
- Service quality management processes must be in place to ensure a seamless delivery of service through the new technology.

In sum, companies adopting new technologies need to ensure that all parties understand how those technologies affect the operation and the customer experience.

The study proposes the following four questions to examine how customer-facing technology influences the traditional full-service dining experience:

- Research Question 1a: What is the relationship between guests' belief that a tabletop device improves their service experience during a full-service meal and their liking for the tabletop device?

- Research Question 1b: What is the relationship between guests' desire to return to the restaurant and their liking for the tabletop device?
- Research Question 2a: What is the relationship between guests' belief that the tabletop device improves the service experience during a full-service meal and the tip percentage paid to the server?
- Research Question 2b: What is the relationship between guests' desire to return to the restaurant and the tip percentage paid to the server?

Method: Participants and Procedure

The study began with 23,640 point-of-sale transactions from the 21 casual-dining restaurants from July 2014 through September 2014, along with 13,476 email survey responses from restaurant guests who used a tabletop device during their meal. The tabletop device in question allows guests to view menu items, play games, order food and beverage items, and settle the bill. After matching the POS transaction data to guests' email responses, excluding cash transactions and those with no tip on the credit card, the final sample was 1,358.

Dependent Variables

To determine how well guests liked the technology, the email survey asked them, "How did the tabletop device improve your dining experience?" Although this was an open-ended question, a pilot test of 306 diners' responses allowed the researchers to assign the answers to one of five categories, as described next. The other key outcome metric was tip percentage relative to total sales measured per transaction, which helped control for the number of guests at each table. Tip percentage was used a proxy for the guest satisfaction with the service experience.

The five response categories were as follows:

(1) Did not like the device. This category included guests who stated that they missed the contact with the service personnel, the device was in the way on the table, or that the device diminished the service

experience. This category of responses indicated that the use of the device diminished their service experience (coded as 1);

(2) Device malfunction. In addition to an actual malfunction, this category included operator issues, such as guests' wanting more information about how the device worked, or complaining about charges for the games, about a lack of connection to the restaurant's loyalty program, or about problems with applying coupons (coded as 2).

(3) Neutral. This category included relatively neutral or mixed responses, such as when guests reported both a positive and negative response to the device (coded as 3).

(4) Convenience. Answers in this category expressed guests' overall positive reaction to the device, citing ease of use, convenience, speed, functionality, control of credit card information, or reduced wait times in placing and receiving orders (coded as 4).

(5) Great experience. This category included those who enjoyed using the device. They said it was fun to use, appreciated the self-service aspect, and found that it enhanced their service experience greatly (coded as 5).

The coders found that a high level of agreement emerged in categorizing the survey responses, supporting the classification scheme developed in the pilot study. The researchers had to examine and reclassify only 41 of the 1,358 responses that the two coders did not completely agree upon.

Independent Variables

Participants also responded to questions regarding whether the table device improved their experience and increased or decreased their likelihood to return to the restaurant. With a code of 2, the "Increase" response would have a higher value than the "Decrease" response, which was coded as 1.

Analyses

The statistical analysis included multivariate analysis of variance to test the mean values of guests' liking for the tabletop device and the tip percentage (as the dependent variables) compared to the guests' assessment of whether the tabletop device improved their restaurant experience and whether they intended to return. Independent t-tests were conducted to test the magnitude and significance of the differences uncovered in the dependent variables.

Multivariate Analysis Results

The multivariate analysis indicated that guests generally liked the tabletop technology, and many reported that it improved their restaurant experience. Those happy guests cited the technology as a reason to return, and they left better tips than those who were not so keen on the technology. The multivariate model further found that guests' reactions to the tabletop device were connected to varying levels of why or how they liked the tabletop device, as well as their tip level. For the effect-on-experience variable, the Hotelling Trace Statistic was significant in the model,[1] as was the return intent variable.[2] The interaction between effect on experience and return intent was not significant, however.

TABLE 9.1. Response frequencies for categorical and interval study variables (N = 1,358)

Categories of likeability	Frequency	Percentage
Did not like	132	9.70
Device malfunction	189	13.90
Neutral	72	5.30
Convenience	868	63.90
Great experience	97	7.10
Improve experience	**Frequency**	**Percentage**
No	288	21.20
Yes	1070	78.80
Return intention	**Frequency**	**Percentage**
Decrease	233	17.20
Increase	1125	82.80

Between Subjects Effects: Likeability

Restaurant guests' perceptions that the tabletop device improved their experience in the restaurant was significantly related to their liking for the tabletop device.[3] The t-test was also significant,[4] showing that restaurant guests who reported that they liked the device overwhelmingly reported that the tabletop device improved their experience in the restaurant.[5]

Restaurant guests' perceptions that the tabletop device influenced their desire to return to the restaurant were significantly related to their liking for the tabletop device,[6] showing that guests who reported that they liked the device overwhelmingly reported that the tabletop device influenced their desire to return to the restaurant.[7]

Tip Percentage

Respondents' perceptions that the tabletop device improved their experience in the restaurant were not significantly related to the tip that they left for their server.[8] While not significant in the between-subjects model, however, the t-test was significant and showed that restaurant guests tipped their server more when they reported that the tabletop device improved their dining experience.[9]

Restaurant guests' perceptions that the tabletop device influenced their desire to return to the restaurant also were significantly related to the tip that they left for their server.[10] The t-test was also significant, showing that

TABLE 9.2. Correlations and descriptive statistics for study variables (N = 1,358)

	M	SD	(1)	(2)	(3)	(4)
(1) Effect on experience[a]	1.79	.41	—			
(2) Return intent[b]	1.83	.38	.83***	—		
(3) Likeability	3.45	1.12	.65***	.66***	—	
(4) Tip percentage	15.42	7.24	.14***	.17***	.09**	—

Note:

[a] "Decrease" was coded as 1, "Increase" was coded as 2;

[b] "No" was coded as 1, "Yes" was coded as 2;

** Correlation is significant at p =.01 level (2-tailed);

*** Correlation is significant p < .001 level (2-tailed).

restaurant guests who tipped their servers more overwhelmingly reported that the tabletop device influenced their desire to return to the restaurant.[11]

Discussion

Over 70% of the customers liked using the tabletop device. Approximately 79% of customers reported that the tabletop device improved their dining experience, and nearly 83% said that they would return to the restaurant as a result of using the device (see table 9.1). Likewise, the dependent variables—liking for the device and tip percentage—were positively and significantly correlated with customers' reports of the tabletop devices having a positive effect on their experience in the restaurant and their desire to return to the restaurant. These findings are consistent with the 2016 National Restaurant Association study, where 79% of customers reported that technology options increased convenience and 70% said that technology options speed up service and improve order accuracy.[12]

Minority Report

In the midst of the good news that the large majority of customers found the tabletop devices to be a useful addition to the service experience, however, it's important to note that slightly more than 20% of the respondents were not so pleased. This group of customers should not be ignored. In full-service restaurant settings (or any service-based setting) restaurant operators need to be sure that their service staff members determine whether customers are interested in using the technology, offering them the support to do so, and not shaming them if they take a pass.

The study underscores the common-sense principle that the customers who reported that they did not like the tabletop device, either for reasons of affect in the service episode or due to some element of functionality, should be given the option to not use the technology or to discontinue its use at any point during the meal. This will require operators to train their staff to monitor each customer transaction to ensure that the customers get the service they expect, regardless of their involvement with the technology.

It may also be that the minority of users who did not like the tabletop technology may warm up to it as they learn more about its use. This learning curve generally occurs with the adoption of technology. Wang, Harris, and Patterson, for instance, found that customers over time will become familiar with customer-facing technology, learn how to use it, see the benefits from it, and become satisfied with it.[13] Once satisfied with the technology they will use it regularly, as in the case of airline check-in kiosks. Needless to say, the restaurant situation is different from airlines, in part because the service providers are mostly tipped employees. In that vein, servers should be aware that guests who reported a negative experience with the tabletop device left on average a 2% lower tip and reported they were less likely to return to the restaurant. Knowing this, both managers and their line-level staff again should understand the need to closely monitor customers' progress with technology. That includes working with customers who enjoy using the device and who as a result left larger gratuities on average and reported an increased desire to return to restaurant.

Limitations and Suggestions for Future Research

This study is limited by the fact that its data come from a single multiunit restaurant company. Despite the relatively large sample size, one should be cautious in generalizing these findings. They may apply to other full-service restaurants but studies should also examine the effect of technology in other restaurant companies and service-based businesses. Also, due to data limitations, this study could not consider guests' sociodemographics or their evaluation of the food, service, ambience, or servers' reactions to the technology. In conclusion, as customer participation in service experiences and the related use of technology becomes more prevalent in service-based experiences, business owners, their staff, and their customers should continue to learn more about how technology can be used to add value to service experiences.

Notes

Original citation: Susskind, A. M, Awan, S., Parikh, R., & Suri, R. (2014). Guests' reactions to tabletop technology in full-service restaurants. The New Science of Service Innovation. Symposium cochaired by C. E. Enz and R. Verma, conducted at the Cornell Hospitality Research Summit, Ithaca, NY, October.

1. HTS = .48, $p < .001$, with an F statistic of F (2, 1353) = 32.19, $p < .001$, η2 = .05.

2. HTS = .41, $p < .001$, with an F statistic of F (2, 1353) = 27.71, $p < .001$, η2 = .04.

3. F [1,1354] = 63.72, $p < .001$, η2 = .05.

4. t [1356] = −31.42, $p < .001$.

5. M = 3.83, SD = .76, for "improved," and M = 2.05, SD = 1.13, for "did not improve."

6. F [1,1354] = 50.33, $p < .001$, η2 = .04; t-test: t [1356] = −31.96, $p < .001$.

7. M = 3.78, SD = .81, for increased intent to return, and M = 1.84, SD = 1.01, for decreased intention.

8. F [1,1354] = .42, $p = .52$, η2 = .00.

9. t [1356] = −5.18, $p < .001$; M = 15.94, SD = 7.61 for "improved," and M = 13.48, SD = 5.28, for "did not improve."

10. F [1,1354] = 4.38, $p = .04$, η2 = .004.

11. t [1356] = −6.22, $p < .001$; M = 15.97, SD = 7.54, for "increased" and M = 12.77, SD = 4.74, for "decreased."

12. National Restaurant Association (2016), *Mapping the technology landscape*, Washington, DC.

13. C. Wang, J. Harris, & P. Patterson (2013), The roles of habit, self-efficacy, and satisfaction in driving continued use of self-service technologies: A longitudinal study, *Journal of Service Research*, 16(3): 400–414.

The Influence of Tabletop Technology in Full-Service Restaurants

Alex M. Susskind and Benjamin Curry

From an operational perspective, tabletop technology affects several elements of a restaurant experience that can benefit both the operator and the guest. First, the ability to limit meal duration has two main benefits: the ability to turn tables more quickly for operators and the ability of guests to finish their meals at their discretion. Because restaurants essentially have a fixed capacity, reducing table turnover time increases the number of guests served each day, assuming a demand for the additional seats. For example, using a conservative estimate of a restaurant achieving $2.5 million in sales, and achieving a 15% reduction in table-turn time, there is the potential for an additional $375,000 in sales from unmet demand.[1] Irrespective of potential sales gains from improved table turnover, research has shown that restaurant consumers value more control over the payment process and the service elements afforded by customer-facing technology during their meal.[2]

The next benefit for operators is potential labor savings. If the tabletop technology reduces the amount of time servers need to attend to their guests, operators can use that "excess" service labor to improve service delivery by giving guests more attention or make each server responsible for a larger number of guests. This presents a choice to each operator on how to use the potential labor savings per guest or table. The last benefit from customer-facing technology in full-service restaurants is the potential for higher guest checks, through the sale of add-ons to the customers' meals.[3] Additionally, guests who use the tabletop technology do not need to wait for a server to place orders for additional beverages, refills, or food, such as appetizers and desserts. To put this in perspective, if the tabletop technology can improve the average guest check by just $3, that would result in a 20% improvement considering a restaurant average check of $15. From a theoretical perspective, the addition of technology into the service experience for restaurant guests affects the traditional interaction between servers and their customers.[4] As all participants in the service process adjust to these changes, research has shown how and why individuals gravitate toward or away from new technologies. Specific studies have shown that sociodemographic characteristics, usage characteristics, and usage outcomes are key influences in decisions for adoption, use, and enjoyment of a new technology.[5]

With these findings in mind, we seek to quantify the value of using tabletop technology for restaurant operators through two studies. The first study involved observations using a single restaurant in a chain operation before and after tabletop technology was added to their restaurants. The second study used point-of-sale (POS) data from a larger sample of restaurants within the same chain to confirm the results from Study 1 after the tabletop devices had been fully implemented. Through Study 1 we investigate how the introduction of tabletop technology influences table-turn time in the restaurants and how the tabletop technology influences front-of-house labor usage. Through Study 2 we confirm the relationship between tabletop device use and table-turn time, and also examine the relationship between the tabletop device use and consumer purchasing behavior.

To frame our analyses we present the following two research questions for Study 1:

- Study 1, Research Question 1: Does the introduction of a tabletop device in full-service restaurants affect the overall efficiency of the restaurant as measured by average table-turn time for all tables in the restaurant (not just the tables using the technology)?

- Study 1, Research Question 2: Does the guests' use of tabletop devices reduce front-of-house labor needs measured as server time spent serving guests with or without the technology?

To frame our analyses for Study 2 we present the following two research questions:

- Study 2, Research Question 1: Does the introduction of a tabletop device affect the overall efficiency of the restaurant as measured by average table-turn time for all tables in the restaurant (not just the tables using the technology)?
- Study 2, Research Question 2: Does use of a tabletop device influence guest spending?

Study 1 Data, Methods, and Findings

In a pre- and post-adoption research design, we collected data with the cooperation of a restaurant chain one month before and one month after the company installed tabletop devices in their restaurants. At the time of installation, the tabletop devices allowed guests to view food and beverage menus, order food and beverage items, summon their server, and pay for their meal.

All observations were recorded at a single location from a chain restaurant over two Fridays and two Saturdays (one each pre-adoption and post-adoption) between the hours of noon and 10:00 p.m., when the restaurant operated at or near capacity. To collect the observational data, the researcher was positioned near the POS terminal, where he could accurately observe server time spent on the terminal and where he could view two sections of the restaurant that had 15 tables that we selected to observe. The average number of guests at the table in the pre-adoption condition was 2.80 (SD = 1.08), and in the post-adoption condition it was 2.83 (SD = 1.15).

During each of the four observation sessions we measured and recorded key dining moments during the meal: start time, ordering, food delivery, payment, and check closing, along with the amount of time spent by the server doing specific activities, such as taking orders, using the POS system, delivering food, and consulting with guests. The dining time for each table was recorded as starting once the guest was seated and considered closed when the guest left the table. In the pre-adoption session we observed 115 table-turns and in the post-adoption session, 103 table-turns.

Meal Duration: Research Question 1—Findings from Study 1

The average dining time in the pre-adoption period was 1 hour, 2 minutes, and 58 seconds (N = 115, SD = 13 minutes, 41 seconds). In the post-adoption period dining time was classified in three ways: (1) for those who did not use the tabletop device, (2) for those who used the device to pay, and (3) for those who used it both to order and pay. For those who did not use the tabletop device the average dining time was 1 hour, 1 minute, and 8 seconds (N = 63, SD = 16 minutes, 8 seconds); for those who used the tabletop device for payment only the average dining time was 50 minutes and 33 seconds (N = 33, SD= 12 minutes, 43 seconds); and for those who used the tabletop device for ordering their food and beverages and payment the average dining time was 42 minutes and 4 seconds (N =7, SD = 7 minutes, 28 seconds). The total average meal duration across all three post-adoption conditions was 57 minutes and 40 seconds (N =103, SD = 8 minutes, 27 seconds (see table 10.1 and figure 10.1).[6]

When compared to the pre-adoption period, there was a significant difference in meal duration in the post-adoption period, of 5 minutes and 18 seconds (p < .05), which represents an 8% reduction in meal duration. When we analyze the post-adoption period based on how the tabletop device was used (or not used), we found no significant difference in meal duration for guests who did not use the tabletop device (difference = 1

TABLE 10.1. Average meal duration, Study 1

Condition	Pre-adoption	Post-adoption	Post-adoption	Post-adoption	Post-adoption
	No device	Average all three conditions	No device	Payment only	Order and payment
Meal duration	1:02:58 (13:41)	57:40 (8:27)	1:01:08 (16:08)	50:33 (12:43)	42:04 (7:28)

Note: Standard deviations are reported in parentheses after the means: pre-adoption N = 115 table observations; post-adoption N = 103 table observations.

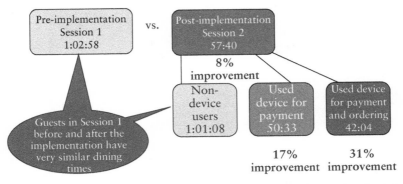

Figure 10.1. Comparison chart of dining time pre- and post-implementation, Study 1

minute and 50 seconds, p > .05). We did find significant differences for guests who used the tabletop device for payment only (difference = 12 minutes and 25 seconds, p < .05) which represented a 17% reduction in meal duration and for guests who used the tabletop device to order and pay (difference = 20 minutes and 54 seconds, p < .05), which represented a 31% reduction in meal duration.

Service Labor Usage: Research Question 2—Findings from Study 1

Building on our findings from Research Question 1, we examined the influence of this technology on service time and how it relates to potential service time or cost savings. To create the baseline for this set of analyses, we compared the guests who did not use the tabletop device during their meal and relied on their server to those who used the device. For the baseline group (non-users) the server would invest 10 minutes and 16 seconds on average in visits to the table (N = 63, SD = 2 minutes, 17 seconds). We then compared this baseline group to those guests who used the tabletop device to settle their bill or to both order and settle their bill. For the guests who used the tabletop device for payment only, the server would invest 6 minutes and 30 seconds on average in visits to the table, a decrease in 36% from baseline (N = 33, SD = 2 minutes 25 seconds). For the guests who used the technology for both ordering and payment the server would invest

TABLE 10.2. Applied variable labor analysis per guest check, Study 1

	Ordering time	POS tTime	Check-ins	Total labor	% change
Non–device users	2:30 (1:29)	2:46 (0:46)	11 (3.44)	10:16 (2:17)	—
Used device for payment	1:50 (2:04)	1:40 (1:12)	9 (2.80)	6:30 (2:25)	–36%
Used device for ordering and payment	0:00	0:00	7 (3:17)	3:30 (1:57)	–65%

Note: A check-in is defined as anytime the waiter interacts with the guests at the table (e.g., discussing the menu and specials, taking orders, delivering food or drinks, and socializing with the guest). Standard deviations are reported in parentheses following the mean.

Dining time spent at the table for the guests

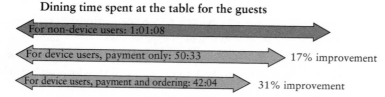

Figure 10.2. Table-turn efficiency gains from device usage, Study 1

3 minutes and 30 seconds on average in visits to the table, a decrease in 65% from baseline (N = 7, SD = 1 minute, 57 seconds; see table 10.2 and figure 10.2). This shows that servers invest less time on average managing their tables when their guests use the device. In short, the more the guest uses technology, the less labor is needed to deliver proper service.

Study 2 Data, Methods, and Findings

To verify and build on the results of Study 1, we gathered point-of-sales data from an additional 45 restaurants in the chain operated by a single franchisee in Southern California from January 1 to 31, 2016.[7] To gather the data, the technology company monitors the POS and collects information about each guest check. This information allowed us to identify each guest check's server, table number, check open and check close time, and total dollar amount spent.

To make this an accurate comparison we made sure we were only comparing checks that could have involved using the tablet had the customer chosen to do so. As a result, we excluded to-go orders and checks that originated at the bar. After collecting all of the checks we then cross-referenced the check numbers with a list showing whether that customer used the device to play games, order any food or drink item, order an entrée, and pay the bill. After marking each check we then subtracted the game-playing charge, when appropriate, from the total bill. This was to ensure that we measured the check average increase from food and drink purchases, not from games on the device.

We then excluded a number of checks that appeared to have faulty data, such as those with 0 minutes meal duration, $0 total, or a negative total. For the meal duration test, we eliminated all checks showing meal times of fewer than 15 minutes and more than 180 minutes. In the check average test we excluded bills less than $15 and greater than $200, given the average entrée price is about $10. In both instances filters are used to prevent outliers from skewing the results (typically caused by a device malfunction or improper use of the POS by the server). In the end, 265,414 transactions were collected. For the meal duration test there were 243,301 transactions, and for the average check test there were 231,495 transactions.

We used the data in two ways to answer the research questions in Study 2. First, to answer Research Question 1 the data were used to identify each check's open and close time. This measurement acts as a proxy for meal duration, similar to what was observed in Study 1. The next step was to separate the checks based on whether the guest used the tabletop device to pay for his meal. We then compared these cases to those who paid through their server. This allowed us to examine how using the tabletop device to pay is connected to meal duration compared to those who did not use the tabletop device to pay.

Because we had only aggregate check-level data for the restaurants and we had no measure of server time spent at the table from the POS (as we collected in Study 1), we were unable to test Research Question 2 from Study 1. Instead, we tested a new research question that examined the differences in guests' total spending on food and beverages by looking at the guests who used the tabletop device to place an order for an entrée and those who did not. In effect, we selected customers who stayed in the restaurant for a casual meal and used the device to order an entrée and those who did not use the device to place an order. These data allowed us to examine the differences in the guests' average check for those who used the device and those who did not.

Meal Duration: Research Q1—Findings from Study 2

When we compared the check open and close time for these guest checks, we found that guests who paid with the tabletop device had a table-turn time of 45 minutes and 21 seconds (N = 66,016, SD = 17 minutes and 40 seconds), compared to 53 minutes and 45 seconds for those who did not pay with the device (N = 177,282, SD = 26 minutes and 2 seconds). This 8-minute, 24-second difference, or 15.5% reduction in table-turn time, is statistically significant (p < .05) and close to the 17% reduction we observed in Study 1, showing that meal duration is consistently reduced when guests use the tabletop device (see figure 10.3).

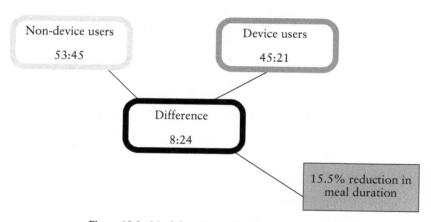

Figure 10.3. Meal duration and device usage, Study 2

Is Guest Spending Affected? Research Q2—Findings from Study 2

By examining the POS data we were able to determine whether guests who used the device to order an entrée spent more than guests who did not. On average, guests at tables who used the tabletop device to order a meal

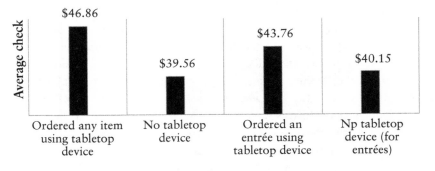

Figure 10.4. A comparison of guest checks with and without the tabletop device

spent $3.61 more (M = $43.76, SD = 20.43, N = 13,320) than those who did not (M = $40.15, SD = 20.92, N = 218177), which was significant at the $p < .05$ level. Using this same set of guest checks to extend beyond the threshold of at least ordering an entrée, we expanded this analysis to examine whether the incidence of device-using guests purchasing any items using the tabletop device differed from guests who did not use the device. Guests who used the tabletop device to order any item spent $7.30 more on average (M = $46.86, SD = 22.75, N = 25,106) compared to those who did not use the device (M = $39.56, SD = 20.54, N = 206,389), showing that using the tabletop device during a restaurant meal is associated with higher check averages (see figure 10.4).

Discussion

Through our two studies we showed that the use of tabletop devices in full-service restaurants is connected to key efficiency gains: reduced table-turn time, reduced need for a portion of service labor, and increased spending under certain circumstances. We showed that when restaurant guests used the device to pay for their meal they spent less time in the restaurant. For restaurants that normally have long waits for their tables, guests' use of this technology is yet another revenue management tool to help operators improve table-turn time. In restaurants where demand for tables exceeds the supply, controlling and monitoring meal duration is a key issue. If operators can use technology to better control this aspect of the service experience, they may be able to serve more guests each day. Of even more significance, as Millennials become the largest demographic group in our economy, and hence the largest group of restaurant consumers, we need to understand what is important to them. We do know that Millennials favor the use of technology in nearly all aspects of their lives, particularly the convenience that it offers.[8] Given our findings, the influence of tabletop technology on meal duration is beneficial to both guests and operators going forward. Additionally, based on reported consumer profiles and preferences of technology users, tabletop devices give restaurant operators a better chance when competing for younger guests and patrons who spend less time while dining.[9] While not the focus of this study, guests in previous studies reported that this technology improves the dining experience through greater convenience, faster delivery of food and drink (which we did measure), and improved security.[10]

Next, we found through Study 1 that when guests use the tabletop technology to order or pay, it reduces the amount of service labor needed for the table. This enables restaurant operators to reassign service labor and either increase the level of service delivered to the guests or reduce staffing levels by giving servers more tables in their stations.

Last, we showed that the use of the tabletop devices is connected to higher sales when compared to when the technology is not in use. Assuming the demand exists, restaurant operators can increase profits through this technology by increasing the number of guests they serve or by having their guests spend more while they are in the restaurant. Both outcomes are central to every operators' strategic and tactical plans. We look at these issues separately because we believe the tabletop device's ability to influence check size is not dependent on someone paying on the device, and similarly the time-saving benefits of paying on the device are not restricted to people that also ordered on the device.

Practical Implications

This new layer of technology has the potential to improve restaurant performance for guests, servers, and managers. For guests, there is more control over the dining experience; they can order when they are ready to, get refills on beverages when they want them, settle the bill at their convenience, and summon their server when needed. Hence, giving guests more control over parts of their service experience is likely to increase their satisfaction with the service experience and, as we have shown, can increase their spending.

For servers, the tabletop devices may reduce the number of steps needed to do their jobs. Labor can be reduced or reapplied to different elements of customer service, such as upselling, increased attentiveness and care to each table, and cross training to improve servers' abilities. While these noted uses of saved labor are different, each approach can benefit the guest and the restaurant alike. Managers benefit from the technology by having more flexibility with the use of service labor in the dining experience, although this new technology also puts a burden on managers to ensure their guests are receiving the service they need. This will likely require additional training and oversight so that all staff members understand how and why the delivery of service is affected by the technology. Managers must understand that about one-quarter of all guests do not like to use the technology, and that all guests require appropriate service regardless of whether they use the tabletop devices.[11] Management must also ensure that service standards do not lapse as a result of the technology being used by guests.

Finally, for all of these benefits to be realized by full-service restaurants, it is crucial that the restaurants' standards for service delivery remain consistent. Any efficiencies gained through labor savings and table-turn time from the self-service aspect of the technology can be lost if any guests are not satisfied with core products: food, beverage, and service. Research shows that standards for service remain a key driver of guest satisfaction in restaurants. Moreover, some 20 to 30% of consumers using guest-facing technology remain uncomfortable with the idea.[12] The bottom line for restaurant operators, when introducing technology and making other changes to their business processes, is to create an excellent experience for their guests.

Ideas for Future Research and Conclusion

While our research represents an important step in examining the impact of guest-facing technology in full-service restaurants, there is much more to do to better pinpoint the costs and benefits of using this technology.

In future investigations, we plan to expand this research to concurrently examine the relationship of guest-facing technology use and other elements of the dining experience, such as guest satisfaction, employee engagement, guest return intentions, and purchasing behavior and spending. These additional factors should further our understanding of how tabletop technology in restaurants influences the entire guest experience.[13]

Notes

Original Citation: Susskind, A. M., & Curry, B. (2016). The influence of tabletop technology in full-service restaurants. *Cornell Hospitality Report, 16*(22): 3–9.

1. Kelsey Printz (2014), Presto by E la Carte improves lunchtime table turn at Genghis Grill by over 30 percent, http://www.businesswire. com/news/home/20141202005140/en/Presto%E2%84%A2-la-Carte-Improves-Lunchtime-Table-Turn#.VeCEjU3JCos.

2. J. E. Collier & S. E. Kimes (2013), Only if it is convenient: Understanding how convenience influences self-service technology evaluation, *Journal of Service Research, 16*(1): 39–51; A. M. Susskind & B. Curry (in press), An examination of customers' attitudes about tabletop technology in full-service restaurants, Service Science; M. White, B. C. Lawrence, & R. Verma, Consumer preferences for US restaurant-based technology, *Cornell Hospitality Report 15*(18).

3. S. E. Kimes & P. Laque (2011), Online, mobile, and text food ordering in the US restaurant industry, *Cornell Hospitality Report 11*(7): 6–15.

4. M. Giebelhausen, S. G. Robinson, N. J. Sirianni, & M. K. Brady (2014), Touch versus tech: When technology functions as a barrier or a benefit to service encounters, *Journal of Marketing, 78*(4): 113–124.

5. V. Venkatesh, J. Y. Thong, & X. Xu (2012), Consumer acceptance and use of information technology: Extending the unified theory of acceptance and use of technology, *MIS Quarterly, 36*(1): 157–178; and Susskind and Curry, Examination of customers' attitudes.

6. While not observed during this set of observations, there are circumstances where a guest uses the tabletop device to order, but pays with cash. This service scenario will obviously require additional service interaction on the part of the server to tender the payment.

7. This single franchisee was selected because the menus and prices were identical across all 45 restaurants. This helped control for variation due to differences in the menu and prices, as franchisees in the system have some latitude on what menu items they sell and how they are priced.

8. Goldman Sachs (2016), Millennials coming of age, http://www.goldmansachs.com/our-thinking/pages/millennials/.

9. White et al., Consumer preferences for US restaurant-based technology.

10. Susskind & Curry, Influence of tabletop technology; White et al., Consumer preferences for US restaurant-based technology; Alex M. Susskind, Saqib Awan, Ron Parikh, & Rajat Suri (2015), Guest's reactions to tabletop technology in full-service restaurants, *Cornell Hospitality Report 15*(18): 20–24.

11. Susskind & Curry, Influence of tabletop technology.

12. Ibid.; White et al., Consumer preferences for US restaurant-based technology.

13. A. M. Susskind, K. M. Kacmar,, & C. P. Borchgrevink (2007), How organizational standards and coworker support improve restaurant service, *Cornell Hotel and Restaurant Administration Quarterly, 48*(4): 370–379; Susskind & Curry, Influence of tabletop technology; White et al., Consumer preferences for US restaurant-based technology.

CONCLUSION

The Human Function

ALEX M. SUSSKIND AND MARK MAYNARD

Alex: We all know that people are an important part of the restaurant business, and we have discussed this idea from many different angles in the chapters above. As our business becomes more dependent on technology, people will remain the source and the mechanism by which we create and deliver hospitality. Our industry has a rich history of "being of service," but it was not always as glamourous, desirable, or acceptable as it is today. The idea of service, or servitude, has a negative connotation connected originally to slavery, but when you fast-forward to today (and tomorrow) and blend in the idea of hospitality, being of service is what allows operators to create and deliver a food and beverage experience of value to and in demand by guests, in a fashion that leads to a profitable, sustainable business for owners and operators. No book on hospitality management should forget the famous E. M. Statler quote that is etched into the DNA of Cornell's Hotel School: "Life is service—the one who progresses is the one who gives his fellow men a little more—a little better service."

We have come a long way. In 1965 Howard Johnson's was everywhere and was a leading food-service and lodging company in the United States; at the same time McDonald's was not much more than a small growing start-up, making a name for itself with burgers, French fries, and shakes. Today McDonald's is a mature, leading global food-service brand, Howard Johnson's has all but disappeared, and Shake Shack is a relatively new kid on the block growing by leaps and bounds selling burgers, fries, and shakes around the globe. What we do as food-service professionals has evolved, and the restaurant industry has grown and changed to a point that no one could have predicted in 1965.

What has not changed, however, is people. People are the driving force behind all we do in food service, starting with the supply chain and ending up in the hands and hearts of our employees and ultimately guests. Everything that happens, good, bad, great, or ugly in your restaurant begins and ends with people. Without well-trained, passionate, innovative, committed, caring, and smart people working in and helping you run your restaurant(s), you will not be able to succeed. Period.

The restaurant business sits in a unique place in our economy as far as labor is concerned. Based on recent data from the National Restaurant Association, the US restaurant industry directly employs 15 million people. Under even the best circumstances, compared to other industries, the turnover rate in the hospitality business is high, estimated at 72.1% in 2015, up from 66.7% in 2014.[1] It seems that there is a constant need for talent at both the line-level and supervisory/management levels. The restaurant business relies heavily on part-time labor, and many restaurant workers are transient, using restaurant work as a stop along their way to pursue work interests or careers in other industries. The restaurant labor market also seems to improve when unemployment rises, as workers can readily find employment in the restaurant space when other industries are contracting and are not hiring. Conversely, when unemployment is as low as it is at the moment (around 4.3%), recruiting and retaining talent becomes even more challenging.

At the moment there are a few hot-button topics that are connected to the labor force: minimum wage, wage equity, and health care/benefits. Ironically, none of these are new as issues of debate and discussion, but they have worked their way to front of the line, again.

The key to success in the service business is built on the ability to understand people and how to make them happy. In my time, I have found that the attitude, disposition, and outlook of employees and managers are what drives success.

When I think of the challenges of managing a service-based workforce, I am reminded of a two-part study called the *Industry of Choice*, conducted by the National Restaurant Association and Coca-Cola in the mid-1990s.[2] I first read the report nearly 20 years ago, but the findings and insights in that report still make sense today. In the report, four groups of workers were identified based on their career orientation, or how committed they are to their work. Career orientation of food-service employees in the *Industry of Choice* report was defined in four ways, highlighting unique challenges to operators as they try to build, develop, and maintain an effective workforce.

The first career orientation group is called "Careerists." *Careerists* have identified the restaurant industry as their career of choice; as such they have made a commitment to be in the restaurant business and plan to stay. Most operators would say that these employees are the best for the operation, and I would agree. Where operators miss the mark is when they take *Careerists* for granted. While only 18% of the sample, *Careerists* need to be commended for their commitment to your operation and the profession, given opportunities for growth and development, and given the motivation, tools, resources, and rewards to be successful at their jobs. Having committed and motivated employees is an aspirational goal; therefore, do everything in your power to make sure *Careerists* stay *Careerists*.

The second group of career orientations is called "Undecided." *Undecided* workers are currently working in the restaurant business, but have not made a longer-term commitment to the business as a career. As an operator, this group of employees can be very important to building and maintaining a base of competent employees. This group of employees (which made up 22% of the sample in the report) will be performing well on the job, so just like with the *Careerists*, they will need full support and motivation to continue to perform well in their jobs. In addition, this group of employees will need to be honestly and appropriately encouraged to stick with the industry and make a longer-term commitment (that is, convert them to becoming a *Careerist*). Making sure this group builds a passion for the business is important, or you risk losing them to another sector of the economy.

The third career orientation group is called "Passing-Throughs." Members of the *Passing-Throughs* employee group are currently working in the restaurant business, but they have clearly defined career goals in another industry. *Passing-Throughs* will likely be very good employees, but they have a defined period of time they will remain in the restaurant business. We see this all the time with employees who are currently in school earning degrees (high school, post-secondary, or graduate school) or aspiring to enter some field such as entertainment. This group represented 35% of the sample in the study, and made up the largest group. As noted, these employees will be in the restaurant business for a defined period of time . . . sometime less than forever. As noted, these employees should be dedicated and good employees while they are working with you. While they view the industry as a temporary stop along the way, they have chosen it in the short-term. As a result, they will need support and motivation to be successful, but it is unlikely that they will become *Careerists* because of other well-defined career objectives (although we have all seen *Passing-Throughs* stay longer than planned). An example comes to mind from McDonald's, who tries to appeal to workers with the saying "America's Best First Job." McDonald's knows that many of its workers will be transient. It does its best to hire and retain employee talent for as long feasible, knowing they will be moving on to other things.

The last career orientation group is called *Misfits*. *Misfits* unfortunately have little or no interest or desire to be doing the work they are doing. Generally, they do not like the work, they are not suited for it, and they are not particularly good at it. This group of employees should not be hired in the first place, but once they are working for you in the restaurant business they should be un-hired as quickly as possible once it has become clear that they are not suited to the work they have been hired to perform. These employees may be toxic to the work environment and make the work of the other staff members and management more difficult. In the *Industry of Choice* report, this group made up 25% of the sample. This likely occurs because managers and owners let their guard down in the hiring process to fill an open position. I assure you, you are better off not hiring these types of employees in the first place.

Understanding how to attract, motivate, and retain the right employees for your business is one of the most important things you can do as a manager and owner.

From my experience (and the *Industry of Choice* report), here are a few things that can help you hire and retain the best people possible.

1. Make sure you have enough employees scheduled (trained and hired) to handle the workload of your business. When employees are stretched too thin, they cannot effectively deliver on your company's service mission and execute your company's standards. Also make sure that all your employees are viewed by their peers as doing their part. Employees who are viewed as loafers will negatively affect morale.

2. Make sure you offer competitive wages to all employees based on the market in which you operate. All businesses will be competing for the best talent available; competitive wages can help you gain an edge in recruiting, hiring, and retaining talent. In that regard also consider having some form of incentive pay built into the compensation system. Incentive pay can help reward staff for engaging in the workplace behaviors that are important for your success.

3. Your staff will perform better if they believe that the company is managed well and that the company cares for its employees and guests. This should be a top priority to have your staff feel like you are with them or as Danny Meyer would say, "on their side."

4. Make sure you offer a competitive set of benefits for your employees. Understand what each type of employee needs and find ways to support them with benefits. I remember working for a restaurant company that offered an amazing set of options. As a manager, in addition to health insurance, I could choose from a variety of other benefits, such as a group car insurance plan, life insurance, and an allowance for daycare or eldercare. At that point in my life, the car insurance plan was the most attractive to me; at this stage in my life, childcare or eldercare would be more attractive. Yes, all these things (which need to be carefully selected and managed) come with a cost, but having happy, well-adjusted, secure, committed employees will bring financial rewards back to the business time and time again. Remember, employee turnover is very costly. With turnover

you have to start all over with the hiring, training, and motivation processes when you replace staff members. Pay it forward and invest in your people.

5. Make sure that, as you hire new employees, you are always getting better staff members, encourage *Misfits* to move on as quickly as possible, and build and train for your specific company culture.

6. Make sure you develop systems to help ensure your staff is being trained properly. Training is just a tool to teach your staff what is important, what needs to be done, and how it should be done. Training by itself is not enough. You need to have ways to ensure that your staff can effectively and consistently perform the things you teach them. You need to set objectives for learning, develop the vehicles to transfer the desired knowledge, skills, and abilities, and follow up to make sure your staff actually has internalized the learning and can effectively apply it on the job.

7. Lastly, develop systems to help cross-train your staff. This does a few things: it creates growth vehicles for staff, it shows employees how other parts of the business function, and it helps staff members perform their jobs better. I got my start in the kitchen as a dishwasher and was eventually promoted to become a line cook. When my manager at the time had me wait tables and work behind the bar, I couldn't really understand why he had me do that. It was only after working in those positions that I began to fully understand how my role as a cook connected to the other parts of the business. It was a necessary step in my growth and development as a hospitality professional.

Mark: As I consider my career, I wonder if I could have possibly flourished in any other industry as much as I have in the restaurant business. As I noted in the introduction, one of the most special things about the restaurant business is the diversity of people within it. But beyond that, one of the most magnetic forces is the diversity of opportunities available to those people who choose to devote themselves to the industry. I love the term "Industry of Choice," because it can be interpreted in many different ways: does it imply that the people working with us have chosen to be here, or does it imply that there is a lot of choice when considering where to land? Or does it imply that the industry chooses those of us who have made restaurants our profession? Whichever way it may be interpreted, it is clear that there are tons of career options in the restaurant sector.

I would argue that there is no one industry that offers as many options for entry. The classic story is of someone who starts as a dishwasher or backwaiter and becomes a chef-owner, but there are many other ways to initially engage with restaurants, from interning in an accounting firm that specializes in restaurants to working on a restaurant-centric public relations campaign, to joining a technology company that provides analytical support to restaurants, to working for a contractor that builds restaurants. People who have chosen to study restaurants in culinary schools or at the university level are encouraged to spend time in the trenches to complement their academic training. Those people who are able to harness both practical and academic learning are the people who can most readily move from the dining room to the board room. It's notable that both Alex and I started as dishwashers and worked our way through many positions in restaurants before choosing our ultimate professions within the industry. These career stories are remarkably common, which I find encouraging. A challenge for leaders is to recognize the potential in new employees, many times before those employees have realized that the restaurant industry can provide a viable career path, and frequently before those employees have expressed any passion for the work they are doing.

When I started at Union Square Cafe, I had absolutely no interest in pursuing a career in restaurants. I was an example of the *Passing-Through* in the *Industry of Choice* study, and most of my service staff coworkers were in the same boat. I was surrounded by actors, singers, dancers, and artists, many of whom would work just enough hours to be eligible for USC's great benefits package (which was, and remains, one of the best in the industry). In fact, *Careerists* were the minority. In contrast, most members of the culinary team were dedicated to the restaurant industry and were honing their craft so that they could one day become an executive chef. This paradigm has not changed much in the past 25 years, though, as Alex has noted, it is now more acceptable to proclaim a desire to pursue a career in restaurants. Because of this, *Careerists* in both the kitchen and dining room have become much more knowledgeable, versatile, and well-rounded than before. Ambitious cooks who want to become chefs learn early on about finances, marketing, and human resources as a way to differentiate themselves. At the same time, an appreciation of the whole person has arisen as our industry becomes more aware of issues such as quality of life, health, and safety and how to recognize the signs of burn-out and addiction.

Inspiring the different groups within the four walls of the restaurant is one of the most challenging aspects of leading a team. While I may not have been initially interested in pursuing a career in restaurants, I did love the people with whom I worked, and I loved the food and drinks we served. I didn't care whether or not my colleagues were in it for the long haul. They were good at their jobs, and we worked together to make our guests happy. In many ways, it doesn't really matter to which employee group each person belongs. What matters is that the leadership team sets the example and provides support for the team to achieve the business' goals. At USC, the partners created fertile ground for us to grow, whether we would be there for six months or six years. I have witnessed restaurant managers miss opportunities to grow employees because they didn't want to invest time in "out-of-work actors." But early in my career, I was one of those employees (though I was an underemployed designer), and I would not be writing this book without mentorship, especially early in my career. Having leaders who shared their passion, maintained high standards (of both skill and behavior), and invested in me as an individual ultimately converted me from a *Passing-Through* or *Undecided* to a *Careerist*. Three stories from my first decade at USHG help illustrate the sort of investment that is required to help someone flourish, and each story has to do with me behaving in a less-than-enlightened way.

A story that I have told many times centers on a New York strip steak. When I was a junior manager working Sunday nights, a guest once loudly complained that his steak was overcooked and that we should know bet-ter. His tone was less than charitable, and I somehow thought in that instant to ask, "If it was so bad, then why did wait until you had eaten the whole thing before telling us?" Needless to say, this was not the correct response. The guest ended up leaving angry, and, after a couple of phone calls, Danny ultimately convinced the guest to return with his compli-ments. But the story is not about the steak or the guest. The real story is about the patience I was shown, even though I did not really deserve it. Danny took the time to show me the errors of my ways in a manner that involved neither shame nor ridicule. He clearly showed me that taking the long view is more important than trying to prove I was right. It's a lesson that I use regularly, especially with new employees who are not familiar with our culture or managers who may wear their frustration on their sleeves when things are not going their way. I try my best to remember this story when someone on the team does something ill-advised.

The second story involves a personnel matter, and it shows how hard we have to work to build bridges. One afternoon when I was assistant GM (several years after the infamous steak episode), a server did something during service that I thought showed lack of care (I don't even remember what the "infraction" was, but it is now irrelevant). The following day, I chose to call out the server as we were setting up the dining room before service. He felt I had ambushed him, got very defensive, and took issue with my confrontation. Though I could see him getting uncomfortable, I chose to dig in and start to raise my voice. What had begun as a gentle scolding became a yelling match. After a couple of minutes, we were both flustered, and we ended the argument by stomping our feet and storming off. Moments later, I attempted to commiserate with managing partner Paul Bolles-Beaven, with whom I shared an office. But rather than siding with me, he asked one question: "Did you accomplish what you set out to achieve?" I could not have been more frustrated, because his implication was spot on—by losing my cool, I had only made matters worse, and I had potentially broken the trust of not just the server, but of anyone within earshot (which was pretty much the entire team). Even if they had agreed with the premise of my argument, most would also agree that I had not handled myself in a constructive manner. Paul strongly encouraged me to make things right, and after a couple of days, my colleague and I sat down and had a constructive conversation. We honestly shared concerns we had with one another, and our relationship dramatically improved over the next few months. If only I had remained calm and collected (and empathetic) in the first place!

The final story is about remaining open to the world of possibilities. In 2000, I was general manager of USC, which was then the most popular restaurant in the *Zagat Guide*. While I loved my job, I could feel my enthusiasm waning, so I let Paul know that I wanted a change of scenery. Since 1994, Danny and his partners had opened Gramercy Tavern, Tabla, and Eleven Madison Park, all of which had eventually garnered critical acclaim and legions of enthusiastic followers. When I approached the partners about a potential new opportunity, I naturally thought of fine dining. What I did not know then is that Danny was starting to plan a casual barbecue-focused restaurant and jazz club that would ultimately become Blue Smoke and Jazz Standard. Months after I expressed a desire to leave USC, the partners suggested that I may want to consider being the opening GM of this new place. I was concerned, because it was so different than anything I had done before. In fact, it was different than anything that had ever been attempted in New York City. In addition to a general fear of failure, I feared that running a barbecue joint would somehow hurt my credibility and derail my career. I sought the counsel of Michael Romano, USC's chef-partner, who had worked in some of the world's top kitchens. I shared my concerns, and Michael took the time to allay my fears, explaining that it's important to remain open-minded about possibilities and to break out of one's comfort zone. But the kicker for me was his description of, and admiration for, barbecue. He described in great detail the first time he had tasted a baby back rib straight from the smoker of legendary pitmaster Mike Mills. I had only heard that tone from Michael when he was describing the top vintages of Bourdeaux or Burgundy, and it was eye-opening that he would choose to use the same language to describe barbecue. Coming from a chef that I admired immensely, and hearing his passion for the craft of barbecue, it was impossible for me to walk away from the opportunity.

As I think about these three conversations, I reflect on how well-rounded I would become because of the investment my mentors made in me. The steak story taught me early on about guest service, complaint management, taking the long view, and using mistakes to create brand loyalty. The second story taught me how to lead people who are not like me and the importance of self-awareness in leadership. It also taught me that showing vulnerability is important if you hope to develop relationships. Finally, the Blue Smoke story taught me to remain open-minded to the possibilities that may not be evident at the outset. Planning Blue Smoke gave me many opportunities to leverage my design background, and many of the visual aspects of Blue Smoke benefited from my formal training. It was also the first time I could create, not just maintain, a culture. I got to learn a new cuisine and culture that I knew nothing about, I got to travel to the South many times, and I learned a ton about beer and bourbon. So, all in all, Blue Smoke was a great career move, and I am thrilled that I took the leap. But at the end of it all, the most important takeaway is that each one of these lessons was made possible by someone who was willing to make a personal investment in my success. It is easy to forget these formative moments, but it's imperative that we use them for inspiration as we work to improve the lives of the people we lead.

Notes

1. R. Ruggless (2016), http://www.nrn.com/blog/hospitality-turnover-rose-721-rate-2015.
2. *Industry of Choice Executive Overview*, Part I, produced by the Educational Foundation of the National Restaurant Association and the Coca Cola Company (1997); *Industry of Choice Executive Overview*, Part II, produced by the Educational Foundation of the National Restaurant Association and the Coca Cola Company (1999).

Afterword

Alex M. Susskind

So what can we do to make the restaurant business *the* "Industry of Choice"? We need to think about the future and what we can do to ensure our industry grows and progresses. A few challenges always remain that require attention. This is what we signed up for. Mark and I both found the restaurant industry at an early age, Mark at 16 and I at 14. While Mark started on a different path, he found his way to the pinnacle of our business. I imagine he was drawn to the same things I was, whether he knew it or not at the time—being of service. I fell in love with the restaurant industry during my first shift as a dishwasher when a friend of mine asked me to cover his shift on Christmas Eve in 1980. The fast pace, the camaraderie, all the moving parts—I had never seen anything like it, and was fascinated by it. At the time, I had no idea what I was getting into. Since that evening, I have spent the last 37 years working in, with, and for restaurants.

As noted in the *Industry of Choice* report, attracting, hiring, compensating, training, motivating, and evaluating staff should always be a priority. As an operator, you need to be clear on what your staff should be and do, be diligent in making sure they have all the tools they need to be successful, and pay them fairly. As an operator you hold the steering wheel; set and enforce standards and lead your staff by example. There is nothing more important than this.

As we presented, discussed, and debated in the preceding chapters, our business is complex. We have to conceptualize and design, we have to manage service processes, we have to understand our staff, our guests, our suppliers, our investors, and the communities we serve. As Mark noted when he described how Union Square Cafe found a way to reset itself after 14 years, nothing stands still. It reminds me of a Will Rogers quote: "Even if you are on the right track, you'll get run over if you just sit there."

I will conclude by sharing an amazing lesson I was given about service and hospitality as a new line cook at age 15. It was a busy Sunday night, and I had been cooking on the line for only about month after being promoted from prep cook. I knew the menu, was confident in my abilities, and I was excited to be doing the work I was doing. That evening, the lead line cook, who was dealing with a substance abuse problem, had an issue and couldn't finish his shift. As a result, I needed to step up and finish the work; I received a "line promotion" as he walked (stumbled) off the line. It was busy, I was in the weeds, doing the best I could and moving through the tickets and the shift. Things were going okay, but not great. I was in the process of putting a dish in the window from the grill (a burger ordered medium rare) for a ticket that was running late. The guests had been waiting for 20 minutes longer than expected at that point. The server was asking about the ticket. I knew the burger was overcooked, I had lost track of it. The burger was visibly over-charred on the outside, and I was trying to cover the excess char and terrible appearance with the bun, lettuce, tomato, and onion. Right then, one of the owners looked at the dish and said sharply, "What is this?" I responded and said, "It doesn't look that bad." He laughed and asked me to put another burger on the grill and thanked me for stepping up to manage the line. He knew I was a new cook and 100 % in the weeds; he went out to the dining room for a couple of minutes. He then came back to the kitchen with an apron on and cooked with me for the rest of the shift. At the end of the night he thanked me again and said, "Remember that everything you do will have a positive or negative effect on the guest. We are here for them." He further said,

"You knew that the burger was burnt and you tried to serve to one of *our* guests. We all make mistakes, but it is what we do after our mistakes that defines us. Burning a hamburger is going to happen, but don't try to pass that off as 'not so bad.' If you got that burger would you be happy?" I said, "No." He then said, "Next time, just let me know. We will deal with the guest, and you cook it like you know it should be cooked." I asked what he did in the dining room after I put the new burger on the grill. He told me he went out to the table, told the guests that their food was going to be another 10 minutes, and he bought them a beer while they were waiting. He saw I needed help, and he wanted me to know that it is okay to make mistakes as long as I learn from the mistakes and do my best not to repeat them. That lesson has been with me ever since. From that interaction I learned that restaurants are complex and dynamic, and good things don't happen by accident. I also realized that I worked for an amazing, caring man who cared for me as much as his guests and his business. Is that hospitality defined? I think so.

BIOGRAPHIES

Editors

Alex M. Susskind joined the faculty at Cornell University's School of Hotel Administration in the Department of Food and Beverage Management in 1998. He earned his PhD in communication from Michigan State University, with a specialization in organizational communication, and his MBA with a concentration in personnel and human relations. Alex earned his undergraduate degree at Purdue University in restaurant, hotel, and institutional management and is a trained chef with a degree in culinary arts from the Culinary Institute of America in Hyde Park, New York. Prior to starting his career in academia, Alex was a chef and restaurant operator for both independent and multi-unit restaurant companies in the northeastern and southeastern United States.

At Cornell, Alex teaches undergraduate and graduate courses addressing the operational and strategic elements of the restaurant business. He also teaches in the Hotel School's Executive Education Program to managers and executives, both on and off campus, and has recently developed and launched an eight-course online certificate program in food and beverage management for eCornell.

Through his active research program, Alex is currently examining how: (1) customer-service provider interaction with guests and managers influences organizational performance; (2) technology is influencing/changing the relationship between guests and service-based employees and managers; and (3) nutrition information provided by restaurants on menus (as required by the Affordable Care Act starting in May 2018) is influencing guests' food choices when they dine out in full-service restaurants.

Alex studies Chun Do Kwan tae kwon do and holds a first-degree black belt; he is also an enthusiastic collector of fine wines, with about 1,500 bottles in his wine cellar, and a drummer.

Mark Maynard is a director of operations at Union Square Hospitality Group. A 27-year veteran of the company, Mark began his USHG career as a reservationist at Union Square Cafe, where he ultimately became general manager. He moved on to cofound Blue Smoke and Jazz Standard in 2002. For 13 years, Mark led the strategic growth of Blue Smoke, which expanded to multiple locations, including New York's Battery Park City and outposts of Blue Smoke on the Road at CitiField, Washington Nationals ballpark, and JFK Airport's Delta Terminal 4. For two years, Mark simultaneously served as managing director of operations for Union Square Events, the catering and events services branch of USHG. Mark conceptualized and cofounded Porchlight, USHG's first stand-alone cocktail bar, which opened in 2015. He is responsible for its strategic direction and all day-to-day operations. He also leads USHG's expansion into the bar and lounge category.

Mark is a graduate of Cornell University with a degree in landscape architecture. He is an adjunct professor of food business operations at New York University's Steinhardt School and a member of the Institute of Culinary Education's professional advisory committee.

Contributors

Saqib Awan is vice president of Lightspeed, which he joined in 2015 to oversee the firm's CIO forum, which connects founders from portfolio companies with industry experts who can help them achieve their goals. Previously, he was a strategy manager with Deloitte Consulting and a regional sales manager at General Motors. He earned an MBA from the Stanford Graduate School of Business.

Carl P. Borchgrevink has a PhD in communication from Michigan State University, an MS in hotel, restaurant, and travel administration from the University of Massachusetts, a Norwegian undergraduate degree from the Norwegian Hotel School, a culinary degree from Oslo Vocational School, and a Norwegian Chef's Certificate (*Kokkefagbrev*). Believing that hospitality students need a global perspective and should travel or study abroad, he is highly involved in study abroad and exchange programs in the School of Hospitality Business at Michigan State University's Eli Broad College of Business. Prior to his academic career, he accumulated 14 years of hospitality business experience. The positions he held included chef, restaurant manager, and food-service manager. He is currently the director of the School of Hospitality Business and an associate professor at Michigan State University.

Joel E. Collier, PhD, is an associate professor in the Department of Marketing, Quantitative Analysis, and Business Law at Mississippi State University. His areas of research are in services marketing, service recovery, self-service technology, and relationship marketing. He has published in leading journals such as *Journal of Retailing, Journal of the Academy of Marketing Science, Journal of Service Research, MIT Sloan Management Review, Journal of Public Policy and Marketing,* and *Journal of Personal Selling and Sales Management.* Within the self-service industry, he has served as a consultant for many businesses, such as Time Warner, Muvico, and Cashman Photo.

Benjamin Curry, PhD, is a data scientist at Presto, where he leads analytical projects and extracts practical insights from the company's huge dataset to guide product and business strategy. He earned his PhD in behavioral economics and finance from Claremont Graduate University, where he also earned his MBA with a concentration in finance. His areas of expertise include behavioral economics and finance, consumer behavior, risk management, organizational behavior, financial modeling and analysis, corporate finance, and marketing analysis.

Miguel Gómez is an associate professor at the Charles H. Dyson School of Applied Economics and Management and a fellow of the David R. Atkinson Center for a Sustainable Future at Cornell University.

Sachin Gupta is the Henrietta Johnson Louis Professor of Marketing and Professor of Management at the Johnson Graduate School of Management at Cornell University. He is also coeditor of the *Journal of Marketing Research*, published by the American Marketing Association. His current research focuses on marketing by nonprofit organizations and methods to protect customer privacy. Previously he has worked on measurement of returns on marketing investments, pricing, promotion, and advertising decisions, and marketing research methods.

K. Michele Kacmar, PhD, is a professor and the Fields Chair of Ethics and Corporate Responsibility in the Department of Management at Texas State University. She received her PhD from Texas A&M University. Her general research interests fall in the areas of ethics, impression management, organizational politics, and work-family conflict. She has published over 100 articles in journals such as the *Academy of Management Journal*, *Journal of Applied Psychology*, and *Personnel Psychology*. Michele served as editor of the *Journal of Management* from 2000 to 2002 and as an associate editor of the *Academy of Management Journal* from 2007 to 2010.

Sheryl E. Kimes, PhD, is Singapore Tourism Board Distinguished Professor of Asian Hospitality Management at the Cornell University School of Hotel Administration, where she has served as interim dean and also as the school's director of graduate studies. In teaching restaurant revenue management, yield management, and food and beverage management, she has been named the school's graduate teacher of the year three times. Her research interests include revenue management and forecasting in the restaurant, hotel, and golf industries. She was given the Lifetime Achievement Award by the College of Service Operations Management Society and was honored with the Industry Relevance Award by the Cornell University Center for Hospitality Research in 2010 and 2012. She has published over 50 articles in leading journals such as *Interfaces*, *Journal of Operations Management*, *Journal of Service Research*, *Decision Sciences*, and the *Cornell Hotel and Restaurant Administration Quarterly*. In addition, she has published over 25 Cornell Center for Hospitality Research Reports and has been an invited speaker at numerous international conferences. She has served as a consultant to many hospitality enterprises around the world, including Chevy's FreshMex Restaurants, Walt Disney World Resorts, Ruby's Diners, Starwood Asia-Pacific, and Troon Golf.

Edward McLaughlin, PhD, is the R. G. Tobin Professor of Marketing in the Department of Applied Economics and Management at Cornell University.

Ron Parikh is the chief marketing officer at Genghis Grill Franchise Concepts, LP, managing director for CMG's Twin Peaks and Pepper Smash franchise businesses, and, since November 2004, chief marketing officer at Chalak Mitra Group LLC, where he spearheads all marketing and advertising campaigns for the Genghis Grill. He also is on the board for Pratham USA, Dallas-Fort Worth chapter, which is a charitable organization that benefits children's rights to education. Ron has a bachelor of science degree from the University of Texas at Dallas.

Stephani K. A. Robson, MS, is a senior lecturer in facilities planning and design at the School of Hotel Administration at Cornell University. After working for several years in restaurants and retail food operations in her native Canada, she graduated from the School of Hotel Administration and began her career as a food-service designer, first with Cini-Little International and subsequently with Marrack Watts in Toronto, Ontario. Having designed kitchen facilities for hotels, restaurants, airports, hospitals, universities, and catering halls, she joined the School of Hotel Administration faculty in 1993. Her academic interests and current doctoral studies center on how environments affect customers' preferences and behavior, with a particular focus on hospitality settings. She is a specialist in restaurant design psychology and has presented and published her research in a wide range of industry and academic forums around the world.

Rajat Suri is the founder and CEO of E la Carte. Previously, he was a cofounder of Zimride, now called Lyft, a member of the board of directors of FedS, and the founder and president of the Forum for Independent

Thought. He has a bachelor's degree in chemical engineering and economics from the University of Waterloo and attended a PhD/MBA program at MIT.

Anthony Viccari has most recently served as chief strategy officer with Lick Honest Ice Creams based in Austin, Texas. Previously, he has held positions with Starbucks Coffee Company and Dick's Sporting Goods and as an instructor of hospitality management in the David B. Falk College of Sport and Human Dynamics at Syracuse University. He is a graduate of the School of Hotel Administration at Cornell University and the Whitman School of Management at Syracuse University.

Index